The Business of
Indie Games

The Business of Indie Games

Everything You Need to Know to Conquer the Indie Games Industry

Alex Josef, Alex Van Lepp
and Marshal D. Carper

CRC Press
Taylor & Francis Group
Boca Raton London New York

CRC Press is an imprint of the
Taylor & Francis Group, an **informa** business

First Edition published 2022
by CRC Press
6000 Broken Sound Parkway NW, Suite 300, Boca Raton, FL 33487-2742

and by CRC Press
4 Park Square, Milton Park, Abingdon, Oxon, OX14 4RN

CRC Press is an imprint of Taylor & Francis Group, LLC

ISBN: 978-1-032-10422-5 (hbk)
ISBN: 978-1-032-10421-8 (pbk)
ISBN: 978-1-003-21526-4 (ebk)

DOI: 10.1201/9781003215264

Typeset in ITC Slimbach Std
by KnowledgeWorks Global Ltd.

Thank you to all the fantastic people I've worked with throughout my career in video games. In particular my early business partner, John Foster, who taught me a great deal about people and business. Also, a big thanks to AVL and MB – both good friends and great business partners. Thank you to my mom and, lastly, a big shout out to Malcolm & Roxy – just keep doing what you do!

–Alex Josef

This book is dedicated to my wife, Christina, and son, Theo. Thank you for always smiling and helping me get through long work days. A big thanks to all those that I've worked with in the industry and taught me what I know today.

–Alex Van Lepp

I'd like to thank James Deighan. I learned a great deal about business from working with you, and I am grateful for that. I'd also like to thank my team members – Kayla, Jason, Christian, Ronald, Christine, and Ian – for making our work possible.

–Marshal D. Carper

Special Thanks

This book is possible because we have been fortunate to collaborate with a wide range of people in the games industry. We are particularly grateful for any forum or publication that has pushed to make business knowledge and opportunities more accessible for indies, which includes great organizations like the Game Developers Conference (GDC), Gamasutra, GamesIndustry.biz, GameDiscoverCo, and Indie MEGABOOTH.

TABLE OF CONTENTS

About the Authors xvii

Introduction xix

PART 1 How the Indie Video Game Industry Works

1 Developers and How They Fit into the Games Industry Ecosystem 5

The Broad Definition of "Indie" Developers 7

The Money People: Investors and Publishers 9

How Investors Work 10

How Publishers Work 12

Self-Publishing and Crowdfunding 13

How Money People Keep Making Money 14

2 The Power of Platforms and Stakeholders 15

Primary Platforms 15

Miscellaneous Secondary Platforms 17

Orbiting Stakeholders 18

The Indie Mindset for Platforms and Stakeholders 19

3 The Art of Video Game Revenue 21

Game Sales 23

Minimum Guarantees 24

Subscriptions: Games as a Service 26

Physical Releases 27

Soundtracks 29

Merchandising 31

Licensing Deals 33

Bundle Sales 34

Secondary Platform Sales 35

Revenue Recap 36

4 The Secret Economy of Steam Wishlists 37

Wishlists as a Crystal Ball for Future Sales 37

Wishlists as Currency 39

Wishlists and the Steam Algorithm 40

Are Steam Follows the Next Critical Metric? 41

Revenue, Wishlists, and Beyond 42

PART 2   Pre-Development Choices

5 Project Types and Project Goals 47

Pre-Development Overview 47

How to Use This Section for True Pre-Development 48

How to Use This Section for Retroactive Pre-Development 49

Project Types and Project Goals 50

Hobby Game Projects 51

Self-Published Projects 53

Traditional Publishing 56

Crowdfunded Projects 60

A "Living" Document...63

6   Genre and Market Evaluation 65

Predicting Sales Success.. 66

    The Ins and Outs of Sales Data... 68

    Trends and Traps...71

Stepping Back for the Big Picture 73

7   Scope and Engine Choices 75

Assessing Scope by Genre...76

Assessing Scope by Assets and Length 77

    Scope Exercise 1: Reverse Engineer an Existing
Game..78

    Scope Exercise 2: Prototype 79

    Scope Exercise 3: Ask Another Developer............................79

    Scope Exercise 4: Learn from Your Old Projects................. 80

Translation and Localization 80

Assessing Additional Development Needs 83

The Business Perspective on Engine Selection............................85

    Engines You Should Know 86

        Construct 3.. 86

        GameMaker Studio 86

        Godot.. 86

        Unity...87

        Unreal...87

        CryEngine 87

        Open 3D Engine (Formerly Amazon's Lumberyard).................87

        Other Game Engines 88

    Publisher Preference 88

Genre Trends...89

Licensing Fees and Other Terms of Use 90

Platform Incentives.. 90

Final Words of Caution...92

8 Timelines, Budgets, and Project Management 93

Mapping Scope to Time Estimates.. 94

Picking a Release Window 95

Avoid Q4 and Major Holidays 95

Be Aware of Other Game Releases................................... 96

Release in the "Slow" Season 96

Consider the Good and the Bad of Tradeshow
Launches 96

Launch One Month Later Than You Think. 97

Weigh Potential Exceptions to Our Advice 97

Assess the Timeline Gap or Overage 97

Budget Best Practices...97

Important Budget Terms and Concepts 99

Projected Costs vs. Actual Costs..................................... 99

Burn Rate 99

The Long Tail.. 100

Start with a Budget Template.. 102

Building and Managing a Team... 102

Types of Team Member Relationships............................... 103

Be Cautious with Agreements and Equity 104

Recruiting and Hiring.. 105

People and Project Management 107

Backups.. 107

Version Control 107

Organization and Communication 108

Ongoing Course Corrections.. 108

PART 3   Pitches and Publishing Deals

9   Pitch Deck Perfection 113

Pitch Deck Basics...114

Deck Content: Product Details..117

    Game Concept...118

    Launch Timing 119

    Game Length and Game Price.................................119

    Platforms 120

    Engine..121

Deck Content: Marketing Assets 121

    Game Trailers 122

    Screenshots and GIFs 123

    Other Key Art 124

Deck Content: Roadmap to Launch 125

    Market Analysis.. 125

    The Ask and Budget Breakdown 126

Deck Content: Team Information...................................... 128

Deck Content: Demo and GDD 129

How to Present Your Pitch 130

    Account for Time Constraints 131

    Rehearse Your Pitch..131

    Prepare Your Own Questions..................................131

Pitch Delivery 132

When a Pitch Fails 133

10   How to Negotiate with a Publisher..... 137

Negotiation Overview... 138

Key Background Insights.. 139

Basic Indie Publisher Deal Structure 140

    Milestone Schedule...141

    Recoup 141

Advances 143

Revenue Share 143

Intellectual Property Terms 144

The Negotiation Process 146

Revisiting Your Pitch Deck 146

Pitch Context and Rapport 147

Meeting Context 148

General Sales Tips 149

The Stages of a Publishing Deal 151

Discovery Call 151

General Preparation 151

Preparing for Specific Publishers 152

Preparing to Answer Questions 153

Budget and Timeline Questions 154

Engine Selection and Market Fit 155

Asking Your Own Questions 156

Publisher Review 158

Receiving an Offer or an LOI 159

If the Offer Matches the Ask 159

If the Offer Does Not Match Your Ask 160

How to Counter 162

Shopping Offers and Walking Away 164

Approaching a Publisher Who Has Not Made an Offer 164

Approaching a Publisher Who Has Made You an Offer 165

Walking Away 165

Letter of Intent 166

Working With an Attorney 168

Proven Industry Experience 168

Fair and Clear Rates 169

Responsive and Available 169

Relevant Regional Credentials 169

Managing the Client–Attorney Relationship 170

Taking Changes to the Publisher 170

Advocating for Yourself 171

Juggling Business Development with Game Development 172

PART 4   The Road to Release

11   Quality Assurance............................. 177

The Business Implications of QA 179

Managing QA for Indie Games.. 180

Sourcing Game Testers 182

Gathering Feedback 184

Implementing QA Feedback.. 186

    Recognize Your Own Biases and Limitations 187

    Revisit Your Comparable Title Research 187

    Seek to Understand the Root Issue 188

    Run Tests 188

QA as a Skill 189

12   Translation, Localization, and Porting ... 191

Best Practices for Preparation 191

    Get the Tools You Need 192

    Routinely Assess Your Workflows... 192

    Flag Potential Obstacles 192

    Test It Out... 193

    Plan for the Unexpected 193

When to Change Your Plans... 193

Opening New Porting Opportunities.. 194

    Being Open to the Outlandish 195

    Wishlist Momentum 196

        Establish Relationships 196

        Talk to Your Network 196

        Ask Your Platform Representative for Help.................... 197

Follow up a Splash with Another Splash..197

Think Bigger than Minimum Guarantees..197

Launch Day Is Not Always Ideal 198

13   Marketing from Zero 199

Hello, World! Hello, Twitter!..200

Key Assets: How to Create Memorable Marketing..201

On-Property Digital Marketing: Attract and Retain Interested Players............203

Off-Property Digital Marketing: Injecting Your Game Into Player Communities 205

Gaming Events: Entering the Epicenter of the Industry..207

Press Engagement: Earning Media Coverage..212

Pre-Release Accolades: Building a Body of Social Proof..216

Other Marketing Channels 218

Paid Advertising..218

Influencer Marketing..219

Curators and Key Distributors..221

Giveaways..222

Charity Activations..223

Example Calendars and Schedules 224

Example Launch Calendar..224

Example Social Media Calendar..225

Budget and Measurement..226

Example Marketing Budget Breakdown 226

Crash-Course in Marketing Metrics..228

An Extension of Your Game 231

PART 5   Post-Release

14   What about Second Launch?.............. 237

Discounts and Bundles 238

A Launch Discount Is Probably a Good Idea 238

Gradually Increase Discounts over Time.................................239

Steam Sales Are Not the Only Sales....................................239

Account for Sales Fatigue...239

Be Strategic with Bundle Promotions..................................240

Charity Activations 240

Secondary Platforms...241

Unlocking Additional Revenue Channels 241

The Size of Your Customer Pool..242

Player Demand..243

Assess Your Level of Access to Players.............................243

Listen to Your Players...243

Start with Small Tests...243

Find a Partner...244

Deciding Scope...244

Understand the New Business 244

Open for New Opportunities..245

15   The Next Game 247

Stay Lean. Stay Scrappy. 247

Get a Headstart..248

The Merits and Pitfalls of a Sequel.......................................248

Reconsider 248

It's Dangerous to Go Alone 249

We Want That to Change...250

References 251

Index...259

ABOUT THE AUTHORS

Alex Josef and Alex Van Lepp

Collectively, Alex Josef and Alex Van Lepp bring more than 40 years of industry experience to their work as video game educators. As the founders of VIM Global, a video game PR agency, they have worked with clients ranging from solo indie developers, notable indie publishers, and AAA studios to bring their games to market.

Some of those games include:

- *Super Mario Galaxy 2*
- *Guacamelee! And Guacamelee! 2*
- *Super Mega Baseball 1, 2, and 3*
- *Surgeon Simulator 2*
- *Portal: Bridge Constructor*
- *The Flame in the Flood*
- *The Saints Row Series*
- *Darksiders II*
- *Human Fall Flat*
- *Runbow*
- *Metal Gear Solid Series (select titles)*
- *Diablo II*
- *Silent Hill*

As the founders of Graffiti Games, they have published more than a dozen indie games, which means that they manage the careful balance of serving our investors, coaching indie developers through the development and release of their games, and then interface directly with major gaming platforms like Steam, Nintendo, GOG, Epic, and Stadia to negotiate deals and placement.

Some of the releases from Graffiti include:

- *Turnip Boy Commits Tax Evasion*
- *Blue Fire*

- *Cyber Hook*
- *The King's Bird*
- *Mable and the Wood*
- *Joggernauts*
- *Double Cross*
- *Trident's Wake*
- *REZ PLZ*
- *Adventures of Chris*
- *Bite the Bullet*

Marshal D. Carper

Marshal's first step into the creative world was at 19: He wrote for the Nintendo DS RPG, *The Black Sigil*. Today he is a career marketer and the author of more than 15 books. With his work spanning journalism, video games, combat sports, and a variety of client industries, he brings a nuanced perspective formed over years of working with innovative creators at the top of their fields. From launching indie games to helping a nonprofit like No Kid Hungry collaborate with Wizards of the Coast and GIANTS Software, his work has touched many corners of the games industry.

Either as the founder of the marketing agency Carper Creative or in the trenches as part of a development team, a few notable clients include:

- Zen Studios
- Mega Cat Studios
- Graffiti Games
- Playtra Studios
- Studio Archcraft
- Synersteel Studios
- No Kid Hungry
- Project Pinball
- hedgehog lab

INTRODUCTION
Indie Games Feel Different

As the escalator whisks you down to the showfloor, you look out over PAX East. Giant booths from AAA developers are in the immediate front, their scale that of small fiefdoms, towering over the throngs of gamers weaving between them. Their blockbuster booths are game worlds brought to life by staggering creativity with an event budget to match.

The convention hall pulses with electric excitement as you push past long lines and through dense crowds. Coming out the other side is like being spit out of a wave.

In this part of the convention hall, the energy changes. The booths here fit only a few people, and many of them are not more elaborate than a few Kinkos banners and PCs on folding tables. Players are still beaming with enthusiasm for the controllers in their hands, but no one is looking up at a stage. Every player and every developer are at eye-level, and they're talking the way your friends do at a basement LAN party. At a glance, you can't tell who are the developers and who are the players.

They all just feel friends you didn't know you had, hanging out because you love games of all kinds. From the massive open world AAA titles to the 45-minute platformer produced entirely by one person, you just love great gameplay, and so do they. Dozens of iconic indie games started in booths just like these at an event like PAX. You have the chance to discover the next indie sleeper hit.

We love indie games. And getting to be even a small part of the industry that makes these games possible is incredibly rewarding.

The three of us have industry experiences that encompass the publishing, marketing, public relations, and development of indie games, and we each observed a trend: For all of the openness and collaborative spirit that drives indie development, few shared the business side of games. The community was happy to talk about how to make a game, but guidance on how to get published and how to launch a financially successful game was not a common topic nor was this knowledge readily available in any centralized format.

Instead, many aspiring indies jump in headfirst not anticipating the rocks beneath the surface. These are often amazingly creative developers with great game ideas, but the business of indie games is a total unknown to them. It's not their fault. They simply had no way to learn about the steps of launching an indie game before making the attempt. As a result, many indie projects fail because of business mistakes they did not know to avoid.

We hope to change that.

Everything in this book draws from our in-the-trenches professional experience as well as the insights we've gleaned from working directly with major industry stakeholders. We consolidated our knowledge on the business of indie video games to capture all of the lessons we learned through trial and error and through successes and failures.

We want you to have the tools to skip over common obstacles so that you do not have to improvise your own path through the rocks like so many developers before you.

How to Use This Book

Though this book is designed for beginner and experienced indie game developers alike, we organized the material as though we were giving an indie developer a crash course on the industry prior to their beginning development. They haven't spent any money. They haven't started development. They have an idea, and they want it to be the first of many ideas to come to life and go to market.

If you are already developing your game, the material we cover here can help you to prioritize your production plan and give you insights into what problems to solve first and what problems you might save for later.

Regardless of where you are in your process, we recommend exploring the lessons in the order they're laid out so that you can see how each piece fits together and how the various components of your business plan support one another. Of course, you're welcome to skip to the sections you feel are most relevant to you and your game, but we don't want you to miss any valuable information or tips and tricks.

Here is the overview of the journey you are about to take.

Part 1: How the Indie Video Game Industry Works

- Developers and How They Fit into the Games Industry Ecosystem
- The Power of Platforms and Stakeholders
- The Art of Video Game Revenue
- The Secret Economy of Steam Wishlists

Part 2: Pre-Development Choices

- Project Types and Project Goals
- Genre and Market Evaluation

- Scope and Engine Choices
- Timelines, Budgets, and Project Management

Part 3: Pitches and Publishing Deals

- Pitch Deck Perfection
- How to Negotiate with a Publisher

Part 4: The Road to Release

- Quality Assurance
- Translation, Localization, and Porting
- Marketing from Zero

Part 5: Post-Release

- What about Second Launch?
- The Next Game

This is your manual for the business of indie games. Use each chapter as a framework for mapping your business, working backward from clear creative and revenue goals to create an effective plan for this game and the ones that follow. At various points, we suggest that you revisit previous plans, notes, and research to either update your plan or to lay the foundation for the next stage of the business process.

Even when you have finished reading this book, you should review your business and production plans regularly. When you are nose-to-nose with making a game, you cannot see the angle of your trajectory. You have to step back from the tasks immediately ahead of you and evaluate the bigger picture, seeing how the pieces of your development and your business intersect. Every choice and dollar within your business is like a gust of wind to a sailboat.

With your hands on the rutter and an eye on the compass, you can use that wind to move closer and closer to your destination. Left unattended, though, your ship will drift.

That means you are never truly done with the material you are about to learn. It will be relevant for every day you are in business, so come back to it often and never stop learning how to be a more effective developer, business owner, and team leader.

PART 1

How the Indie Video Game Industry Works

DOI: 10.1201/9781003215264-1

Supergiant Games and Bastion

Meeting an Industry Insider
Tired of Playing Bad Games

Supergiant Games was founded in 2009 by Amir Rao and Gavin Simon, and started in Rao's father's house. In the beginning, there were only seven people working on *Bastion*. They started with the idea of creating an action-RPG where you could also build the world yourself. The concept evolved into a core part of the game, with the world building around you as you venture through each level.

Bastion is a celebrated indie game, and for good reason. The art and story are memorable, the action feels tight and engaging, and the stylistic choice of creatively incorporating a narrator wowed players and critics.

The game is great, but Supergiant also made some key business decisions early in their studio's history. One of the biggest is that they put themselves in a position to make a critical industry connection.

When the original team at Supergiant got deep enough into development, they knew *Bastion* was a game that they loved, but they didn't know if other people would also love it, so they decided to take it to PAX to get player reactions and to meet publishers.

At PAX, Supergiant met Michael Leon, who was the Director, Business Development & Developer Relations of Warner Brothers Games at the time.

After playing *Bastion*, he took Rao aside and said, "You have no idea how much shit I play and how little of it I like."

Rao hoped that meant that Leon enjoyed the game, and it turned out he did. A lot.

Back then, you couldn't get your game onto the Xbox Live Arcade unless you had a publisher, so the chance meeting with Leon played an important role in opening a door for *Supergiant*. With the support of Leon and Warner Brothers Games, Supergiant was able to release *Bastion* on the Xbox Live Arcade. Warner Brothers also provided marketing support, bringing awareness to *Bastion's* release by showcasing the game at events like E3.

When *Bastion* officially launched on July 20, 2011, it did well enough that they were able to leave Rao's father's house and move into their own studio space in San

Francisco. A decade later, *Bastion* is still an indie legend, and Supergiant has gone on to produce several more highly praised indie games, with the latest being *Hades*.

If Supergiant had not gone to PAX with *Bastion*, they may never have made the connection that ultimately gave their game a well-supported indie launch.

Noclip. (2019, December 23). The Making of Bastion - Documentary. YouTube. https://www.youtube.com/watch?v=uo7TcJ2E0-I.

J. Michael Leon's LinkedIn. LinkedIn. (n.d.). https://www.linkedin.com/in/j-michael-leon-4388731/.

Developers and How They Fit into the Games Industry Ecosystem

Part of the magic of indie games is that players can feel very close to the developers. Indies are often solo creators or working in close-knit teams, so that demo they played at an event with a developer eagerly watching their every button press could become the next hit indie game.

And they got to meet the developer. Maybe the developer replied to them on Twitter. Maybe they answered emails with thoughtful replies.

The community element of indie games is powerful, and it's one of the reasons we love this side of gaming, but the power of that magic can also be misleading. That sense of proximity to other indie developers and players can give aspiring developers the impression that the path between a new game and a new player is short and direct.

Make a great game. Show it to players. Then enjoy the wild success of being an indie developer celebrity.

But that's not really how it works for most projects. When you release a game, you are engaging an ecosystem. Players are a foundational part of that ecosystem, naturally, but if you want to give your game the best chance possible of finding financial success, you also need to account for a myriad of factors; publishers, investors, platforms, journalists, content creators, and so on. All roads eventually lead to players, but launching your game with a full understanding of the industry can open more doors for your game.

Sometimes those doors lead to funding. Sometimes they lead to platform exclusivity and support. Sometimes they lead to a devoted fan community who will love your game.

The precise way you leverage the ecosystem around indie games will be unique to you and your project, and you may ultimately decide that some parts are more important to you than others, but you still need to understand the pieces and how they fit to make smart decisions for your project.

We drew a picture to help.

DOI: 10.1201/9781003215264-2

Overview: The Indie Ecosystem

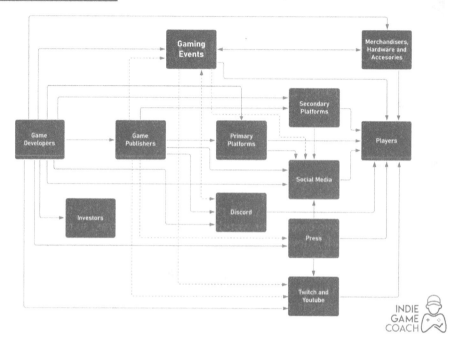

We dig into each component in more depth later in this section, but here they are at a high level:

- Developers – Individuals or teams who make the games themselves
- Investors – Provide funding for a project, but typically do not take an active role in the development or release of a game
- Publishers – Help developers bring their games to market, usually through a combination of funding, developer support, and marketing
- Platforms – Storefronts and consoles where players access and/or buy games
- Press – Publications and journalists who review, promote, and break news about games
- Events – Major gatherings for players and industry leaders
- Streaming Services – Content platforms such as Twitch and YouTube, where content creators broadcast gameplay and commentary
- Content Creators – Streamers, YouTubers, and social media influencers who create independent content about games
- Merchandisers – Brands who make gaming-related products and may license a game IP

- Outside Brands – Non-gaming companies or organizations who have an interest in gaming

If you look hard enough, you can find nuances that our summary illustration doesn't capture, but this overall structure of the industry should help you to see that the games industry is far more complicated than developers connecting with players. Ignoring that complexity is one of the first big mistakes indie developers can make. Again, you may decide that certain elements are not a fit for your project, and that's okay, but you should have as much information as possible when you make those kinds of choices.

For most indie developers, understanding this ecosystem makes it easier to pitch to investors, to secure deals with publishers and platforms, and to see the many paths indies might take to get their games into the hands of more players. The first step in that process is to better understand how you (and possibly your team) fit into this puzzle.

The Broad Definition of "Indie" Developers

When most people think of indie developers, they picture Phil Fish anxiously watching players stumble through a demo of *Fez*, a scene from the popular documentary *Indie Game: The Movie*. One developer with a singular vision for what their game can be, pouring their heart and soul into bringing it to life – that's the classic indie game persona.

Springing from this persona is an expectation for indie games to perhaps be more stylized, to take more creative risks, and to explore ideas that large game developers might avoid.

This is largely true of indie games, but in practice, many companies are "independent" but do not fit into this stereotype of indie developers. Technically – and even this definition is debatable – an indie studio is any entity not attached to a large publishing entity. Indie developers are probably working with tighter budgets or even trying to juggle every aspect that goes into releasing a game themselves.

Just like the definition of an indie studio, the exact definition of a AAA (or triple-A) studio is debatable as well, but most industry experts agree that AAA video games are akin to blockbuster Hollywood films: large production budgets, massive teams, long timelines, big partners. In the case of games, AAA developers often function as their own publishers as well, instead of needing to seek outside support or funding.

We are hedging a bit here because official definitions in this space are murky, at best, but understanding that the indie game industry is more than solo developers or really small teams is important for finding your own success. Here's why:

- Industry stakeholders are approximately familiar with how much scope varying team sizes can reasonably accomplish in a set window of time
- The size of your team is a first glimpse into what a potential development budget might be for your game, or what might be needed to help support your release

- The structure or nature of a team could have an impact on a game's development process as well at its potential reception at launch

If you misunderstand the expectations the industry has for a team of your size, you can easily talk your way into a corner. You might have a good reason for being the exception, but you will still need to address the expectation.

For example, *Hades* from Supergiant is an incredible indie game, but the makeup of Supergiant as a company and as a team is, today, very different from a small team or a solo developer.

They are still very much indie – let's be clear about that. However, if you, as a solo developer, pitch a publisher on a game similar in scope to *Hades*, that publisher will justifiably be skeptical and may outright doubt your credibility. Supergiant credits 64 people for the development of *Hades*, and that doesn't include the voice cast. Even accounting for the fact that some of those credits are independent contractors who were not present for the full development process of the game, that's many people working on a bevy of content that one person could not possibly accomplish in a reasonable timeframe.

Written out like that, the conclusion of how much one developer can reasonably do seems obvious, but this is a persistent problem for many indie developers who are planning, scoping, and pitching their projects. They don't understand their own capacity – where they fit in the ecosystem, how a game can generate revenue, and how to properly communicate to other stakeholders.

An indie studio might fit into one of the following size categories, which again may vary from person to person:

- Solo developers: 1 person who does the majority of the design, art, programming, and music
- Small teams: 2 to 5 people dividing tasks but still sharing many duties
- Mid-size teams: 6 to 25 people, each with clear specializations and duties
- Large teams: 26 or more people, each with more granular specializations

At any size, indie studios may also seek outside support for some or all of the following (where a AAA studio will do most of it in-house):

- Quality assurance (QA for short)
- Porting to additional game systems
- Translation and localization
- Distribution
- Marketing (Public relations and advertising)
- Production management

From the outside, no one can say for sure how exactly resources were used internally on a project like *Hades*, but savvy members of the video game industry can do the "envelope math" to approximate what a budget might look like, using industry best practices and their own business experience as a guide. You can do something similar as a developer planning your own project, which we will talk about in a later chapter, but for now, you should be raising your own red flags if the size of your team is radically different, in either direction, from a comparable title.

You should also start to see that even large, experienced indie teams often need outside resources. Sticking to our Supergiant example, a partnership with Warner Brothers was a major component of their early success with *Bastion*, helping them to unlock funding and access to a larger player base on the Xbox Live Arcade. Even today, when Supergiant is about as indie as indie developers can get, they still credit outside resources for facets of their development.

That doesn't make them less indie. It makes them smart developers and savvy business people.

Lastly, we should define contract or "work-for-hire" development studios. These are hired guns who work on games for clients and build according to the specifications of the client. Contract studios are incredibly common in the games industry at all levels. Though contract work does not fall into the typical bucket of indie game development as a subsection of the broader industry, many indie studios are hybrids, using contract work to maintain consistent revenue and capital while they also work on their own projects.

As an indie developer, you might pursue this path to keep the bills paid and your team fed while you work on your projects, or your publisher may recommend a contract studio to help fill a void in your development, such as console porting.

For many indie developers, regardless of their team size or internal capabilities, securing funding is a critical next step toward bringing their game to life. Better understanding your team will make that process easier as it makes your planning more concise and better equips you to connect with other leaders in the industry, such as investors and publishers.

The Money People: Investors and Publishers

Even if you plan to fully fund and self-publish your game, you can't completely escape needing to understand how investment or publishing works in games. If you self-publish, you take on the burden and responsibilities of an investor or publisher internally, so you still need to know what investors and publishers do and how they function if you want a successful launch.

Investors typically provide funding with little to no additional support or participation. They can either provide capital for an individual game or in the studio itself. In either case, investors give developers a set amount of capital in exchange for a stake in the returns. For most indies, investors will likely fund an individual project.

In some cases, an engaged investor may take a more active role in the process, helping to connect a developer with additional resources or opportunities to increase the likelihood of the game being a success, but generally, investors write a check and step out of the way to let the developers do the work.

Publishers, on the other hand, often collaborate shoulder-to-shoulder with developers to help bring the game to life. They aren't directly developing the game, but they are in frequent communication with developers to ensure that milestones are reached and to support the project with expertise as well as resources. Beyond funding development, a publisher may also coordinate QA and localization, bring in additional staff to aid development, and provide ongoing feedback on the project as it develops.

How this looks in practice will vary from publisher to publisher, but you can expect a publisher to be a much more active and vocal participant in the development of your game than an investor.

As to which is ideal, well, that's a big question full of wrinkles, considerations, and preferences. We will explore this side of investing and publishing in more depth in later chapters when we discuss deal terms and negotiations, but for now, let's focus on the function of these different stakeholders over what may or may not be right for your game.

How Investors Work

As we said, investors are typically not engaged participants in the development process itself, but if you better understand the typical motivations and background of an investor, you will be better equipped to pitch them your game and to get the most out of a potential investor relationship.

People who invest in video games are similar to that of any person investing in a creative project: They likely have a passion for the industry but probably do not have the skillset or the motivation to create their own games. These folks could just as easily invest in any number of less risky businesses or ventures, so some love for gaming usually attracts them to participate in the space.

If you explore this path for funding, these are the types of investors you may encounter:

- Private investor – an individual who does not invest in games professionally but may fund projects from time to time
- Professional investor – an individual who invests in games as a career
- Investment scout – similar to an agent, these professionals fill a business development and advisor role, making recommendations to investors (usually attached to a firm or fund)
- Investment firm or fund – a collection of investors who pool their investments to maximize their returns; often, this is the type of investor that takes a more active role in development

An investment itself can come with a variety of terms, but generally investors make two types of investments in gaming:

1. Project funding – investing in specific titles under a studio's umbrella for a share of revenue while not taking an ownership stake in the studio: for example, investing in *Risk of Rain 2* as a product rather than Hopoo Games, the team that made the game

2. Company funding – investing in the studio itself for a share of ownership and, therefore, a potential share of all future game profits: for example, an investor in Epic Games stands to gain from every facet of the company's success and not just a singular product in its offerings

The most common investment type in video games is project funding. Investors bet on individual titles rather than studios. A hit-based industry like games lends itself to specific games or IPs that end up driving the bulk of the success for a company, and it can also feel less risky to both sides. Tethering your money to a single game likely takes less of an investment than funding the whole of a company and spares the investor the complexity of being wedded to the overall business indefinitely.

No two investors will behave exactly the same way in terms of the dynamics of the relationship. Whether you work with an individual or a fund, you can expect investors to participate in the game process in at least one of the following capacities:

• Require a periodic report on the progress of game development, delivered monthly or quarterly

• Negotiate terms around revenue sharing when the game releases

• Request follow-on rights, such as having the option to invest in a sequel or taking a stake in potential licenses of the IP (more on what licenses are later)

• Incorporate recoup into the relationship, which means that some or all of the investor's money is "paid back" before profits are shared between the developer and the investor

• Provide varying levels of support – from none at all to a great deal – for the project itself, such as inviting other investors or providing key industry connections

Expect the scope of investment to vary wildly as well. Investment preferences are just as broad and varied as the industry itself, so you are likely to encounter investors who prefer investing at particular stages of development over others or have specific criteria about the monetization model of the game and other strategic elements. These details are often covered in the series of conversations that lead up to an official relationship. Those details matter, but we have incorporated into the later section on deals and negotiations so that we can spend more time unraveling the nuances and the pros and cons of different relationships.

How Publishers Work

Publishers are technically investors as well, but they typically take a far more active role in developing and releasing a game. Many indie developers prefer working with publishers over investors because they recognize that they need more resources or expertise than they have alone or within their team. Sometimes that's marketing. Sometimes it's console porting. Other times it's store support and distribution to international audiences. In all cases, the developer benefits from the additional resources and access a publisher brings to the table.

No two publishing deals will be alike, but publisher relationships generally fall into one of the following categories:

- Full-scope publishers: They bring funding and all the resources needed to support a project
- Royalty-only publishers: They provide some level of development or launch support but do not fund the game's development
- Porting publishers: They specialize in bringing PC games to consoles and typically provide technical resources for completing ports in exchange for a revenue share of game sales on those consoles
- Regional publishers: Some publishers specialize in bringing games into specific markets, more commonly seen in larger titles and with certain territories such as Asia

Publisher-to-project fit is critical, so we devote a good many pages to it in our later discussion about deal structures, but for now, know that some types of publishing are more ideal for certain circumstances than others. Funding is typically the preference for indie developers, but the size of your game or the nature of the genre could make the right-royalty-only publisher the best fit for your project.

All of the facets an investor may require of a relationship apply for publishers as well, but in this case, the publisher is usually also committing to some level of performance in terms of what resources they contribute. The exact capacity varies, but usually publishing deals include a mix of the following:

- Marketing support
- Press engagement and public relations
- Event marketing support
- Quality assurance
- Translation and localization
- Console porting
- Ongoing promotional and platform management
- Occasionally additional development resources, including talent acquisitions

Classically, a publisher is a developer's bridge to successfully bringing the game to market by leveraging a myriad of industry connections. A publisher who specializes in Switch porting, for example, likely has fostered a relationship with Nintendo and may be more likely to successfully negotiate an exclusive promotional window or a minimum guarantee of sales (more on what that means in a few pages). The professional track record a publisher develops can be an incredibly powerful tool for a newer indie developer. They can open doors that a new indie can't, and they can anticipate (and solve) potential problems well before they become disastrous.

Your challenge as an indie developer will be to determine what kind of publisher relationship is ideal for your game so that you can target the right partners for your pitch. The actual business agreement between you and a publisher is loaded with nuances as well – development milestones, intellectual property rights, revenue sharing, payment schedules, platform commitments, resource allocation, sequel rights, and on and on. Part 3 will give you a deep dive into deal structure, but for now, your takeaway should be that publishers can take several approaches to making games in their portfolio (like yours) profitable.

Self-Publishing and Crowdfunding

When digital distribution for video games gained market traction, doors opened for indie game developers around the world. Where publishers and platforms used to be the gatekeepers, indies could now release their games under their own terms, setting the stage for a Renaissance of game types and styles that may not have fit into the old business model for video games.

Self-publishing is about as independent as you can get in the industry, but just because it's easier than ever does not mean that it's the right path for your game. It could be, but don't allow the simplicity of uploading a game to Itch.io or Steam cloud your judgment.

We often see indies underestimate the difficulty of releasing a game because they misunderstand how much a publisher can actually contribute to the success of a title. If you choose to self-publish, you should be prepared to fulfill all of the functions of a publisher yourself or within your team. Refer to the list of publisher functions we outlined in the previous section, and assess your ability to execute those responsibilities. If you find that you are missing even one of those skills or resources, you should have a plan for filling that void before you bring your game to market.

And that thinking should apply to crowdfunding as well.

Like uploading a game to Steam, setting up a Kickstarter or an Indiegogo campaign is relatively straightforward, which sometimes gives developers the illusion that "if they build it, they will come." That's simply not how it works for the majority of indies.

Successful crowdfunding campaigns can take as much planning, effort, and resources as a full game launch, and then you're still on the hook for making and releasing the game afterward.

Self-publishing and crowdfunding are both book-worthy topics in their own rights, but the goal of this book is to teach you to be a successful indie developer, not to teach you how to be a publisher. We'll cover a myriad of information by necessity, but if you choose to self-publish or crowdfund, you should devote more time to learning the intricacies of those particular corners of the industry.

Kickstarter, for example, is incredibly active at gaming conventions, giving talks and sharing resources on how best to use their platform to fund and promote your game. Digging into those talks and exploring successful, as well as unsuccessful, crowdfunding campaigns will help you to better decide if crowdfunding is the right path for you or if you should focus your efforts on pursuing a publisher.

Pivoting is always possible, but we encourage you to make these considerations early in your planning process so that you can match your development schedule to your launch path.

How Money People Keep Making Money

As our original diagram highlighted, the games industry is a network of stakeholders all depending on each other to varying degrees for finding success. Developers need the resources and funding publishers provide. Publishers need the content and ideas that developers provide. And for that relationship to result in financial success, the result of what developers and publishers build together needs to also serve the goals of other industry stakeholders.

The ripple of a successful game release will eventually touch the whole of the games industry, but the next immediate link in this chain is platforms, the services, and storefronts that directly interface with players. Like investors and publishers, platforms have certain mechanisms for generating revenue, and they are motivated to work with developers and publishers who are the most effective at pushing players to purchase their products.

The Power of Platforms and Stakeholders

Distribution platforms play a major role in the success of a game for a myriad of reasons. Their business development and marketing teams can influence your game's visibility in a storefront. Their algorithms can influence where and how often your game appears in searches or customer recommendations. Differences in consumer preferences from platform to platform can make one platform a better target for your title than others.

In some cases, platforms can also serve as publishers, providing funding and support for select projects.

Primary Platforms

Understanding the differences between major platforms will help you to target the right publishers to reach the right players and can also guide your development process. A Nintendo Switch audience, for example, is generally different from a PlayStation one. If you recognize that your title is a better fit for the Switch, you can structure your development with Switch porting in mind, and you can use your marketing to target Nintendo communities early on. Those decisions could, in turn, help you attract a Nintendo-savvy publisher and increase your chances of getting amplification via the Nintendo marketing team.

Here are the major platforms that might be relevant for your game:

- Steam
- Nintendo (eShop)
- PlayStation
- Xbox (Microsoft Store)
- GOG
- Epic Games Store
- Itch.io

DOI: 10.1201/9781003215264-3

And then there are dozens of tertiary platforms that can also be relevant, especially as you leverage your title later in its lifecycle for bundle sales or special promotions, but these are the core platforms that tend to matter the most for indies.

Like publishers and investors, platforms look for high-traction titles to earn more from their revenue share – the fee associated with each sale in their store. For every platform except Steam and Itch.io, the strategy for maximizing profits takes the form of a curated selection process. Not every game can be released on PlayStation, and the games that are released are filtered through assessment teams tasked with making sure the right content lands on the platform. After that, each game has to pass a battery of technical tests (called console certification) to confirm the game runs well on the hardware and uses the right visuals (displaying PlayStation buttons to PlayStation players in a tutorial rather than buttons from another console, for example).

Different platforms will look for different kinds of games.

Those exact preferences are ever-evolving because our industry is in a state of constant change, and platforms are adjusting rapidly as well, but speaking generally, platform preferences tend to look like the following:

- Steam – Nearly all games end up on Steam eventually, and releasing on Steam is accessible for most indies. The Steam algorithm automates much of the discoverability on the platform, but taking part in Steam events or festivals that have a Steam component can give your game extra visibility.

- Nintendo (eShop) – Beyond meeting the requirements of the hardware, Nintendo audiences tend to favor colorful games, pixel art, platformers, and titles with mechanics that have deep retro roots. First-person shooter (FPS) and real-time strategy (RTS) games or games with darker themes are less likely to find success on the eShop.

- PlayStation – PlayStation has developed a reputation for big cinematic experiences and fast-paced, high-fidelity shooters. Indies have still found success here, of course, but a PlayStation release is rarely the first stop for an indie developer.

- Xbox (Microsoft Store) – As a platform, Xbox has a long history of helping indie games find success, so while some of the player preferences for FPS titles like *Halo* and *Call of Duty* apply here, Xbox players and Xbox executives seem much more open to indie experiences as well.

- GOG – Originally a second chance for aging PC titles, GOG has become an indie-friendly platform with a heavy emphasis on curation. For indies, GOG is an especially good home for rich, story-driven games and for highly detailed, strategy-heavy games (likely a carry-over from the depth of retro PC RPGs that first made GOG popular).

- Epic Games Store – Aiming to be a Steam competitor, titles on the Epic Games Store are diverse and serve several types of player preferences. Currently, they seem most interested in using exclusives to bring users to the platform, so games with large communities or developers with significant track records of success could find opportunities here.

- Itch.io – Even more accessible than Steam, Itch.io hosts a variety of content beyond games (such as development assets and tabletop resources). The community around Itch.io seems especially open to betas or experimental projects and for being less formal than Steam. You probably won't release exclusively on Itch.io, but it could be a part of your early marketing strategy and your later monetization strategy.

We need to say this again: All of this information could very easily have changed by the time you read this book. At the time of this writing, Microsoft has made aggressive moves to bolster their Game Pass service, acquiring companies like Zenimax (the parent company of Bethesda) in the process. A change in that service could create new opportunities for indies, or the response of a competitor like PlayStation could create opportunities as well. Do some extra research in addition to what we cover here to make sure you are thinking about the present of the platforms, not the past.

Miscellaneous Secondary Platforms

For Graffiti Games – and this is true of many publishers – releasing on secondary platforms is a core part of driving sales post-release. Once the fanfare of the launch has died down, Graffiti titles end up in game bundles and are periodically put on sale on a variety of storefronts, not just the major platforms we covered previously.

Humble Bundle is the major player here, and they are at times selective about what titles they include in their promotions, but the strategic opportunity of being in a Humble Bundle promotion applies to other platforms as well. It's another opportunity for your game to be purchased by players who may have missed the initial release.

The legwork it takes to upload to these platforms or to negotiate special promotions is typically a function of a publisher, but even if you work with a publisher, you should be aware of these opportunities so that you can advocate effectively for your game. If your publisher does not have a process for these late-cycle activations, you should request that they do it for your game. As part of the partnership, they should be taking these efforts off your shoulder. If you decide to self-publish, then know that all the legwork is yours and plan your post-launch roadmap accordingly.

For the way that we think about games, secondary platforms are a piece of a game's revenue cycle, so we will revisit the strategic implications of secondary platforms in the next chapter.

Orbiting Stakeholders

Large industries tend to spawn a variety of businesses that serve the same community, even if they don't directly produce the core offering.

The National Football League (NFL) in the United States makes football content. Their function is to create entertainment for fans to view and consume. Orbiting the NFL are a slew of other businesses, ranging from sports analysts to betting services to merchandisers. All of these businesses depend on the audience that the NFL attracts but have separate functions for the community and different ways of generating revenue.

In the games industry, those orbiting stakeholders may include the following:

- Gaming publications
- Independent games journalists
- Event organizers
- Streaming services (Twitch, YouTube, Facebook Gaming)
- Streamers and independent content creators
- Community management platforms (Discord, Reddit, Facebook Groups)
- Community organizers
- Charity organizations
- Merchandisers

With the widespread adoption of gaming, nearly every business could touch gaming at some point. The NFL is a quasi esports organization because of the *Madden* franchise, and a variety of professional sports teams have incorporated esports into their venue experiences or formed partnerships with esports teams.

That said, this is a core list that is most likely to be relevant to the typical indie game, and a comprehensive launch strategy will address each of these stakeholders directly. While these are independent businesses, think of them more as gatekeepers to communities or access points for additional revenue opportunities that might be a fit for your project.

In other words, successfully connecting with one of these opportunities could lead to more reach, more revenue, or both.

An example indie launch strategy for these stakeholders might look like this:

- A press blast to a targeted list of relevant journalists
- Direct relationship building with key journalists or thought leaders to garner more targeted coverage of your game
- Presence at gaming conventions such as PAX East or PAX West
- A Twitch integration in your game to attract the support of the Twitch Developer team

- Sponsored streamers and organic streamer outreach
- Building your own Discord community
- Engaging existing community leaders to rally interest for your title
- A post-launch charity activation to support a good cause and to generate a fresh round of press attention
- A merchandise partnership to generate additional revenue for your title and engage with your community

The exact plan for your game will vary, but we are again emphasizing that there is more to the launch of a game than finishing development and uploading it to Steam.

Returning to our Supergiant example, their team has done a masterful job of managing the symphony of variables that surround the release of a game. From early in their history, they have attended events, engaged press, worked tirelessly to build and manage a community, and have served that community with additional merchandise, including T-shirts and vinyl albums to extend the profitability of every title they release.

They make great games, yes, but they have also spent a great deal of time addressing the full scope of the indie game ecosystem.

Where a team like Supergiant manages much of these elements in-house, most indies look for support, especially when their teams are newer to the industry. Publishers can address many of these opportunities, but even if you are working with a publisher, we encourage indies to take an active role in this big-picture strategy development and in building these relationships with orbiting stakeholders.

Contributing your own energy to engaging the press or to building a community will enhance the impact of the publisher's efforts, and it will also give you more momentum for your next title as well.

The Indie Mindset for Platforms and Stakeholders

The best indie developers we have worked with over the years approach games with an integrated mentality. Where some developers separate game development from the rest of the business of gaming, such as what it might take to effectively engage a platform or to connect with stakeholders that might boost the reach of a game, the best indie developers see how the pieces of the industry connect.

While the temptation to lock yourself in a room and not leave until the game is finished can be strong, especially for a natural creator, the more consistently successful path means constantly touching and nurturing the other facets of the business. Yes, your game still has bugs that need fixing, but a big gaming event is around the corner and being there could mean a big boost in Steam Wishlists and more connections with industry insiders.

And as part of attending that event, you should probably send an update to the publishers and investors you have talked with previously. They might be there also, and that in-person connection could give you another shot at securing funding for your project.

For developers with this mentality, the business of games is just another component of development. In the same way that you devote specific time, resources, and talent to design, art, and music throughout the production of a game, so should indies devote time, resources, and talent to business development and business management.

That comprehensive mindset and thinking about the broader IP will bring more opportunities to your project and enable you to be proactive about unlocking the full revenue potential of your game, which is much more complex than selling your game to players.

The Art of
Video Game Revenue

Indies make money by selling games. Yes, this is true, but the Supergiant story we've been telling should already help you to see that the reality is much less simplistic than "make game; sell game." For the effort you invest and the risks you take as an indie developer, you should pursue as many opportunities for generating revenue from your work as possible. Not every potential option will be the right option, but you need to be aware of what *might* be viable in order to make educated decisions for your project. If you wait too long, you might also miss a potential option completely.

The real revenue potential for an indie game is unlocked with diversification. Being a fan of video games is so much more than just playing games, and all of those ways that fans participate in their passion can be potential profit drivers for your project. When you talk to a publisher or an experienced games investor, they are doing this analysis and math as you pitch, so you should do your own math well ahead of those pitches.

You have a cute, fuzzy protagonist? A plushie product might sell well in parallel with the game.

You hired a fantastic composer to score your game? A companion soundtrack and maybe even a vinyl release could be possible.

The style and design of your game lends itself to DLC? That increases the potential value of any new player because they might also buy your follow-up content.

Revenue opportunities should be a part of your planning process as early as the initial game design document (GDD), but we have sometimes been met with sour faces when we suggest that to indies. With so many indies believing deeply in the artistic power of games, mapping a revenue strategy to the design of a game can feel like handing your paint brush to your accountant. That's not what should be happening here, however. And that's not how you should be thinking about this side of game development.

Instead, think of revenue opportunities as a two-way street. In many instances, your creative vision will unlock other business opportunities for your game and

DOI: 10.1201/9781003215264-4

your team, and simply being aware that those opportunities exist makes them available to you. In other circumstances, the thought experiment of applying a potential revenue opportunity to your game could inspire new ideas.

If you didn't know that video game soundtracks can be highly successful as digital and physical releases, you might choose to use stock music rather than something original. You might still ultimately choose to go that route for a number of reasons, but if you are aware of this opportunity, you might spend more time talking to that chiptune artist you met at a convention and invite them to lend their talent to your project.

That music could then influence how your artist crafts a setting to set a certain mood or tone for a level, which could ripple into several other positive enhancements for your game.

And the first domino in that process is the simple question of *what if we wanted to sell a soundtrack with our game?*

This kind of open mindedness can lead to incredible moments. The raw creativity that indies bring to the table coupled with their inherent scrappiness can unlock some very cool opportunities, so don't let the stereotypes of the "bean counter" or the "sellout" hold you back from fully exploring your options.

Before we dive into individual revenue channels, let's look at the bigger picture of what the revenue lifecycle of a game might look like and the components that might be included:

The Indie Revenue Life Cycle

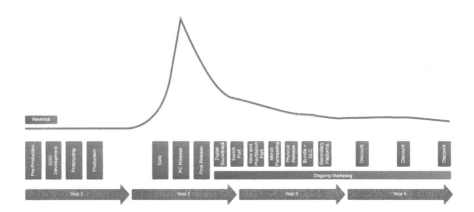

The elements and timing listed in our illustration are broadly applicable to all indie games, but as it is with anything we discuss in this book, think of these as guidelines rather than rules. Where we recommend pursuing one kind of revenue at a particular point in a game's life, you may have a perfectly viable reason for doing something completely different. Instead, our intention is to illuminate blindspots so that you don't look back on your game two years after its release and kick yourself for not thinking of something we cover here.

Let's break down each of these revenue channels.

Game Sales

The cornerstone of revenue in the games industry, indies can make money by selling their games to players. That's a groundbreaking insight; we know. Like everything we have discussed to this point, more happens beneath the surface of this transaction than might be immediately apparent.

When a player buys your game, the math for the actual profit may be influenced by the following:

• The percentage of the sale that goes to the platform
• The percentage of the sale that goes to the publisher or investor, if applicable
• The percentage of the sale that goes to the developer
• The percentage of the developer revenue that goes to taxes

The total revenue of a sale can also be influenced by discounts, promotions, and refund policies.

Technically, all of this revenue gets taxed, but you are responsible for the tax on your personal income as well as the income of your studio or team, depending on the legal structure you develop games under. We've heard and seen horror stories from creatives in a number of fields–from streamers to writers–who didn't consider taxes in their business planning, so even if that seems obvious to you, we want to make sure that everyone is aware.

With that out of the way.

The math is boring, but it tells a very specific story about your game and the business surrounding it.

Let's say you retail your game for $9.99. When it sells a copy on Steam, Valve takes 30%, which leaves $6.99.

If you have a 40/60 revenue split with your publisher, they will take 40% of that remaining profit, leaving $4.20. In the United States, the average tax rate is 22.4%, so after taxes the net profit is $3.26 per unit sold – and that doesn't account for potential discounts or promotional pricing.

This also may sound silly to you, but indie developers often overlook how big the difference between gross profit (the raw total of how much revenue you generated) and net profit (the total revenue remaining after accounting for expenses) when they set their budgets and make projections about their potential game sales.

If your development budget is $100,000, you could easily think that you need to sell 10,010 units at a $9.99 price point to breakeven. If you look at the reality of revenue sharing, however, your real recoup will come at 30,675 units sold. That's a significant difference in sales volume and that's assuming everyone is paying full price for the game. The reality is that in the current gaming landscape, a large number of consumers will only purchase an indie game when it's on sale, so that 30,000 figure will actually need to be more.

We will talk more about how to predict total sales of your game based on market data and metrics like Steam Wishlists later, but for now, you should start using this math as a two-way street for your decision-making.

If a moderately successful title in your chosen genre can expect to sell 30,000 units in its first year of release and your anticipated price point matches the pricing for games of a similar scale and polish, you are likely on a good path, provided your overall budget is roughly in line with those sales expectations. If you do this math and discover that you need to sell far more units than the average success in a genre, you should pause and think more deeply about the choices you're making.

When your budget is dramatically different from your projected return, there's a problem. You may need to reconsider the overall scope of the game. You may need to look for more budget-friendly resources. You may need to adjust your design to incorporate mechanics from a larger genre so that you can pull in more players. You may need to rethink your monetization strategy in its entirety.

The exact response will vary, of course, but this mental exercise is critical for your long-term sustainability. If your indie career plunges you deeply into debt, and your teammates quit because they need paying jobs and can no longer work for free, you are unlikely to make more than one game. You might not even finish your first.

Minimum Guarantees

Minimum guarantees (or MGs as they are commonly called in our industry) are largely unknown to new indie developers and to consumers, but the Epic vs. Apple court battle briefly shined a light on this common industry practice.

A minimum guarantee is a baseline commitment to a payment. No matter how many units you actually sell, the MG ensures that you get paid at least the amount specified in the agreement.

If you negotiate an exclusive pre-order period with GOG, for example, they might offer an MG of $10,000 for that privilege. Once your game makes them more than $10,000, you start to receive a share of the profit. The win for GOG in this purely hypothetical scenario is that they get a level of access to your content that's unique to the GOG platform, which can be a marketing advantage that helps them convince players to buy a title through GOG instead of through other stores or be a store with exclusive access to the game.

The win for the developer (and the stakeholders invested in the developer's success, such as a publisher) is twofold:

1. The revenue is guaranteed, often well-ahead of the games official release or shortly thereafter.
2. A partner that commits to a minimum guarantee is motivated to market and promote a game in order to make a return on their investment, extending the overall reach of the game.

MGs are incredibly common in the games industry in general, but many indies often lack the savvy or the access to negotiate minimum guarantees themselves. After all, if you don't know it's an option, you can't ask for it. Or, as is often the case, you simply don't know who or how much to ask for in the first place.

When court documents for the Epic vs. Apple became public, many gaming fans were shocked that minimum guarantees existed and were perplexed by how wildly they could vary.

For the Epic Games Store, minimum guarantees were offered under a "buyout" format, a one-time fee to offer a game for free during a set window of time, at which point Epic could conceivably distribute as many free copies as they wanted (though actual terms may have varied for specific games; we can't know for sure).

Axiom Verge, the surreal Metroidvania title from Thomas Happ Games, received an $80,000 minimum guarantee, while *Celeste*, the atmospheric platformer from Matt Makes Games, received a minimum guarantee of $750,000. On paper, *Celeste* might be the more popular game overall, but the actual performance of the titles on the Epic Games Store doesn't reflect the extreme difference in minimum guarantees.

Axiom Verge was downloaded a reported 1,292,299 times and facilitated 52,037 new Epic accounts, according to the documents.

Celeste, on the other hand, was downloaded a reported 2,705,525 times and facilitated 62,523 new Epic accounts.

For a little more than double the total units distributed, and roughly 20% more in new Epic accounts, the Epic Games Store paid Matt Makes Games 937.5% more than it paid Thomas Happ Games.

We weren't behind the scenes on these deals to say for sure – and as players, we are fans of both games – but we can reasonably deduce that *Celeste* had more bargaining power due to the success and reach of the game. Where *Axiom Verge* has 3,796 Steam reviews at the time of this writing, *Celeste* has 33,397. If you don't have your calculator handy, that's 879.8% more reviews for *Celeste*, which roughly aligns with the disparity in the minimum guarantee.

Epic could only make educated guesses as to how big of a draw a game would be for its platform, and they likely used existing metrics around game sales, Steam Wishlists (more on this in the next section), and community activity to make those guesses. Ultimately, nearly all minimum guarantees are determined with a process like this. The platform reviews the available data on the game, even if it has not been released, and benchmarks its potential performance against their internal data, using the performances of past minimum guarantees to inform how they approach new ones.

On top of the math, platforms will consider other factors for a minimum guarantee, such as genre relevance, the quality of the game, and the timing of the release. These factors are much more abstract than the financial and conversion data, so the science is not exact and is open to persuasion and negotiation.

For indie developers, understanding and leveraging minimum guarantees is a way to insulate the revenue potential of your game. Yes, minimum guarantees are ultimately a version of game sales, but since many minimum guarantees happen pre-launch, you may be able to recoup a great deal of your expenses with minimum guarantees. In some cases, a game can be profitable before it even releases because of the minimum guarantees in place.

Making a deal with a platform is not easy, but it's an important part of the business of indie games and should, therefore, be a part of your revenue plan.

Subscriptions: Games as a Service

With the rise of Xbox Game Pass and Google's efforts with Stadia, a game-streaming service, a portion of the games industry is leveraging the Netflix model for content distribution. Instead of buying games individually, users pay a monthly fee for unlimited access to the titles on the platform.

The nature of these deals is a work in progress as the industry continues to evolve, but this revenue channel for an indie developer can be much different from a traditional sale. Currently, a developer can make money from these relationships in one of three ways:

1. **A minimum guarantee:** As explained in the previous section, the platform pays a flat fee for the right to distribute a game

2. **Adjusted revenue share:** Just as Steam gives a developer a percentage of a sale, a subscription platform may pay a royalty per download of a game, but that exact percentage and total is likely to be different from a traditional platform

3. **Pay-per-hour:** While this is rare, a few platforms, including Utomik, pay developers based on how long players actually play a specific game

Netflix might be the easiest comparison point in terms of user experience, but the monetization potential for games is not the same.

In March 2021, Mincrosft's Sarah Bond told *Forbes* the following: "When you subscribe to a channel that enables you to watch a video, like Netflix [...] that's kind of the end of the monetization cycle that you have with that piece of content. In gaming it's the opposite: there are items that you can buy in the game, there are extensions you can buy, there's a next franchise you can purchase, there are other genres that you can leap to."

Bond also shared in that interview that Game Pass subscribers also do the following:

- Spend 20% more time playing games
- Play 30% more games
- Play 40% more genres
- Spend "about" 20% more money on gaming overall

Game Pass and other subscription services might not be the best fit for your game, but you should at least consider them as you explore the revenue potential of your project. Traditional premium experiences – such as single-player titles with a clear beginning and end – have found success on Game Pass and so have multiplayer titles.

Currently, subscription services are an opportunity for indie developers to extend the life-cycle of their games, which means that an indie title likely gets a traditional PC and console release first and later makes its way onto a service like Game Pass to reach players who might be deterred by risking a purchase on a new game but are happy to try it as part of a subscription experience.

In the future, though, subscription services are likely to be platforms unto themselves.

Microsoft announced in January 2021 that it had 18 million members using the Game Pass service. A few months later, in April 2021, Microsoft announced that the service had grown to 23 million subscribers.

That's a lot of players!

Just as the Epic Games Store negotiates exclusivity with publishers and developers to bring more players to their platform, subscription services are likely to do the same with more frequency as these services grow. At a minimum, indie developers should be exploring getting their games listed on these platforms at some point in a game's life. Beyond that, the popularity of subscription services may begin to influence game design for better and for worse.

For instance, you may be more motivated to optimize the file size of your game to make it more rapidly accessible to new players, or you might think more about DLC and cosmetics to give players more content and to create more opportunities for monetization.

Keep an eye on these services. They are likely to be more and more important for the success of your game.

Physical Releases

Similar to subscription services, physical releases are often a part of the long-tail for a game's revenue, occurring well after the initial launch. Where physical distribution was the only way players could get new games in the 1990s and early 2000s, digital distribution is now the norm for the majority of games. AAA titles releasing on consoles still get physical releases, but for the thousands of indies in the industry, digital distribution is the most cost-effective release strategy.

That's not a groundbreaking insight for anyone reading this book, but what's old has a way of becoming new again.

If a game attracts a loyal fanbase, the appeal of owning a collectible version of the game goes up, so many indie titles that find success in a digital release eventually see a limited physical release as well. Switch titles are particularly popular in this corner of the industry, perhaps because of Nintendo's long history with physicals, but PlayStation releases have also done well with this format.

Here's how it usually works.

If a game is popular enough, a partner that specializes in physical releases (Such as Strictly Limited Games) will approach the developer or the publisher and pitch a partnership. Though it is slightly less common, physical distributors can also be open to receiving a pitch and can be convinced to release a physical version of the game. We've worked with games that received offers from physical distributors, and we have also worked with games where the developer negotiated the deal themselves or the publisher negotiated the deal on the developer's behalf.

A physical release usually gets the "collector's edition" treatment, packing maps and manuals and figurines into an oversized collectable box, the kind of thing a superfan would be excited to put on a shelf or in a display case.

The business relationship itself is akin to a publishing deal where the parties involved agree to share revenue, but due to the high-cost and high-risk nature of physical production, the distributor may have a minimum recoup clause and may take a sizable portion of the revenue. This is typical in almost all business deals where one party takes considerably more risk than the others, so don't let a big revenue split spook you if you have the opportunity to take this path.

Since physical releases are often bought by existing fans of a game, physical releases are largely an opportunity to remonetize your superfans by giving them something special, but we have also seen a successful physical release drive more digital sales because that physical release gives superfans an excuse to talk about a game again. They share links to cool collectibles with their friends as part of a fan conversation and take photos of the box and collectibles when they arrive, and those photos ultimately end up on Instagram and Twitter.

So, in addition to the revenue on the physical sales, the noise a good physical release makes can also bring you new players and additional digital sales.

Technically, an indie developer could manage a physical release themselves, but unless you have a background in manufacturing or ecommerce, we caution against it. The advantages of working with a partner usually include the following:

- **Access to a built-in customer-base:** In addition to fans of your game, there are large pools of collectors who buy nearly every release from their physical producer of choice

- **Physical marketing experience**: Promoting a physical product is an art in itself, from great product shots to great timing, positioning, and pricing
- **Manufacturing experience:** What's the best kind of paper and printing process to use for a game insert? Most people won't know and won't know where to start looking for the answer, but a physical specialist will have a process for every component in a release
- **Economies of scale:** A business that solely produces physical games will have a network of partners to get the materials they need at bulk rates, making their cost-per-unit far lower than anything an indie could hit with a single release
- **Fulfillment:** Storing, packing, and shipping physical products is not only a logistical challenge, it can also play into economies of scale in terms of efficiency but also in terms of shipping and material rates

While we mentioned most games have a physical edition release post-launch, we have noticed a trend of more developers offering a limited-edition incentive for Kickstarter campaigns. This is a great incentive to help meet your goal and build excitement among the community. However, be aware that the physical partner will likely have the rights to the physical version. If your game ends up being a huge success, you may miss out on being able to work with a massive partner that can get your game in stores. Ultimately, you'll need to decide what's best for your game.

Not every game is a fit for a physical release, but this is a consideration you should make as you get a sense for the reach of your game at launch and post launch. The additional revenue can give you a greater return on your investment, and you might attract some new players along the way.

Soundtracks

Video game music has a long history of fostering its own parallel fandom which today has evolved into a multifaceted experience that, for fans, includes symphony renditions of video game music, hundreds of YouTubers performing their own covers of game music, and active remix communities where musicians from a wide array of backgrounds exchange tracks. OCRemix has 4,030 such tracks, an estimated 230 hours of remixed music made entirely by fans of video game music.

In an earlier chapter, we briefly mentioned that some indies have found great success in releasing soundtracks from their games digitally and physically as CDs and vinyl record albums. As far as digital distribution is concerned, Steam has made it relatively easy to list a soundtrack alongside a game release, so many indies sell a soundtrack with their game simply because it's easy to do.

As a revenue strategy, a game soundtrack is rarely successful if the game it's attached to is not also successful, so your priority should still be on making your game as fun as possible. but as you make choices around your budget and development, knowing that a great soundtrack is a product unto itself might change how you approach the music to your game.

There is nothing wrong with using creative commons music or using royalty free music. These are cost-effective ways to get music into your project, but you won't own the original rights, and the music in your game might appear in a dozen other indie games. If the music is entirely original and transcends the game itself – being good enough to listen to outside of playing the game – there's a chance to sell the soundtrack.

Unfortunately, data on soundtrack sales are much harder to find and is reported on far less often than game unit sales, but consider this: *IGN,* as part of its coverage of the PlayStation 3 and PS Vita release *Hotline Miami* by Dennaton Games (published by Devolver Digital), reported that *Hotline Miami* had sold 300,000 units by that point in 2013. From day one of its release, the music of *Hotline Miami* was one of the standout parts of the game experience and was highlighted in nearly every review or story about the game.

Today, that soundtrack is sold on Steam for $9.99. If 5% of *Hotline Miami* fans loved the music enough to buy the soundtrack, that's 15,000 units in soundtrack sales alone, or $149,850 gross profit, or $104,895 after Steam takes its platforms cut.

That's just based on the units sold by 2013, and that's revenue generated from an asset that was included in the game anyways, yet many players were happy to pay for it again as a standalone soundtrack because they enjoyed the music that much.

We highlight the *Hotline Miami* story for a few reasons:

1. The *Hotline Miami* soundtrack is likely one of the most financially successful indie soundtracks of all time, by our estimation.
2. The music selection was a fantastic complement to the gameplay, making the entire experience inherently more interesting and engaging for players.
3. The *Hotline Miami* soundtrack was not produced for the game but rather licensed from several individual independent musicians or bands.

That last point is important. Somewhere along the way, Dennaton Games (the developers) or Devolver Digital (the publisher) recognized the value of the soundtrack and ensured they had secured the proper licenses to not only use the music in a commercial game but also to sell the music as a soundtrack.

What a fantastic example of the crossroads between scrappy indie developer creativity – scouring the internet for relatively unknown artists making great music with affordable usage terms – and indie business savvy – recognizing early on that the music of *Hotline Miami* was special and that fans would want more.

Licensing music and being careful about the rights you secure could be the approach that helps to make your game more profitable, but you might also consider commissioning an entirely original soundtrack. This path is likely more expensive, but the vast majority of breakout game soundtracks (from *The Legend of Zelda* to *Bastion*) are wholly original compositions made specifically for the games they accompany.

Sabotage Studios, the indie team behind *The Messenger*, hired *Chrono Trigger* composer Yasunori Mitsuda to contribute music to their upcoming game *Sea of Stars*, a pixel art title heavily inspired by retro RPGs like *Chrono Trigger*. They announced this collaboration as part of the game's Kickstarter campaign, triggering a wave of news coverage and excited fan reactions centered around Mitsuda's role exclusively.

The entirety of the Kickstarter was a masterful piece of games marketing, of which Mitsuda's music was one strategic piece, but even before the release of *Sea of Stars*, its music has helped to make it a financial success. 25,589 backers crushed the goal of CA$133,000, contributing CA$1,628,126 by the end of the campaign.

Whether your soundtrack is a cornerstone of your game experience or a small stream of additional revenue, how you leverage music should be part of your business planning process.

It's worth noting here that if you choose to go the physical music route–selling CDs or vinyl record albums or collectable thumb drives – the considerations we shared around physical game releases also apply. Typically, working with a partner who specializes in those products is the most cost-effective approach for indies, but there are many more indies who have self-published vinyl soundtracks than there are indies who have self-published physical game releases.

Merchandising

Technically, a physical game release or a vinyl release of a soundtrack fall under the category of merchandise, which are physical goods related to the intellectual property (or IP) of a game. For our purposes, we break these into separate considerations because, as a strategy, how you approach a soundtrack release or how you approach doing a custom Switch box set will often be different from a broader merchandise strategy.

Before we get too deep, a merchandise push for an indie game could include any of the following:

- T-shirts
- Hoodies
- Socks
- Pins
- Posters
- Mugs
- Art books
- Keychains
- Plushies

- Statues
- Trading cards
- Jackets
- Hats
- Stickers
- Stationary

Merchandise, like the other items we have covered in this chapter thus far, are opportunities to expand the revenue potential of your project and to serve your fans in new ways. Anyone reading this probably has at least one piece of video game memorabilia in their collection, but more likely, you have several and a trove of video game t-shirts mixed into your wardrobe as well.

The fan experience lends itself well to merchandise because fans love to express their love for games. When you provide great merchandise to a great fan community, everyone wins. Indies get more revenue to fund future projects, and fans get to celebrate something they enjoy.

Despite the significant revenue potential of merchandise – and indie games like *Stardew Valley* and *Hollow Knight* are great success stories – this is not always a great path for indie developers to take, so tread carefully. Beyond the potential investment you have to make in actually producing and fulfilling product for orders, all of these items are products in their own right. They need to be promoted. They need to be marketed. They need to be well designed and released at an appropriate time.

The trap here is to assume that indie fans love t-shirts (they do) and that they, therefore, will buy a t-shirt based on your game (they might not). What is more likely to happen is that you end up with a box of t-shirts rotting in the corner of your closet because you couldn't find enough people to buy them. For an indie, that can represent precious budget that is ultimately wasted. This is especially true for items such as plushies that cost thousands of dollars to produce correctly and often require a minimum order.

While many indies manage their own merchandise strategy, recognizing how many don't is also important. Fangamer, The Yetee, Sanshee, Gaming Outfitters – the major merchandise companies you often see at events like PAX – are the exclusive merchandise pipeline for several video game IPs. Part of the benefit of that relationship is in the value of exclusivity because it pays to be the only store carrying merchandise associated with a popular indie game. The other part of the benefit is that these partners shoulder the massive burden of executing an effective merchandise strategy.

Running a merchandise company is hard and requires a skill set that is different from the skill set you need to make games. That's why, for many indies, the best merchandise strategy is one that passes the bulk of the responsibility to a trustworthy third party. Negotiating a deal like that can be difficult and requires a significant amount of indie popularity, but the upside is that you can generate more revenue from your game without adding yet another responsibility to your internal team's bandwidth.

The tradeoff is that a merchandise partner is likely to take a larger revenue split as a result, but the reduction in risk and time usually justifies that concession.

For smaller indie developers that want to experiment with merchandise but may not have the bargaining power of a game like *Undertale*, small merchandise runs are available as are services that offer print-on-demand style experiences. These companies only make shirts when customers order them, make it relatively simple to set up your own storefront with your own designs, and manage all of the fulfillment for you. Teespring is one such example (though that is not an endorsement, so do your own research).

More creative approaches to indie merchandise are on the rise as well. For example, we've found success with plushies via a company called Makeship, which uses a crowdfunding approach for generating a minimum interest in a new plushie before actually sending them out to be produced. Makeship gets a new product they know fans want. Fans get an awesome new plushie. And indies get an additional source of revenue without upfront costs.

For the average indie, merchandise won't unlock a windfall of profit, but it can be profitable, making it a worthwhile consideration for driving even more of a return from your game.

Licensing Deals

A license is the official permission to do or use something, usually in exchange for a fee, a share of revenue, or a combination of the two. If The Yetee prints a bunch of t-shirts for your game, you would first grant them a license to do so.

In the world of content – books, movies, television, and video games – licenses can be an opportunity to extend a universe and to generate more revenue from an IP that fans love. The television version of *Game of Thrones* was made possible because someone negotiated the purchase of the television rights associated with the original book series.

At the AAA level, licensing has been common for years and has given us gems like the *Super Mario Bros.* movie, and more recently (and thankfully), the *DOTA* and *Castlevania* anime series on Netflix. Licensing for adaptations and derivatives is still not common in indie games, though, but given the trends in all other forms of media and at the AAA level of games, we expect that to change over the next few years.

For book authors, these rights are often sold at a flat rate and rarely executed on. Sometimes media companies will buy the television and film rights in a bundle, and in other cases they split them or focus on one type of license.

Despite the sale of indie licenses for use in television or film being relatively rare in indie games, their inclusion in publishing agreements is not so rare. Even if it's a longshot, many publishers recognize how big of a lottery ticket those rights can be and scoop them up when they sign a game. That might sound nefarious, but that exchange is not always predatory.

What's actually important is that you are aware that those rights and licenses have potential value and that you should think carefully about what you believe is fair compensation. If your publisher takes the television and film rights to your game but commits to clear terms on revenue sharing and shares their plan for pitching a series based on your game, that exchange might be perfectly worthwhile from a business perspective.

Too many indies, however, sign agreements without realizing that they are also signing over these rights. Their exact value is difficult to estimate, but they should be a part of your contract negotiations, so we'll cover that topic in greater depth later on.

Bundle Sales

Bundle sales have become a mainstay of the indie game life cycle. At some point, nearly every indie game is featured in a bundle of some kind, packaged alongside several other titles and sold at a huge discount.

Humble Bundle conquered this corner of the games industry with a thoughtful approach to engaging indies blended with altruism: a portion of the proceeds went to charity. Today, there are several game bundle services of varying sizes and reach. Itch.io also often features bundles, and bundle sales are also possible on Steam, though they are usually more narrowly curated and less frequent.

The downside of bundles is that the profit per unit is much lower than what a developer could make selling through Steam, but that steep discount is also what makes bundles attractive to players.

Here are the upsides:

- Bundles are a way to wring more sales out of a game long after the hype of a launch has died down, bringing you new sales that may not have ever occurred through traditional channels and platforms.

- A well-timed bundle can help to drive interest in a sequel or a DLC release as it gives players a low-risk way to discover your game just in time to pick up your next offering at close to full price.

- Bundles naturally generate an additional marketing moment for your game, giving you an excuse to re-promote your game through several channels alongside the built-in marketing that most bundle services provide.

If bundles aren't a part of your business plan, they should be, especially if you plan to release several games and aim to build a long-term community around your work. Bundles will bring you more revenue and more players at a moment when traditional channels will continue to slow.

Secondary Platform Sales

Earlier, we defined the idea of a platform in the games industry and talked about the major players that represent the top tier of game platforms (or first party platforms as they are commonly called), including Steam or the Nintendo eShop. The games industry, however, is expansive and new storefronts are constantly opening and closing, attempting to capture a share of the market.

Many indie developers overlook the revenue potential of these platforms because they are generally smaller and less popular than mainstream platforms or serve lesser known regions or markets.

Some of the secondary platforms we've worked with include:

- GOG
- Green Man Gaming
- Fanatical
- Genba
- Buka
- Plug in Digital
- Nuuvem

Similar to a bundle sale, the profit potential of engaging a secondary platform is much smaller than the profit potential of a launch, but there is still profit to be gained. Because they are smaller, secondary platforms can also be more open to exclusive campaigns and promotions, giving your game a much more focused marketing push than most first party platforms would ever provide.

That might mean frontpage placement on their storefront, a dedicated blast to their email list, and a full social media campaign to promote the availability of your game on their platform.

In some cases, these secondary platforms will also offer minimum guarantees.

The advantages here are akin to the advantages we covered in the previous section on bundle sales: secondary platforms can bring new players to your game that you likely would not have gotten otherwise, and they give you a chance to make more of a return on a product you've already finished and have already released.

Pursuing these opportunities does take time, however, so many indies lean on publishers to do this diligence and to negotiate these opportunities. Whether you're chasing the opportunities yourself or relying on a partner to capture them for you, they are an essential piece of a well-rounded revenue plan for an indie game.

Revenue Recap

Seeing the full scope of revenue possibilities for your game is an essential piece of the business of indie games. Your game is an asset that has the potential to open the door to several kinds of revenue channels, but you have to know to look for them and may need to make key choices early in the development of your project to make some of those revenue streams a possibility.

Again, not every revenue stream is a good fit for every game, but as you map the plan for your project, you should ask yourself, *If I wanted to generate revenue from doing X with my game, what choices can I make now to make that more likely?*

X can be any of the revenue opportunities covered in this chapter, and your answer to this hypothetical is likely to range from potential game design choices, assets you may need to create, or relationships that you need to make. If you decide that a revenue channel is not a fit for you, that's fine, but make that choice a conscious one. Too many indies don't fully realize the value of what they create and miss out on a great deal of profit as a result.

We don't want that to happen to you.

The Secret Economy
of Steam Wishlists

The stated function of Steam Wishlists is well known to indie developers. If a Steam user wishlists your game, they will get a notification when the game is officially released, and depending on the size of the discount, Steam may also send them a promotional email when the game is on sale. For players, Wishlists are an easy way to keep track of games that caught their attention and to take advantage of future promotions. For indies, Wishlists are a way to capture and retain future customers.

Steam Wishlists are incredibly valuable because of how players use Steam as a service and storefront. For industry insiders, though, Steam Wishlists are a form of currency in their own right that can be leveraged as negotiating tools and as predictors of revenue. Publishers and platforms rely on Steam Wishlists to maximize the potential of a game in several ways, and all of those business activities hinge on the consistent performance that makes Wishlists valuable.

Wishlists as a Crystal Ball for Future Sales

Indie developers and publishers have known for years that a higher Wishlist count translates to a higher volume of sales in a game's lifetime, but what percentage of Wishlists actually convert to sales was hotly debated, with estimates ranging from 10% to 50% of Wishlists becoming paying customers.

In 2020, Valve shared official data with video game industry media outlet *GamesIndustry.biz*. The entire article is worth reading for anyone in indie games, so check our sources for the URL, but here's the element that makes Wishlists powerful: According to Valve, on average, 19 percent of Wishlists convert to sales in the first 12 months of a game being live.

That data means that anyone can predict, with a significant degree of accuracy, the profit potential of a game by looking at the number of Wishlists alone.

To Valve's credit, Wishlists have retained their value because they are incredibly hard to fake. Where you can fluff a Twitter account with bot followers or buy upvotes to force your Reddit post to the frontpage (and for the record, we discourage

DOI: 10.1201/9781003215264-5

both practices), the nature of the Steam platform makes it difficult to spoof. In a world full of smoke, mirrors, and posturing, Wishlists are a reliable beacon of truth.

For indie developers, Wishlists are a leading metric that can be mapped to your budget and sales projections. If you know what it costs to make your game and how many sales you will need to recoup those costs before making a profit, you can use the 19% Wishlist metric to determine your target goal for Wishlists.

For game marketers, Wishlists are a key benchmark for ensuring the success of a launch, which is why so many marketing campaigns rely on the call-to-action of "Wishlist today!" in promotional materials, but the Wishlist goal can also be used as a way of estimating market budget. You may learn, for example, that your Facebook ads can generate Wishlists at a rate of $1 per Wishlist, which can then be factored into a game's total launch and development costs.

If your game needs to sell 30,675 units to break even – like in our example from the previous chapter – but you only have $5,000 set aside for marketing and are currently generating Wishlists at a rate of $2 per Wishlist, the math is not in your favor and you should consider adjusting course as soon as possible. At that rate and with that budget, the likelihood of your game turning a profit is slim, even if you get a splash at release.

What you should do is use your sales goals to set your Wishlist goals. If you need to sell 30,675 units, that means you likely need 161,447 Wishlists, based on the average conversion rate of 19%.

Example Wishlist Math

Development Budget	$100,000
[($9.99 – 30% for Steam) – 40% for publisher] – 22.4% for taxes	$3.26 Net Profit Per Unit
Budget of $100,000 / $3.26 Net Profit Per Unit	30,675 Units Needed for Recoup
30,675 Total Units/.19 Wishlist Conversion Average =	161,447 Wishlists

All indies should do this kind of math in the planning phase and also during development to assess progress. You will not need to hit your Wishlist goal before release, necessarily, as a great launch campaign will increase your Wishlist momentum. However, many indies don't realize that investors, publishers, and platforms use this same math to decide what bets to make in indie games.

Wishlists as Currency

In Chapter 3, we shared that savvy indies negotiate minimum guarantees for their projects, but how do you convince a platform that your game is worthy of a minimum guarantee? Part of that answer is salesmanship and your track record as a professional, but Wishlists are the largest bargaining chip in these conversations pre-launch.

Because Wishlist performance is so consistent and predictable, platforms outside of Steam can use this number to judge how well a game might do on their platform. Hypothetically, a platform like GOG can look at your 161,447 Wishlists (to continue our example math), recognize that the volume of Wishlists is likely to translate to 30,675 in sales on Steam, and then apply their historical data to make an educated guess about how many of those units can be converted on GOG instead.

Post-launch, Wishlists remain relevant but now available data like unit sales, coverage volume, and Metacritic score become negotiation tools as well.

No platform is likely to capture all of the sales that might have occurred on Steam, but with hundreds of game releases giving them a historical perspective on what to expect, a platform like GOG could look at the performance of other games in the genre, assess the reaction the game is getting from fans and news outlets, and then apply their own evaluation criteria to make an educated guess about what their profit is likely to be. If that profit potential is exciting, they may offer a minimum guarantee in trade for a limited window of release or pre-order exclusivity in addition to premium store placement.

We don't have the exact numbers of what percentage of Steam sales a competing platform expects to capture, so this is purely for the sake of education, but let's say that they are confident they can move 20% of sales to their platform with an exclusive launch promotion.

Therefore, those 30,675 predictable Steam sales translate to 6,135 units sold for GOG, or roughly $18,386 if GOG takes a 30 percent cut of a $9.99 list price for a game.

As a result, GOG might be willing to commit to a $8,000 minimum guarantee to secure the total revenue. If their bet is correct, they generate $12,386 in profit on top of the value of potentially attracting new users to GOG or the value of ensuring that current GOG users stay on GOG.

If this sounds a bit like a dark art to you, you aren't far off. The games industry is full of incredibly intelligent people capable of synthesizing all sorts of data points to make decisions, but the business isn't an exact science. Time and time again, the industry has seen games that, on paper, should have been a huge financial success sputter and collapse at launch. Likewise, the opposite is also true. Many games that no one ever expected to be hits suddenly catch fire and gain cult followings.

The variability and unpredictability of the games industry is also present in any space where creativity is the driving force behind successful projects. As scary as that can be when it's your money on the line – such as investing in the development of your indie game – that grey area also opens the door to negotiation and persuasion.

Getting that pre-launch $8,000 minimum guarantee from GOG is often not where that story ends. Experienced indie publishers will have several minimum guarantee conversations simultaneously in order to secure the best deal possible for a game. If GOG is willing to offer $8,000 for an exclusive pre-order, maybe Xbox or Nintendo will offer $15,000. Seeing the interest from other platforms, maybe the Epic Games Store swoops in and offers $200,000 to secure a year-long exclusive for the next hot indie game.

By the end of negotiations, the publisher may be able to secure an exclusive pre-order minimum guarantee, a first major discount minimum guarantee (a post-launch activation), and maybe a DLC minimum guarantee (also a post-launch activation).

All of these negotiations hinge on the predictability of Steam Wishlists. Everyone at the table can look at Wishlists, assign a value to those Wishlists, and then jockey for position to get the best deal for their respective businesses.

With so many of these deals happening pre-launch, this insight may help you to see why many game marketing campaigns begin a year or more ahead of launch. That longer marketing timeline gives stakeholders more time and more opportunities to build up the Wishlists they need to have leverage in these big conversations.

Wishlists and the Steam Algorithm

The less surprising and better-known side of Steam Wishlists is the relationship between Wishlists and placement on Steam. Even this, though, is shrouded in mystery because Valve does not share the exact specifics of how their algorithm works. If you talk to three different successful indie studios, you are likely to hear three different stories about what made them successful on Steam.

Some indies change their game tags daily so that they appear more often in popular searches. Some indies focus on frequent updates with great graphics to keep their audience engaged and returning to their Steam page time and time again. Other indies set their Steam page and barely update it, ever.

Here is what we know for sure:

- Wishlists alert Steam users when a game on their Wishlist is released
- Wishlists alert Steam users when a game on their Wishlist is discounted
- Wishlists are a factor for where games appear in searches
- Wishlists are a factor for what games are featured or promoted by Steam and when

- Wishlists are a factor for how likely a game is appear as a recommended title alongside another game in the genre
- Wishlists can be a selection factor for the Steam representatives who manage events and partnerships
- Wishlists are a factor in the Steam selection process for featured sales opportunities (Daily Deal, etc.)

We don't know exactly how Wishlists impact any of these items, and in all likelihood, the algorithm changes with some frequency. Google's search algorithm, for example, is under constant improvement, seeing sometimes daily tweaks and receiving major updates every few months. Most tech companies take a similar approach because the constant stream of incoming customer and usage data gives them more opportunities to improve the experience of a platform. Google wants search to be as effective as possible for users and advertisers. Amazon wants to drive more sales. Apple wants to drive more app downloads.

Steam wants to sell more games and retain users for as long as possible. As a privately owned company, we have very little access to the specifics of what happens behind the scenes, but we're confident in what we've shared so far.

Where analysis gets murky is the fuzzy line between a best practice and a superstition when you're trying to game a mystery algorithm.

For any game, frontpage placement on Steam is a massive opportunity to increase sales, so AAA titles to indie titles are constantly looking for ways to get that placement. We know that Wishlists can make this placement happen organically, but how many Wishlists does it take to get your indie game on the frontpage at launch?

No one outside of Valve actually knows, so you'll hear a variety of anecdotes from a number of industry folks. The minimum threshold we hear most often is 20,000 Wishlists, but even this isn't a guarantee based on what other titles might release around your launch.

The reality, however, is unlikely to be so clearcut. Storefront algorithms in other industries take into account several factors to reach an outcome, so Steam is also likely to take into account current customer trends, the Wishlist counts of other games releasing that day, and a mix of manual human curation.

If you bank on a mystical minimum Wishlist number getting you to the frontpage at launch, you may be disappointed, so balance that effort with other considerations around marketing, positioning, and timing, all of which we discuss later.

Are Steam Follows the Next Critical Metric?

Steam changes constantly, and the introduction of the Follow feature has shifted how some indies market their games. Where a Wishlist will trigger launch and sale emails for Steam users in the future, a follow means users will receive notifications about updates throughout the lifecycle of the game, pre- and post-release. In other words, a follow is a much bigger expression of interest in a game and represents a more significant commitment to seeing the news and updates about a title.

For indies with active communities and frequent updates, a follow can be a powerful way to turn interested players into advocates for your game. Where a user who Wishlists your game may not think about–and therefore not talk about–a game until they get the email announcing its release, a user who follows a game might see an exciting piece of news in your Steam updates and share the feature with their friends, who, in turn, visit the Steam page and Wishlist or follow the game for themselves.

With Steam gradually giving indies more tools to curate and customize pages about their teams and their games, follows are likely to become more useful and more powerful in the future. The economy around Wishlists is almost certainly here to stay, but follows might become a part of those negotiations in the future as well.

Revenue, Wishlists, and Beyond

As we near the close of Part 1, you should have a much clearer understanding of how your game can generate revenue and the ways in which investors, publishers, and platforms think about the revenue potential of your game. In an ideal scenario, all of the knowledge we packaged up here becomes a part of your planning process, considerations you make before spending your first dollar on production or writing the first line of code.

We know, though, that won't be the case for many readers. If your game is already in development and even if it has already been released, you can potentially unlock new revenue channels and opportunities for your work now that you see the bigger picture of the games industry.

For the readers who are preparing to make a game, use these ideas to map the business case and plan your project. This part of game development is much less sexy than designing characters or building the lore for a new universe, but it still requires creativity and ingenuity, especially for new indies trying to break into the scene.

The sooner you incorporate business considerations into your process, the more likely you are to have a sustainable career as an indie, finding success not with just your current game but all the games that come after it.

In the next section, we connect these ideas around revenue and Wishlists to your development planning, integrating the business of indie games into the fabric of game development itself.

PART 2

Pre-Development Choices

DOI: 10.1201/9781003215264-6

Moon Studios and *Ori and the Will of the Wisps*

An 80-Person Indie Studio with AAA Talent

Ori and the Will of the Wisps has already risen to the status of indie game icon, continuing the success of its predecessor, 2015's *Ori and the Blind Forest*, and catapulting Moon Studios to new heights.

Though Moon Studios is considered an indie studio, the makeup of their team is a far cry from the solo or small team stereotype for indie video game development.

Thomas Mahler, the CEO and Game Director for Moon Studios, wanted to collaborate with talented people all around the world. It didn't seem feasible and reasonable to ask people to move into a different country for the sake of a project.

He told *Gameindustry.biz*, "It isn't that easy to just acquire talent. Really great people who have 10 or 15 years of experience, most likely they're going to have a family. They're most likely going to have kids at school. For them, it's not easy to uproot their family and say they're going to do this or that. That's a hard thing to ask someone to do."

Prior to Moon Studios, Mahler worked on *Starcraft II* at Blizzard. Witnessing the success of games like *Castle Crashers* and *Super Meat Boy*, he saw an opportunity to shift his focus and make smaller games. He moved to Austria after leaving Blizzard and sought out a very talented programmer who lived in Israel.

Gennadiy Korol joined the team, and not seeing the practicality of asking Korol to move to Austria, the two began collaborating remotely.

Then, they started prototyping and seeking talent from all around the globe. Riot, Blizzard, and Disney are just some of the studios where they found new team members. With no need to relocate for the opportunity, Moon Studios started gathering international talent with serious industry experience. The studio even hired Milton "DoctorM64" Guasti, the sole developer of a *Metroid II* fan remake that was in development for more than a decade.

After 2015, Moon Studios grew from 20 employees to 80, representing 43 different countries.

Many indies have found success in using world-renowned apps for their remote work – Zoom, Discord, Slack, Trello. Moon Studios, however, has gone a step farther than most. They developed Apollo, their own internal development management tool. They still use Skype and Microsoft Teams, but they want to expand Apollo into featuring everything they need without relying on any outside software.

Moon Studios has earned every bit of the praise heaped upon their team and their work.

The creativity, polish, and professionalism of Moon Studios is well-worth emulating and learning from, but aspiring indies should also temper the urge to compare their own games to *Ori and the Blind Forest* or *Ori and the Will of the Wisps*. For the latter, 80 talented team members hailing from some of the most competitive gaming companies from around the world sets a standard for scope and development that will be largely inaccessible to the first-time team learning Unity as they go.

https://www.gamesindustry.biz/articles/2020-03-10-building-ori-and-the-will-of-the-wisps-with-80-people-working-from-home

https://www.jp.square-enix.com/company/en/news/2020/html/df9995782da2d516db9ebac425d02d4019665f70.html

https://www.nintendolife.com/news/2021/01/feature_moon_studios_on_ori_and_the_will_of_the_wisps_journey_from_xbox_to_switch

https://www.nintendolife.com/news/2020/02/the_project_am2r_creator_now_designs_levels_for_the_ori_developer_moon_studios

Project Types and Project Goals

The fate of many games is decided before the first line of code is ever written.

We made this assertion in Part 1, and it bears repeating because underestimating the importance of the choices around your project, especially in planning phases, is all too easy for indies. The fun part of indie game development is making the game. Bringing your characters, story, and world to life is magical, and then seeing players experience that content is even more magical. Most indies begin developing games because they are passionate about a game idea, not because they are passionate about the business merits of a digitally distributed interactive product.

These planning choices are not just about budgets and sales projections either. Everything from the genre you choose to the engine you use to the timing of your release can impact the financial success of your game. Each choice in the development process ripples into the others, and while you can't anticipate every possible decision you will have to make as an indie, our hope is that this book helps you anticipate the options that many indies overlook.

Pre-Development Overview

In this part of the book, we will explore the myriad of pre-development decisions you will encounter as an indie. Just as it was in the previous section on the ecosystem of the games industry, this is not about right or wrong answers. Rather, our goal is to help you make the right choices *for your project*. In that spirit, we will walk you through the hidden implications around choices that might seem inconsequential – such as whether you use GameMaker or Unity for your engine – and how those choices could influence how you work with publishers, how you work with platforms, and how you ultimately engage players.

At a high-level, this section explores the following:

- Setting project goals based on your means and your aspirations
- The types of projects you might explore as an indie

- How to assess the business potential of a particular genre
- How to evaluate the market potential of your game concept
- How choosing an art style impacts development and pitching
- Establishing a scope for your development
- Choosing an engine and how engine-selection affects the business of a game
- Determining development timelines and milestones
- Accounting for translation and localization
- A practical approach to budget planning for indies
- Building and managing an indie development team

We will not be able to give you a full tutorial on all of these topics because subjects such as product-market-fit and development management methodologies are full genres of books in their own right, but we will cover the basics with an emphasis on the business considerations.

How to Use This Section for True Pre-Development

You probably have an idea for the game you want to make, or more likely you have several and might be trying to choose where to start. If you are at this stage in your indie journey where you haven't actually started making your game, or are very early, this section will give you a step-by-step guide for a thorough indie game planning process. In each section, you can work along in a notebook or a GDD (game design document) to write out an initial plan for your game.

Think of this initial plan as a rough draft. A development plan for a game is rarely perfect in its first iteration. A choice in one area, like a target release date, can trigger a cascade of adjustments in other areas. If you want to release in Q1 of a particular year, as an example, all of your development milestones will need to align accordingly.

That could mean adjusting the scope of your game to fit that timing, or it could mean hiring additional team members so that you can complete the full scope of the game as planned and still hit your release window. Changing the scope of your game or opting to expand your team also triggers follow-up considerations. You may need to adjust the pricing for your game to better reflect the total content, or you may need to pursue publishers with larger funding budgets.

Planning is a fluid endeavor. That is to say, most plans will need updating during the development process. Part of your planning should be to imagine a variety of outcomes, obstacles, and opportunities so that you can revise your plan as you take in new information. You might not be able to anticipate everything, but the more you do anticipate, the easier it will be to adapt to the real surprises.

As you plan, conduct thought experiments with your project, and ask yourself questions such as the following while you work through each element of your plan:

- What opportunities do I create with this choice?
- What obstacles am I likely to encounter that I should plan for?
- What other areas does this choice affect?
- How would the project change if I changed this variable?
- What elements am I willing to change and why?
- Under what circumstances am I willing to change them?
- How would this plan change if the project funding changed (self-publishing vs. working with a publisher)?

If you have a team, these questions can help to drive group discussions around how you want to bring your game to life and bring to market. If you are a solo developer, these questions will help you to reflect on your plan and uncover perspectives that might not have been immediately obvious.

These exercises, for as abstract as they might feel, can prevent many of the most common project-killing problems for indie developers.

How to Use This Section for Retroactive Pre-Development

If your project is already underway – and we expect this to be the case for many readers – do not despair. Aside from the budget you may have already invested or contracts you may have signed, few development decisions are truly permanent. In cases where it is impractical to turn back, like a year of development in a particular engine, the ideas we explore in this section can help illuminate potential opportunities that may have been otherwise hidden.

Likewise, you may still have time to avoid critical landmines.

With the timeline of development for the average indie game – ranging from one to two years in most cases – the real importance of pre-development choices is understanding what they mean in the long term, so even if the choice is already made, you have much to gain by seeing more clearly what path those choices can put you on.

If you are an indie and your project has already begun, all of the knowledge we impart in this section will still apply, but how you use it will be somewhat different than if you started your indie journey with this book.

For the indies, already in development, here's how to apply pre-development concepts:

- Map the choices you have made around your project already to clearly see where you are and what has been decided
- Identify the aspects of your development that were deeply deliberate and outline your reasoning for making those choices

- Identify the aspects of your development where your choices were less intentional and you did not fully consider the consequences

- Based on what the material we review, brainstorm on what those consequences might be and what that means for your project

- Review your development map with this new clarity and look for weaknesses and strengths that were previously hidden to you

- Update your plan to address the weaknesses and to capitalize on the strengths

For example, you might have chosen GameMaker as an engine because you found it accessible and easy to use, which is completely reasonable. However, you may not have known that some publishers prefer to publish GameMaker titles and that certain genres of GameMaker titles are likely to do well on Xbox and Switch because of player preferences. You also might not have known that the community around GameMaker can be a marketing opportunity in its own right, spanning Reddit communities and Facebook groups in addition to GameMaker's own Showcase efforts.

There might be cons, of course, to having chosen GameMaker as an engine (which we will talk about as well), but in this quick example, we have touched on several points that could have a big impact on your business plan. You could, today, start to target GameMaker-friendly publishers and become more active in GameMaker communities with the hopes of unlocking new potential benefits.

Your inherent creativity as an indie will serve you well here. Use your current trajectory as a springboard for imagining possibilities and for ideating on how you might seize the most worthwhile of those possibilities. While planning earlier is always better, you can almost always open new doors for your work no matter where you are in development.

Project Types and Project Goals

Before you build the details for your grand development plan, defining your basic goals and aspirations can help frame the other choices you make around your project. The plan for a game that funds the overhead of a 10-person team and builds the runway for funding a follow-up title will be a much different plan from the plan for a solo indie working on their game on nights and weekends.

In the world of indie games, both paths are perfectly viable, but the plans will tackle unique problems.

We tend to put indie game projects into five different buckets:

- Hobby projects – Game jams or small side projects that might have commercial value but are really more about learning and experimentation

- Self-published projects – A full game designed to succeed without the support and funding of a publisher or investor

- Traditionally published projects – A full game designed to require publisher funding and support to be successful
- Early Access projects – These titles could ultimately be self-published or released in partnership with a publisher, but the development includes leveraging Steam's Early Access community
- Crowdfunded projects – Ranging widely in scope, these projects are designed with the additional beat of finding traction on a crowdfunding platform well before the full launch

The needs of each project will necessitate a unique plan on top of all of the other choices you have to make about the game itself – genre, art, scope, engine, and so on. Let's explore each of these in greater depth to fully illustrate how varying goals lead to different kinds of plans.

Hobby Game Projects

Indies often make the mistake of trying to make their first game their best game. While this can sometimes be the case, the more likely reality is that your first game will be your worst game. Game design and development are difficult skills to learn and master, so most successful indies start their journeys with smaller hobby projects. Instead of spending three years on 10 hours of platforming content, they might spend a day (as is common in the "Game Jam" format) or a few weeks to bring a simpler game to life.

Hobby projects give you room to fail. Without going too far into being an over-the-top motivational speaker, failure is actually an overwhelmingly positive outcome for a creative. Failure means you tried something new and learned in the process.

Most game jams – which is a format where developers try to make a game in a set amount of time, often a day – create a slew of games that are objectively "bad" from a commercial perspective. Even if the developers execute on their initial concept, the art is usually janky and the controls are a bit wonky, but making a commercial game isn't the point.

The point is to learn so that your next game can be better as a result.

The common missed opportunity for hobby projects is to also practice your planning skills. The stakes might feel so low that doing a full GDD and a business plan for your goofy *Mario* ripoff is unnecessary, but these are actually the best ways to hone your ability to anticipate and address challenges. The scale of the project means you have less to wrangle overall, but all of the considerations you have to make are the same.

If you apply the planning ideas in this book to your hobby projects, you will find it far easier to scale up into a commercial project.

Edmund McMillen, a name you might recognize from games like *Super Meat Boy* and the immensely successful *The Binding of Isaac* series, is a glowing example of how starting with small hobby projects can lead to a successful career as an indie.

McMillen, who went by Bluebaby on Newgrounds, got his start making games in Adobe Flash. By most standards, Flash games are much simpler than commercial games. Fans of this medium – most of whom are counting grey hairs as Flash fades from memory – expected quick experiences, and developers obliged. Most Flash developers were making projects for fun anyway, and the nature of Flash meant that large file sizes were impractical.

As a result, most Flash games lasted a few minutes at most, and McMillen's work fit this mold.

Meat Boy, the precursor to *Super Meat Boy*, began as a Flash game in 2008 and took only three weeks to make. Though it was not a huge game, it was fun, and as the views of the game ticked into the hundreds of thousands, Nintendo and Microsoft took notice. They both wanted a full-fledged version of *Meat Boy* for their platforms, which were WiiWare and Xbox Live Arcade at the time.

Super Meat Boy launched in 2010. By 2012, the game had sold more than a million copies.

In 2018, *Super Meat Boy* got a Switch port–another example of the long-tail sales potential of an indie game that we discussed in the previous section–and a spokesperson told *Kotaku*, "I don't know if I'm allowed to give out specific numbers, but I can say that for Team Meat, SMB Switch made more money on it's day one than our XBLA launch on Oct. 20th, 2010."

That's not bad for an indie game that was 8 years old by the time it got a Switch port, which was also after several other platform releases and years of bundle sales and promotional discounts.

The DNA that made *Super Meat Boy* a commercial success is clearly visible in the Newgrounds version of *Meat Boy*. Yes, *Super Meat Boy* is much bigger. It has more levels. It has more mechanics. The art and controls are more polished. But the hobby version gave McMillen room to explore the core ideas. Three weeks of work is a lot of effort, but if the game had flopped after that, it would have been far less painful than if he had worked for three years only to discover that players had no interest in a game like *Meat Boy*.

Additionally, McMillen's Newgrounds profile is still live, and his upload history has 34 content submissions before the 2008 upload of *Meat Boy*, with his first uploads starting in 2001. If you browse through these uploads, you can see glimmers of the ideas that would evolve into *Super Meat Boy* and *The Binding of Isaac*, but there are also a lot of out there uploads as well.

Blood Car 2000! Looks and plays nothing like the games that made McMillen an indie legend – it's a game about running over zombies with your car – and it was not a breakout success either. One reviewer wrote, "this game is shit, good to play without fingernails though."

If you look hard enough, you can find indie stories where the developer's very first game was their breakout success, rocketing their career into orbit. Practically speaking, though, most indie success stories align more closely with McMillen's. Seven years of small experiments and small projects built up to *Meat Boy*, and because McMillen was so active on Newgrounds, we can more clearly look at the path he took to become the force he is today.

That story for other developers is largely obscured because most one-off experiments never leave the developer's hard drive. They are born and die with no real public release, giving players the illusion that an indie's first commercial game is their first game ever. That's simply not how it usually happens.

Because our goal for this book is to help you become a successful indie, we feel we need to emphasize how important hobby projects can be in your career. If you are new to making games, start with small manageable projects. Don't worry about them being good in the *Metacritic* since of the idea of good.

Experiment. Practice. Fail. Learn. You are likely to find that one of your hobby projects blossoms into your first commercial success. We saw this firsthand with *Turnip Boy Commits Tax Evasion*. The Snoozy Kazoo team made the first iteration as a game jam project with no real intention of making it a full-time project, but as happened with *Meat Boy*, the reaction from players was too big to ignore.

And now they too are an indie success story.

Self-Published Projects

Technically, as soon as you upload your game anywhere, it has been "published." For our purposes here, though, we are focusing more on the intention. If you upload a game jam project to Itch.io because you want to share it with friends, we would still consider that a hobby project.

If instead you are uploading a game to make a profit to offset the time and money you invested into development, that is more in line with what we mean by self-publishing. You made the game with the intention of making a profit on it, presumably so you could continue making games.

For indies, self-publishing is only getting easier. Releasing a game on Steam is relatively painless, and solo developers have successfully self-published on consoles like Switch, PlayStation, and Xbox as well.

As we discussed in Chapter 1, self-publishing ultimately means taking on all of the responsibilities of a publisher and executing on them yourself. If you don't account for that workload in your planning, you may discover significant holes in your budget with no funds available to fill them. Another common problem in not planning for these responsibilities is many will focus on development first before then marketing the game just before launch. This does not give time to build an audience and will likely have a launch fall flat.

Self-publishing should be a strategic business choice. Here are some of the signs self-publishing might be the right path for your game:

- You have the budget to self-fund the project
- You or your team have significant technical and marketing expertise to cover the majority of the responsibilities a publisher would take on

- You are focused on one to two platforms for the initial release
- Your sales expectations are unlikely to justify a publisher commitment
- You have the financial resources to grow slowly overtime
- You have a behind-the-scenes partner to connect you with the right industry insiders

Self-publishing could also be the wrong choice for your game. If you ignore key signs that this is the case, you could doom or severely hinder your project by pursuing self-publishing. Some of those signs are as follows:

- You do not and will not have the budget to complete your game in its current scope
- Your team has very little marketing experience and no existing fan community
- You have little experience with engaging games journalists and streamers to get press coverage
- You or your team are missing key technical skills, especially as it relates to porting
- You can clearly see how an injection of resources or supports would dramatically improve the sales potential of the project

Put another way, these are considerations that indies often overlook when they self-publish. We emphasize that perspective because you may be able to address these points to clear a path to self-publishing.

From a business point of view, self-publishing has a few big advantages over publishing that make it strategically attractive. When you are in complete control of the game launch, you can retain the majority of the profits as well as all of the rights to the intellectual property tied to the game. The big danger, however, is overestimating how much profit you can generate with no help beyond what you or your team are capable of doing.

This takes us back to our profit math from Part 1. The natural reaction for many indies is to recoil when they think about how much of *their* profit a platform or a publisher takes from a sale. It can immediately feel unfair, and the nature of the indie spirit has a built-in willingness to go-it-alone. So, faced with those numbers, why wouldn't you just self-publish and keep all of the profit for the people who actually built the game?

Well, the short-term win could mean giving up on long-term profits that might be substantial.

Let's say that, hypothetically, you are running an incredibly lean development timeline. If a publisher gave you $20,000 in additional funding, you could add four months of development to your game, taking it from a small hobby project to a full-fledged game experience. On top of that, the publisher commits a $10,000 marketing budget.

If that enables you to retail the game at $9.99 instead of $4.99, that alone expands the profit potential of the game significantly, but if we return to the math we started in Chapter 3, we can see more clearly how this story might play out:

Remember that Steam takes 30% for a platform fee, leaving $6.99 in profit per sale. That means that you need to sell approximately 4,292 units for the publisher to recoup their investment (make their money back), at which point you start to get a share of each sale.

Is that reasonable for your project? Maybe. Maybe not. You would need to benchmark your game against similar titles in the genre to get a realistic view of what sales potential might be, and then you would need to find the right publisher who has the performance track record your game needs.

At the same time, though, you should be highly critical of your own ability to drive game sales. For example, if you find that your Wishlist numbers are barely moving after a few months of your Steam page being live, the averages around Wishlist conversions (19 percent on average become sales, as discussed in Chapter 4) could reveal that your game is heading toward a failed launch and it might be wise to revise your strategy.

The revision could still mean self-publishing but with a much larger marketing effort–a new hire or an outside consultant–or it could mean pivoting the project and hunting for a publisher.

The Steam store is littered with the corpses of self-published indie games that never found a playerbase, and the real tragedy is that many of these titles aren't bad games. They might have found real success if they were better prepared to navigate the challenges of self-publishing or if they had the support of an experienced publisher.

Again, this is where the glamor of what indie games appear to be from the outside cloud the realities of the business of games.

Gone Home is an iconic indie title from The Fullbright Company and it has the hallmarks of what players have come to expect from indie games. *Gone Home* is visually compelling with a deep story and the gameplay is a departure from the tropes and cliches of AAA titles. The game itself is wonderful, and the size of the splash it has made since its release in 2013 is so substantial that the importance of the team behind the game can be easy to miss.

Fulbright co-founder Karla Zimonja told *Vice* that the Fullbright team worked from savings and credit card debt to self-finance *Gone Home*. Zimonja and the other two Fullbright cofounders, Steve Gaynor and Johnnemann Nordhagen, had worked together at 2K Marin in San Francisco where they worked on *Bioshock 2* and the Minerva's Den DLC.

The team rented a house, moved in together, and used the basement as the Fullbright office:

"Renting the house together meant we could take a year and a half to make a game and not take out a loan, or go to venture capitalists, not that a venture capitalist would have ever given us money for this," Zimonja told Vice. *Zimonja*

also said, "But we're pretty lucky. We had a fall back—if it didn't work out, we could have gone back to AAA and got jobs again, which isn't an option that everyone has."

From Zimonja's story alone, we can already see that *Gone Home* was a risky project in the minds of the original development team, and the team was also candid about their unique financial and industry advantages. They had the financial runway to bet 18 months of their lives on a strange indie game, and they had AAA development experience that likely helped them navigate game development and the business of games.

Additionally, shortly after the release of *Gone Home*, co-founder Steve Gaynor launched *Tone Control*, a games industry podcast that featured guests like Jonathan Blow, Tim Schafer, Ken Levine, Neil Druckmann, and Derek Yu. While *Gone Home* wasn't the focus of the podcast, Gaynor's connection to the game was a natural part of many of the conversations.

Tone Control was immensely popular in its time (bring it back, Steve!), and one can safely assume that its reach helped to extend the momentum of *Gone Home* as well. The podcast also demonstrates that Gaynor has an incredible network in the industry, hinting at more Fullbright advantages that may not be available to typical indies who haven't worked at AAA studios.

With that lens, a success story like *Gone Home* should look very different. Fulbright had funding, experience, and industry access. So, while a game like *Gone Home* might be a self-publishing success story, make sure you look at the whole story before you decide that self-publishing is right for your project.

Traditional Publishing

Our discussion around self-publishing naturally covered many of the reasons why working with a traditional games' publisher may be right (or wrong) for your project. Funding, marketing, development support, industry access, press relationships, quality assurance – we have talked about all of these variables, as they relate to working with a publisher, already.

If you see even one of these gaps in your planning, engaging a publisher should be a serious consideration for your project. If you decide that a publisher is essential to the success of your game, that choice should directly influence your planning process:

Here's why:

- Your game and development process need to align with publisher's portfolio
- Finding and pitching publishers are demanding tasks and take ample time
- Publishers often request specific materials from indie studios when they pitch
- Having an attorney review agreements will also require additional budget

Whether you self-publish or work with a publisher, we recommend that you follow best practices around the whole of the development process, such as working from a well-maintained GDD, carefully managing budgets and expenses, and applying project management principles to improve efficiency. When you self-publish, though, no one but your own team is looking at the inner workings of your project.

If you sign with a publisher, a third party of experienced game professionals will look at your plans and your processes on an ongoing basis. They start this part during the vetting process to first decide if they want to work with you in the first place, and they do this periodically to ensure that the investment they made in your game is on its way to market as scheduled.

Therefore, if you don't build your planning and project management to account for this outside set of eyes, you could be creating new obstacles for yourself if you intend to work with a publisher.

In our work as publishers, we see this happen to many indies. Their demo looks great and the pitch sounds exciting, but when we look at their GDD and their budget plans, we uncover big red flags that make us hesitate to commit to the relationship. If an indie is not accurately tracking expenses and is projecting unusual numbers for anticipated costs, then we are usually more critical about investing in the project. In this situation, a publisher often asks themselves, "If the indie isn't careful with their own money, can I really expect them to be careful with ours?"

Budgets, development planning, and pitch creation are later topics in this book, so don't fear. We will equip you with tools to keep this from happening to you.

For now, if you plan to pursue a publisher, here are the tasks and objectives you should incorporate into your planning:

- Create and maintain pitch materials
- Reach out and connect with publishers
- Participation in key showcases and industry events to gain awareness for your title
- Market your game in parallel with your publisher search
- Develop a clear plan for why you need a publisher and how you would use their help and funding
- Create a development roadmap synced to budgets
- Produce a high-quality demo

When you are focused on bringing your game idea to life, many of the items in this list can be easily overlooked. A bad pitch can kill a great game, and actually finding a publisher often takes time and money. Indie budgets are often limited, and as the Fullbright story we just shared illustrated, those budgets are often personally funded, at least in part.

Many people would struggle to quickly find $1,000 (or more) to pay for an attorney to review a publishing agreement. Similarly, the budget to attend a major gaming convention, pay for entry into a networking event at that convention, and also cover booth and travel costs would be difficult to amass with any amount of speed.

If you decide in pre-development that your project needs a publisher, your plan should then account for how you are going to find that publisher, allocating all of the time and resources you might need ahead of time so that you have as few surprises as possible to navigate later.

If you identify PAX East as a great place to meet publishers – and it can be – what steps do you need to take to make that happen?

Your plan might look like this:

- Complete a polished pitch deck
- Complete a demo build
- Complete a trailer
- Allocate budget for travel, booth rental, and booth materials
- Identify the publishers likely to be in attendance at PAX
- Reach out to publishers one month in advance of PAX
- Reach out to publishers one week in advance in PAX
- Reach out to publishers on day one of PAX to catch last-minute meetings
- Reach out to the PAX press list when it is available
- Plan for booth coverage so that you (or your business development lead) can take meetings without leaving your booth unattended
- Fill the gaps in your schedule with "cold knocking" publisher booths to pitch your game
- Follow up with the people you met each evening as appropriate (giving them access to your deck and demo, for example)
- Follow up with everyone who replied to your emails after the event, whether you had a meeting or not

Fully preparing for an event like PAX can absorb a month of development time for some developers because every item we listed above ripples through the whole of the project. If you want to have a complete pitch deck and a shareable demo, your team will need to meet specific development milestones to bring those items to life. And then you need to devote time to creating event materials, including posters and displays for your booth, and you also need to set aside time for managing your outreach and pitches.

Even if you elbow grease your way through many of these tasks, the event will still cost you money. If those costs are not well managed, the drain on your budget could threaten the project as a whole.

Fortunately, indie-friendly industry hacks exist. Organizations such as Indie MEGABOOTH have done a great deal to make major gaming events accessible to new indies, and initiatives like PAX Rising do the same. There is also a shifting landscape of contests, scholarships, and grants available to indies that can defray expenses, give you extra help, and put you in front of publishers.

We recognize that opportunities like access to industry events require a certain amount of privilege. Not everyone has the funds to go to events or lives reasonably close to a major event to make it remotely practical. You can still find a publisher without the benefits of attending an in-person event, but again, your plan needs to account for this obstacle earlier rather than later. In this kind of scenario, you may need to spend more time on cold outreach, participating in digital networking opportunities, and drumming up organic interest in your work to get a publisher's attention.

Snoozy Kazoo and Robi Studios are both examples of how different indie paths – but good planning – can set your game up for publishing success. Disclaimer: We worked with both of these teams via Graffiti Games, so our adoration is rooted in a very clear bias for their work, but we believe their stories are relevant here even if we fanboy over their games.

Snoozy Kazoo is the team behind *Turnip Boy Commits Tax Evasion*. This comical pixel art action adventure game began as a small hobby project that the team showcased at a BostonFIG event. If you aren't familiar, BostonFIG is a nonprofit whose mission is to "support and showcase the efforts of independent game developers, as well nurture young aspiring game creators from diverse backgrounds."

For Snoozy Kazoo, BostonFIG was an accessible starting point for sharing *Turnip Boy* with players. The overwhelming love for the game-jam version of *Turnip Boy* surprised the development team and made them decide to expand the scope and vision for what the game could be. The team went back into development and set their sights on showcasing at PAX East, which they were able to have a small booth at as a result of winning the Mass Digi Challenge.

And that's where we met Snoozy Kazoo. One of our booth workers knew the Snoozy team and told us to check out their game of a turnip committing tax fraud and challenging a corrupt vegetable government. The premise was intriguing, and sure enough, as more of our team members found time to check out the booth, the more excited we were to have a conversation with this indie team.

A year later, *Turnip Boy Commits Tax Evasion* became a true indie success story.

The path to publishing for Robi Studios' *Blue Fire* was much different, however. Robi Studios is based in Argentina, so unlike Snoozy Kazoo, they are not right down the street from events like BostonFIG or PAX East. Their path to connecting with Graffiti Games focused more on building their online presence. They posted some great GIFs and images to their Twitter page, which made us contact them to see if they were interested in a publisher.

Once we connected, we worked with the Robi Studios team in much the same way as we worked with Snoozy Kazoo because all of the games published by Graffiti come from studios around the world. *Blue Fire*, like *Turnip Boy*, did very well at launch and beyond.

In practice, we were looking for the same signals even though both of these stories are about very different games and from developers from very different backgrounds: a game that was interesting to us, a game that had marketability, and a team that we trusted to deliver on their promises. They might have come in through different doors, but they ultimately checked the same boxes.

For Snoozy Kazoo, we could see players reacting to the game in real time at PAX, and we had a similar reaction when we played it for ourselves. As we talked to the team themselves, they were professional and prepared despite *Turnip Boy* being their first full game. They had clearly done their homework and did everything they could to be ready to pitch their game if they had the chance.

For Robi Studios, we couldn't see players reacting to the game, but knew what they were presenting would have interest from a large audience. When we played the demo, our excitement grew. And then when we talked with the Robi team, they too were professional and prepared.

We should emphasize that neither Snoozy Kazoo or Robi Studios knew the answer to every one of our questions or had absolutely pristine pitch decks or complete knowledge of the games industry. No reasonable publisher expects a seasoned indie studio to be perfect, and they definitely don't expect a new indie studio to know everything there is to know about making and releasing an indie game.

However, a publisher does want to see that even a brand new indie team is being thoughtful about the choices they make, are doing everything in their power to anticipate and solve problems, and is using the resources they do have in an effective way.

Publishers can tell when a pitch deck was made the night before or if a budget is based on imaginary numbers, so it says a lot about an indie to see that they are putting significant effort into planning from the beginning.

Crowdfunded Projects

In Chapter 1, we mentioned that finding indie game success with crowdfunding is a very specific path that justifies a book-length explanation on that strategy alone. While we don't have the page count to fully explore crowdfunding in this book, we should address how the decision to crowdfund your game can affect your planning.

Crowdfunding could be your path to self-publishing or it could be your path to attracting a publisher. Because a great crowdfunding campaign has many of the same hallmarks as an actual launch in terms of the noise you need to make and the level of polish that backers have come to expect from promotional materials, putting your game on Kickstarter or Indiegogo is a strategic business choice, a marketing moment, a funding tool, and a revenue channel all in one.

Many publishers use Kickstarter as a scouting tool. If a developer is able to hit a crowdfunding goal independently, that says a great amount about what the appetite for a game might be if the official launch was fully supported.

If a project does really well with crowdfunding and has a great team behind it, the game might have all of the talent and treasure it needs to self-publish.

Crowdfunding is incredible, and the popularity of crowdfunding has been a major boon to indie games of all shapes and sizes, but this path is not without risks. Despite the efforts of Kickstarter and Indiegogo to educate campaign organizers on best practices, many aspiring indies still think of crowdfunding as "easy money." Make a campaign, make some big promises, sprinkle in great art, and voila, you have a few hundred thousand dollars to build your dream game.

That's, of course, not how it actually works, but enough indies are still making this mistake that we feel we need to address the business implications here.

Beyond the lift of running a great crowdfunding campaign, you should also consider the following:

- It can take one to two months to put together a successful Kickstarter campaign
- The first crowdfunding campaign from a developer is rarely a runaway success, especially if the developer is unknown
- A failed crowdfunding campaign can send negative signals to potential investors and publishers
- Breaking promises to backers can permanently harm your reputation in the industry
- Fully accounting for development and perk fulfillment costs is especially challenging for inexperienced indies, so you can reach your goal and still discover you don't have enough budget
- Stretch goals can significantly shift development scope and player experience, which can be difficult to manage post-campaign
- Backers expect regular, meaty updates post-campaign
- Any significant pivot in the game's trajectory that was not addressed in the original campaign can create big community problems (such as signing with a publisher post-campaign)

If you opt to pursue crowdfunding, you should address each of these points in your plan. Depending on your industry experience, you might consider building a small but respectable social media following first and then running a small crowdfunding campaign for a smaller project. For all of the amazing guides and resources out there, learning the ins and outs of running a crowdfunding campaign is largely done from doing one yourself.

If your first campaign is on the smaller side, you will need less fanfare to reach your initial goal while also giving yourself more room to make mistakes that are not catastrophic. For example, misjudging the cost of producing and fulfilling t-shirts for a $4,000 crowdfunding campaign is not as bad as making the same mistake for a $250,000 campaign. Additionally, having successful campaigns tied to your account builds trust, making it more likely for users to believe that you can deliver on your bigger promises when you start making them.

You don't always need to build slowly. It is possible for your game to be a break-out crowdfunding hit, but a good business plan does not rely on being the exception to industry norms. Be reasonable, but also have a plan for how you will capitalize on great coverage and big interest if it comes.

Earlier, we talked about how Sabotage Studios ran an elegant Kickstarter for their game *Sea of Stars*. A great team with a fantastic track record of finding crowd-funding success is not all that surprising. While we can learn a lot from how they approached crowdfunding, many of our readers are unlikely to have the resources and clout that Sabotage Studios had at the beginning of their campaign.

Let's look at a different game that might be familiar: *Undertale*. Today, this indie title from developer Toby Fox is in the pantheon of legendary indie success stories, but *Undertale* actually began from a humble beginning in crowdfunding.

For the millions of units *Undertale* has sold to date, Fox first launched his Kickstarter with a $5,000 goal in 2013. Yes, crowdfunding has changed significantly in the nearly 10 years since the *Undertale* campaign went live, but Fox's initial goal is still worth highlighting because it shows how far small decisions can carry a project.

With a goal of $5,000 and a unique premise for a game, Fox's campaign gained momentum. That manageable goal likely made it easier for early backers to partici-pate because a lower goal meant a higher likelihood for success, and the game Fox pitched to go along with the budget felt like it matched that scope to a reasonable degree. He was not promising an expansive 3D MMO for a small budget but rather a polished, concise pixel art indie game – the kind of scope solo indies have tackled many times before.

And users could try the demo before making a pledge, which turned out to be a critical element as word of the game spread. Prospective players could experience the promises Fox was making about the *Undertale* paradigm, making it real rather than another empty Kickstarter promise.

In sum, 2,398 backers supported the campaign, raising a total of $51,124. Five years after its 2015 release, *NPR* reported that *Undertale* had sold "millions of cop-ies." We can also reasonably assume that *Undertale* merchandise has done excep-tionally well under the stewardship of Fangamer, the merchandise company that has the exclusive *Undertale* rights at the time of this writing.

Millions of units is far from a moderately successful crowdfunding campaign with less than 3,000 backers, and that's one of the lessons hidden in the Fox story: A big success came from a manageable development budget and a relatively small crowdfunding goal not only because the game was good but because Fox kept build-ing momentum for his work one piece at a time.

The *Undertale* campaign has 39 total updates with the last update coming in 2017 (two years after the game's official release). Fox stayed active with marketing and community communication up to and through the release of the game, which included consistent posts to his Tumblr blog as well.

In one of those blogs, Fox wrote, "Though I did work hard, there's definitely a lot of luck involved in having a game become this popular."

Luck may have been a factor for Fox, but the game's trajectory in hindset is a series of well-tempered decisions from an indie developer, and those choices put *Undertale* in position to capitalize on the attention it garnered.

The larger takeaway for indies, whether they plan to self-publish or to use crowd-funding to attract a publisher as well, is that crowdfunding success is not always about big upfront dollars.

A "Living" Document

We have several other planning considerations to cover yet, but this overview of potential project types and goals should already have you thinking about what steps may be best suited for bringing your game to market. That said, the benefit of a thorough planning process is that you can revise and adjust course with relatively little pain.

As we talk about market evaluations, scoping your game, and selecting an engine to work in, your previous choices may warrant an adjustment. Where you thought you needed a publisher, you might realize that self-publishing is a better fit because of how your game fits into its target genre.

Planning is not a linear process. Everything is written in pencil at this point, and you are supposed to go back and make adjustments as new information comes to your attention. A plan is a living document, which means that it changes, expands, and grows over time. It is not a fixed piece of output that you make and never change.

Take notes. Write down questions. Imagine a variety of scenarios. Keep challenging yourself to make your plan better as you continue reading.

Genre and Market Evaluation

In this chapter, we start to step through core considerations in planning the development for your game. This process has several goals, all of which can impact your overall success. Those goals are as follows:

1. Create a predictable and practical development schedule by clearly outlining what you need to make to complete your game.

2. Develop the assets and materials that are likely to be relevant to investors and publishers.

3. Map your plan to a real budget so you can understand the resources your project needs to set Wishlist goals as well as sales goals.

No development plan is perfect. The games industry has a long history of delayed releases, mismanaged player expectations, and cancelled projects. The biggest studios in the world struggle to manage timelines and budgets, so much so that "don't preorder!" has become a meme in the community. If the most experienced people in the industry find this difficult, what hope does an indie have for getting it right?

What we are really aiming to do here is to reduce the severity of planning mistakes. If a AAA team misjudges their release by six months or more, an inexperienced developer can easily miss the mark by a year or more. A delay of that length for a multi-million-dollar game might be painful, but those scale of studios have access to capital and cash reserves in most cases

Adding a year of budget to an indie game is a death sentence for most indies. You will rarely hit your development milestones and your budgets precisely as planned, but you should make every effort possible to get as close as you can with your planning so that you can be in a better position to absorb potential problems.

Asking your publisher for an extra month of development time or taking out a loan to cover payroll for that month is not ideal, but it's not catastrophic. You will still be close to your target launch window, and the relative small amount of additional budget you need could be addressed in several ways.

DOI: 10.1201/9781003215264-8

Missing the mark by several months, on the other hand, puts your game in an entirely new launch window, which could be outright impossible for your publisher to accommodate because of their other planned launches, and your humble indie game may end up releasing at the same time as the next hot AAA title, putting you at a severe marketing disadvantage.

With our process, you can eliminate many of the most common problems that indies face before they actually become problems, and that means deep forethought for the following:

- Your target market
- Game scope (length, complexity, post-launch updates or DLC)
- Engine selection
- Translation and localization
- Development and release timelines
- Building a team
- Mapping your plan to a budget

Even if you already have an idea for what kind of game you want to make, all your development choices will be more impactful if you can clearly see where your game fits into your chosen genre, so let's start there.

Predicting Sales Success

If one of the goals for your game is to find financial success, your planning process should answer the question, "How do I know players will buy my game?"

The answer to this question has implications for every layer of your project, from the features you choose to include to the target development budget to how you market the finished product. Beyond how you and your team will directly leverage that answer, publishers and investors are likely to ask about this reasoning as well. They too want to know if the project they support will be successful, and they will expect to hear your reasoning as they do their own analysis.

No business is a purely scientific endeavor. Yes, we want to rely on data and quantifiable trends as much as we can, but doing something different will always mean venturing into the unknown to some degree. You can make all the best decisions on paper and still not accurately predict the outcome.

The art of business is using a combination of savvy and creativity to fill in the gaps with an educated guess. No matter how smart we are and how much we think we know, we can never know for certain if a product is going to be a success or not.

In the games industry, we often see indies drift to the extremes of this spectrum. Some indies totally ignore the parts of their project that they can quantify–such as the Wishlist math we explored in Part 1 – and put the entirety of their trust in their own creativity. If they are passionate about their game, they assume that the passion they feel will be shared equally by anyone else who plays the game.

At the other extreme, some indies observe a trend in game sales or player preferences and overestimate the implications of that data. If *Among Us* is the most popular game of the moment, they assume that if they make a game that shares the mechanics and features of *Among Us,* they will also be successful.

When we simplify those perspectives to these two extremes, the flaws in the logic of either of these assumptions is likely clear. Of course you can't assume that your personal tastes match the tastes of your target playerbase. Of course you can't expect to be financially successful by ripping off the premise of an already popular game (something that is all too common). Yet, we see indies fall into these traps over and over and over again.

To find the reasonable middle ground, here is the data you need to explore:

- Sales trends for titles in your target genre
- Broader sales trends for the industry
- Metacritic and Steam review data for comparable titles
- Publically available data on social media engagement around comparable titles
- Other market signals that could be impact the performance of your project

The term in this list that might be new to you is "comparable titles." A comparable title is any game that might share your target audience, either in whole or in part. No two games are exactly alike, but a player that likes the action of *The Binding of Isaac* might also like *Enter the Gungeon*. They have enough in common that if you were also making a twin-stick Roguelite dungeon crawler, you could learn a great deal from these two games. Usually your comparable titles are the games that inspired yours or that you reference in your messaging of the game. For instance, we compared *Blue Fire* to *A Hat in Time* and *The Legend of Zelda: The Wind Waker* due to its 3D platforming RPG adventure mechanics.

Discussions around comparable titles and target genres often happen simultaneously, but distinguishing between the two is important for both your planning process and for how you talk about your game to publishers, media, streamers, and potential players.

Genre definitions can be controversial, so while your game might broadly qualify as a platformer, finding titles that are more similar within the genre can help you benchmark player interest and also better communicate your vision for your game (if it is still in development).

Your platformer might more closely resemble *Celeste* than it does *Hollow Knight*, and that's a big distinction because of how players perceive those titles. The gameplay of *Celeste* focuses intensely on contained challenges. The layout of a level is in itself a puzzle, and each level is separated from the others by very clear checkpoints. In *Hollow Knight*, on the other hand, the platforming is also about solving challenges, but it is also a vehicle for exploring a vast branching world, the kind of experience that Metroidvania fans crave.

Even if your game is not exactly like *Celeste* – and it shouldn't be – the data you can find around that game's sales performance will be much more insightful than data from *Hollow Knight*. One is simply more applicable to the kinds of players you plan to target.

Unfortunately, no data are perfect, and your analysis needs to account for what you don't know and what you *can't* know.

The Ins and Outs of Sales Data

Sales data for games is usually derived from the following sources:

- Steam Spy (SteamSpy.com)
- Press coverage (unit sales, if possible)
- Steam user reviews
- Earning reports (from publicly traded companies)
- Sales estimated by reviews
- Data from third party tools or consultants
- Your team's past sales performance (if applicable)

For many years, Steam Spy was the industry standard for analyzing sales performance in the games industry. While Steam Spy is still operational today, the data it provides is very different. Steam Spy relied on access to the Steam API to extract relatively accurate performance data from the platform. When Valve stopped supporting this functionality, Steam Spy lost access to the data it needed.

Steam Spy now uses a model rooted in machine learning, which uses publicly available data to infer conclusions for how many units a title may have sold. According to a 2018 article from *Kotaku*, Steam Spy creator Sergey Galyonkin believes the site has a 10 percent margin for error. That margin for error is likely to be more extreme for less popular titles because of limits on available data, so indies should be especially wary.

To be clear, Steam Spy data were never 100 percent accurate for a variety of reasons, and that caused significant controversy for developers who were judged by Steam Spy data, but even some imperfect data is better than no data at all.

For example, Steam Spy estimates that *Celeste* has 500,000–1,000,000 Steam owners, which is a pretty broad range. For most indies, a shift in sales by 1,000 units or more can be substantial, so we don't have enough data to go on yet.

If we next dig for press coverage about *Celeste* sales, we can find a variety of articles reporting units sold to date. At the time of this writing, the most recent article about *Celeste* sales figures was a March 2020 article from *IGN* that reported *Celeste* total sales had passed 1,000,000 units.

Though the article is light on specifics, total units usually implies that those sales are across all available platforms, not just Steam, so we now have a better idea of how accurate Steam Spy's data was, but if we go digging even more, we can find some insights on how well *Celeste* did on the Nintendo Switch.

Maddy Thorson, the co-creator *Celeste* who worked alongside Noel Berry, told *Destructoid* that "The Switch version of *Celeste* has sold the most, and that's what we were expecting. We feel like *Celeste* and the Switch are a perfect fit for each other."

That's not hard data, but it does give us a big clue: If your game has something in common with *Celeste* and *Celeste* did exceptionally well on Switch in addition to its success on Steam, your development roadmap should likely include a Switch release as well.

We can further bolster this analysis by looking for other data sources. If your game is comparable to an AAA title in some way, you might be able to find public earnings reports that disclose total unit sales or gross profit from a particular title. This is relatively rare in the indie world because most developers and publishers in our corner of the industry are relatively small in comparison to AAA outfits, but there has been a trend of larger parent companies acquiring several indie studios at once.

So, even though the possibilities are slim, you may find one of your comparable titles belongs to a company that regularly shares earning reports, but you won't know unless you look.

The last two data sources available to indies can be controversial. You can approximate unit sales based on the number of Steam reviews a game has received, and you can also use third-party tools to gain extra insights as well.

Steam Spy is a third party tool. It is not officially affiliated with Valve, and it offers a variety of features available only to registered and paying users. Several such tools exist in the games industry, and we are hesitant to officially endorse any of them because the industry changes so rapidly that our recommendation for one tool over another could be outdated by the time you read this. Instead, we'll share that you should tread carefully with third-party tools. They can be incredibly powerful in many respects, but you should also be mindful of their cost (they are typically pricey) and their limitations (what they can actually do versus what they guess at).

That disclaimer aside, estimating game sales based on Steam reviews is a common practice in the industry, but like Steam Spy, you can't completely trust that the conclusion you reach is accurate. It's a hint, another reference point that helps you triangulate roughly how successful a game was.

The best math for this estimate comes from Simon Carless, the author behind *The Game Discoverability Now!* newsletter. In 2020, he polled his readers and used sales data from 237 games to correlate the quantity of public Steam reviews to actual sales. He found that, on average, a game sold 63 units per review.

Carless also notes other key points for consideration:

- The "middle 80 percent of the sample" ranged from 25 to 100 units sold per review
- Compared to survey data published in 2018 by Jake Birkett, average units sold per review is trending downward (Birkett found 82 sales per review in his research)

- Games launched in 2020 averaged 41 units sold per review
- This average is likely to continue trending downward as Steam makes bigger efforts to collect more reviews more often
- The line from total units sold to estimating total profit is not a straight one

For that last point, Carless says, "You've got to factor in average 'regular' price on Steam, how much and how often the game was on sale, and then after the money comes in, Steam platform cut, refunds, and VAT before you even get close to working out the real number. (Realistically, that's 30%–50% of the 'optimistic' gross number, and potentially way less, if discounting is aggressive.)"

To add to this point about revenue being a fuzzy number, don't forget that we're mainly discussing Steam numbers here as it's impossible to find sales numbers for console versions of a game unless a developer discloses them.

Additionally, we have already explored how the revenue potential for a game isn't purely contained in raw sales figures. *Celeste* has been incredibly successful with merchandise, and we also know from the Epic Games report on minimum guarantees that *Celeste* earned $750,000 from the Epic Games Store alone.

Though Carless is transparent about the limitations of this approach, the exact math to use here is hotly debated amongst industry experts. Some publishers still use this approach to guess at a game's total sales while other publishers have seen such radical variability in their own ratio of reviews to sales that they are hesitant to trust any mystical industry average.

If we apply the 63 units per review estimate to *Celeste*, we would conclude that the game sold 2,153,781 units on Steam (based on 34,181 reviews at the time of this writing). Based on the news reports we highlighted earlier, that number feels too large, though it may be possible that the game saw a surge of popularity in 2020 and 2021.

If you use the least optimistic total in Carless' range, which was 25 units per review, the number fits much better: 854,525 units sold.

What do you actually do with this data, especially since much of it is an educated guess, at best?

Here's our recommendation:

- Analyze several comparable titles for your game and try to capture reference points for a reasonable success in the genre (and not just the mega outliers, like *Celeste*)
- In bullet form, perhaps on PowerPoint slides, summarize what you could find for sales and platform performance, note their undiscounted list prices, and also note their Metacritic score and their total steam reviews
- Identify what your game has in common with these titles and what's different (such as art style, game length, theme, and so on)
- Based on the data you collected, make a tentative estimate of how many units a mildly successful title in this genre might move

Emphasis on "mildly successful." We all want your next game to be an iconic indie success story, selling millions of units like *Celeste*, but a sustainable business plan grounds itself in practical realities. If your game is good, if your marketing is good, what is a safe sales projection? What is a pessimistic sales projection?

This exercise will prepare you to talk to investors and publishers about the potential impact of your game, but long before that, you can use those projections to vet your estimated budget. This estimate is easier to make if you have released games before, so if you have a past game to base potential future performance on, factor that in also.

If your development budget exceeds what you can safely estimate for total net profit, you have a problem. The scope of your game could be too large for the market. Your development resources might be too expensive or poorly allocated. Your target genre could be too narrow. Your timeline could be too long.

The source of the problem will vary, but looking at the numbers early on will help to keep these problems from morphing into catastrophes later.

Trends and Traps

In addition to sales data, your market research should aim to capture the direction of a genre as well. This analysis is even less scientific than estimating sales data from Steam reviews, but your diligence matters. Your game needs to strike the strange balance of feeling familiar to longtime fans of a genre while at the same time offering a new and memorable experience. To do that, you need a deep understanding of what has happened in the genre and insights into where the genre might go.

With the benefit of hindsight, we can see that a game such as *Celeste* tapped into several industry trends while also offering a fantastic gameplay experience. Retro pixel art has long been an indie staple, but *Celeste* carefully builds mood and setting with its art direction, level design, and polish. *Shovel Knight* found success here as well, but the platforming of *Celeste* is probably more akin to the *Super Meatboy* experience: move fast, avoid the spikes, die a lot, and keep trying.

The tone of *Celeste*, a deeply emotional narrative of self-discovery, fits into the broad trend of emotional indie storytelling. *Gone Home*, though very different in terms of gameplay, taps into this trend, as do games like *Braid*, *Bastion*, and *Undertale*.

The platformers that would follow *Celeste*, titles like *Katana Zero* and *Blasphemous*, build on these hallmarks in their own way, pushing the idea of storytelling in a pixel art indie platformer to new and interesting places in 2019, which were then followed by titles like *Ori and the Will of the Wisps* and *Spelunky 2* in 2020.

We should note, however, that *Celeste* had a few other key advantages contributing to its success.

Thorson had previously made *Towerfall* and also created several popular levels in *Super Mario Maker*, and the fingerprints of the latter seem to be clearly visible in *Celeste*. Noel Berry, co-creator of *Celeste*, worked on a game called *Skytorn*. Though it had garnered some early interest from players, *Skytorn* was ultimately cancelled not long after the release of *Celeste*.

Celeste itself was born from a four-day game jam project and was first released as a PICO-8 game. Since we are talking about how to predict the potential success of a game, we should highlight the similarities in the *Celeste* development story to other stories we've shared in the book. *Super Meatboy* began as a much shorter Flash game, and *Turnip Boy Commits Tax Evasion* started as a quick game jam project.

So, in addition to broader market signals about what players wanted from an indie platformer, *Celeste* also had the benefit of confirming traction in its core ideas through lessons learned from Thorson's and Berry's previous games, Thorson's *Super Mario Maker* levels, and the PICO-8 incarnation of *Celeste*.

We are going to such great lengths to tell this story because it is important to understand that a game like *Celeste* does not materialize from pure inspiration. Rather, we would argue that *Celeste* is a masterful culmination of the developers' multitude of industry experiences mixed with an artful insight into what would be an original and engaging design for players.

In other words, Thorson and Berry combined two types of data: industry trends and personal experience. We can't explicitly say how exactly that played out behind the scenes and how much of those choices were conscious versus unconscious, but the power of the outcome is clear.

If you base your development purely on broad industry trends, you are likely to fall into three traps:

- Your game will feel like a less interesting version of more successful titles
- Your game will make a big bet on a trend that could die out before you can even launch
- Your game may not stand out when there are hundreds of similar titles trying to take advantage of the trend

Even today, well after the surprise success of *Among Us*, social deduction games of all varieties are launching on Steam each day. Though its initial success was several years ago, we are also still seeing the ripples of *PUBG*'s battle royale success, with many indies trying to put their own twist on the battle royale format or outright cloning existing battle royale games.

From a publisher's perspective, we expect to hear hundreds of pitches in the vein of recently popular games to the point that it can feel like a bad joke (*Hades* anyone?). From the developer's perspective – and we've sat on that side of the table as well – the advice to not look at the latest hits as market indicators could seem contradictory to our previous advice, which was to find comparable titles to bench-mark the potential success of your game.

And you'd be right. There is a potential contradiction buried between those lines, but the real point is to strike a careful balance. If you made a quaint farm manage-ment game with colorful pixel art and a variety of NPC relationships to explore, both players and publishers alike could feel as if this was simply another version of *Stardew Valley*. If instead you took inspiration from those mechanics but reimagined the theme, such as managing a medieval cemetery instead of managing a farm, the conversation you have about your game can talk about why the millions of people who bought *Stardew Valley* would also be interested in your game.

You might know the game we're talking about: *Graveyard Keeper*, developed by Lazy Bear Games and published by tinyBuild.

Graveyard Keeper has a great deal in common with *Stardew Valley*, but what it has in common with other comparable titles is only one piece of the story. Lazy Bear Games took many deliberate steps to make their game fit into the genre while also making it stand out.

If the pitch for *Graveyard Keeper* boiled down to "*Stardew Valley* was successful, so our game will be successful," which is often how a pitch for a social deduction game sounds in a post-*Among Us* market, it likely would not have found a home with tinyBuild. Instead, one can imagine (and this is all speculation on our part), that the pitch for *Graveyard Keeper* touched on a variety of comparable titles while also leaning into its whacky premise.

We will talk more about positioning your game in a pitch in Part 3: Pitch Deck Perfection, but for your early planning, be critical of your own originality. Players who love a game like *Stardew Valley* are often not looking for a slightly better version of *Stardew Valley* (if such a thing could exist). Instead, they are likely looking for games that build on one or several of the ideas that made *Stardew Valley* engaging, taking those mechanics and concepts to very new places.

Stepping Back for the Big Picture

If you conduct a thorough genre and market evaluation for your project, you will generate pages of notes and several rows of data. Once you feel like you have fully explored the market, review your notes, organize them, and start to summarize conclusions. The goals for this stage are four-fold:

- Solidify your broad understanding of and familiarity with your target genre
- Build the case for why players would buy your game
- Establish preliminary sales projections for your game
- Critically challenge your own assumptions about your game's potential

Long before you pitch to an investor or to a publisher, you have to convince yourself that your game has financial potential. Convincing yourself that your project would be intrinsically rewarding to make or that you personally would enjoy playing the game you envision is easy. Building the business case is hard.

The mental exercise here is to step out of your passionate indie dev shoes and to step into the shoes of an objective investor. Can you convince a person that your project has merit using industry data and industry analysis? They don't know you. They don't see the full vision for your game as you do. But they have a budget they are willing to invest.

You may get this right on the first try, but like all of the planning elements have discussed so far, this process is more likely to be a fluid activity that you come back to throughout your project. In the next chapters, we are going to dig deeper into building the development plan for your project–everything from choosing an art style to creating a budget spreadsheet – and a new choice or insight in those areas could influence your market analysis.

That is normal, and in many respects, it is supposed to happen that way. Even if your project does not change significantly in the rest of your planning process, you should still revisit this analysis with the more detailed vision of your plan in hand to reconfirm your initial market analysis conclusions.

CHAPTER

SEVEN

Scope and Engine Choices

Game development is a web of interconnected variables. One development choice in one part of the project can ripple through the rest of the project, impacting timelines, resources, and budgets. For indies, those consequences can be particularly challenging if their development experience is limited and budgets are strained from the start, but the truth is that the games industry as a whole struggles with this process.

If seasoned developers with dozens of games in their portfolio can make a project-killing mistake in their planning, that should tell you that you are entering dangerous waters and should do everything you can to be prepared.

This book is not a guide to game development, though, so know that we are focusing on the business planning side of this stage rather than the technical execution. That distinction is important because while we will talk about milestones and how to use them, we will not drill into the day-to-day process of managing a game under development. Like learning to program or to 3D model, project and team management are skills unto themselves and are well-worth honing alongside your business skills.

We will, however, cover the following in this chapter:

- How to think about the scope of your game (length, complexity, and post-launch content)
- How to think about choosing an art style for your game
- How to approach selecting a game engine for your project
- How to plan for translating and localizing your game
- How to create game development timelines

In the next chapter, we will take everything you learn from this section and create a real budget for your game. That budget process will also touch on hiring talent, managing the equity of your project and your studio, and fundamental recommendations for safeguarding yourself and your work.

DOI: 10.1201/9781003215264-9

For now, though, let's focus on how to connect your game idea to sound business practices.

Assessing Scope by Genre

You may not have realized it, but our genre and market analysis from the previous chapter was the beginning of considerations around scope. The type of game you create fundamentally affects scope even before you start to make additional design choices.

Making a great platformer is hard, but in terms of the resources required to make a platformer, that genre is particular accessible for several reasons:

- Most major game engines have built-in platformer support, meaning that the engine development team already built the code for basic controls, basic movement, basic physics, and basic collision detection.

- The 2D perspective simplifies art needs. With great level design, you can reuse tilesets and objects without hurting the aesthetics of the game, and most characters and enemies only need to be rendered from a profile view.

- Platformers are often easy to port. The broad engine support, the manageability of art assets, and the relative simplicity of platformer control schemes often means that the technical lift for porting a PC platformer to consoles is fairly light.

Already, we can see how design choices are also inherently business choices. Some types of games are, on average, less budget-intensive than other types of games. That doesn't mean you should choose the cheapest genre to develop for, but it does mean that your plan may have to address very different budget needs.

Massively multiplayer online games (MMOs) are some of the most complex and expensive games to make because they require a huge volume of content, which breaks into art, animation, writing, level design, and encounter design. They require robust networking and account management as well as data security to manage player information and to make interactions with other players in the world smooth and enjoyable. On top of that, MMOs need a significant active player base to retain players (an empty MMO isn't fun), so the marketing costs to get new players into the game can also be substantial because you need a lot of them and you need them right away.

You probably aren't making an MMO (please don't), but you should break your project into major systems so that you can begin to assess the complexity of your game. A game that seems simple and elegant on the surface might actually be a large development project.

For example, a retro RPG like *Final Fantasy 6* could look like a manageable project for an indie. Pixel artists are easy to find. Turn-based combat is straightforward. And anyone who has ever played the role of dungeon master can imagine a big fantasy world and dream up dungeons.

But, if you break *Final Fantasy 6* into systems, this project quickly shows its expansive scope:

- Overworld exploration (map, points of interest, and support for different vehicles)
- Town functionality (NPC conversations, buying and selling items, resting at the inn)
- Turn-based combat (deciding action order, calculating hit chance, calculating damage, structuring menus, and managing inputs)
- Player customization (mapping core stat variables to all of the items and choices that can affect a character's abilities in addition to managing level progression with an XP system)
- Unique character design (creating the systems that distinguish characters from each other, like Sabin's button combo attacks or Gau's ability to learn monster attacks)

And then buried within these classic RPG conventions are more systems that integrate into these core pieces. The Esper system of *Final Fantasy 6* is a separate but related experience and ability system that has to mesh with the rest of player customization. Every mini-game or set-piece moment is something different to build, like choosing lines for an opera performance or riding a raft down rapids. And many sprites have overworld as well as combat versions.

Speaking of sprites, the top-down view mandates that if a character (playable or not) moves in the world, you need art for that character standing as well as moving in each cardinal direction, and you might need action or emotion art (such as an attack animation or a surprised reaction).

A game like *Final Fantasy 6* can look like a simple development project because it has been executed so well. The player experience is smooth and intuitive, even today, and that masks how much had to happen behind the scenes for that to happen.

Your job is to identify all of the elements before the project even begins, and understanding the fundamentals of your chosen genre is a great start. Next, we have to answer more specific questions about the kind of content you aim to create and how much of it you aim to create.

Assessing Scope by Assets and Length

The volume and complexity of the systems you need to build to bring your game to life is one part of the development lift that can affect budget. The assets you use and how much playtime you plan to squeeze from them is another major part of development planning.

Art is one of the biggest factors here. The trope of indie games loving pixel art is largely driven by indies having a deep love for retro games, but pixel art is also an accessible art style to learn for a game development beginner and relatively inexpensive to outsource. This is true of most 2D art styles, but 2D does not always mean inexpensive.

According to *Eurogamer*, *Braid* had a development budget of $200,000, and Jonathon Blow, the game's creator, said that he "spent most of the money on hiring an artist." If *Braid* had chosen pixel art over the painted, hand-crafted David Hellman style, Blow likely could have had the equivalent amount of art created for much less money, but we can all agree that *Braid*'s unique art was part of what made the game a memorable experience.

With no simple way for us to say exactly how much one art style would cost compared to another – like the pixel art of *Celeste* compared to the pixel art of *The Messenger* – we need to be more creative about estimating the total scope for a game.

A good scope assessment will prevent snafus in development, and it can even be used to match your volume of content to an accepted pricepoint for games of that genre.

Scope Exercise 1: Reverse Engineer an Existing Game

Revisit your list of comparable titles. If you want to make a retro platformer that players will happily buy for $14.99, you might use a game like *Shovel Knight* as a reference point.

Pick the game that most closely matches the art style you want to use and the rough length of the gameplay experience. Next, break that game down into its project pieces to approximate how much you need to build to deliver an experience of a similar scope.

In other words, recreate a game design document by reverse engineering a game that already exists:

How many levels does it have?

How long does it take to complete an average level?

How many enemies are there?

What are the major mechanics?

And on and on. Depending on the genre, you may even be able to find some of this work already done for you. Many fan communities build detailed Wikis and support mods with extensive libraries of sprite sheets and system analysis. We are not advocating that you take any of this work for yourself, nor are we saying that every fan-driven community is abiding by proper copyright and intellectual property laws. We are saying that you might be able to find a comparable title already partially deconstructed, making it easier for you to see all of the pieces that go into it.

This exercise can be time-consuming, but the practice is priceless. If you can't assess the development scope of an already completed game, you will likely find it very hard to properly scope a game that exists only in your imagination.

Scope Exercise 2: Prototype

We have shared several indie success stories where developers expanded on a game jam project or built on the foundation of what was initially a much smaller game. While we have unpacked how this approach is beneficial for gauging player interest, we have not yet discussed how it can be a planning tool.

Defining scope will always be difficult, and the most experienced developers in the industry still underestimate projects from time to time, but managing scope can be much easier if you have a concrete baseline to base the rest of your plan on.

We can't say this with certainty, but one can imagine that having the playable version of *Meat Boy* on hand made it much easier for Team Meat to assess what a longer version would need. They could reference how much art they needed for the levels they already had. They could use the playtime of *Meat Boy* and the volume of content to approximate how many levels they would need to build to hit a longer playtime metric. And they could tweak and refine a concept that was already playable, a big advantage in a genre like platformers where how it *feels* to play the character is hugely important.

Whether you do your own game jam or simply build a prototype for your project, starting with a much smaller and more manageable development goal can give you insight into your broader project. At this scale, misjudging the needs of your project might cost you an extra week or development time. That same mistake in a full-length game could add months of work or empty your cash reserves long before you actually get to finish.

Art development will be a part of your planning, but if you are not an artist and do not intend to make the art yourself, you can use stock assets as placeholders to estimate the quantity of art your project will need. Many stock assets are available for free or are relatively inexpensive, so this path should be accessible to any indie.

Scope Exercise 3: Ask Another Developer

Sharing your plans with a peer can help you shine a light on the parts of your development you failed to consider or did not adequately explain. Writers, for example, often find it difficult to proofread their own work because their familiarity with the project and its intention unconsciously fills in blanks that are glaringly problematic to a fresh reader.

The same can be true in game development, so regular feedback – even if it is internal to your team or limited close collaborators early on – is useful.

Be critical of the criticism you receive, however.

In many respects, the indie community is generously supportive of other indies, especially developer to developer. The danger of that positivity is that someone's efforts to be encouraging are instead treated as validation that you are making the right choices. While the internet can be harsh and brutal, developer communities can sometimes be too nice. If you want someone to say they like your idea and your plan, you can find someone to say just that if you look hard enough.

An industry mentor is the best resource here, but an engaged and thoughtful peer, an individual willing to be constructive and openly talk about the problems they see, can work as well.

In practice, great indies spend years surrounding themselves with smart, talented people. They take certain kinds of questions to certain people, and they welcome a conversation that challenges their plans and their ideas. That does not always mean they agree with all of the feedback they receive, but their willingness to put their work directly into the fire helps them to see if all of the ideas are strong enough to come out the other side.

Scope Exercise 4: Learn from Your Old Projects

The games industry has a beautiful tradition of sharing "postmortem" project analyses. Postmortem literally translates to "after death," so many of these articles are written by developers sharing the lessons they learned from their mistakes, but you can also find several postmortems about highly successful games as well.

If this practice is new to you, reading postmortems from seasoned developers can help you see how they think about their work in retrospect, the lessons they learned, and how they realized there was a lesson to learn.

Postmortems are a common practice in games, and most of them are never formally made public because they happen behind closed doors amongst team members. Once the fanfare of a launch has died down, a team comes together and reviews their work, both the process and the output. They celebrate what they did well. They identify where they struggled. They discuss what they can learn from those experiences to make their next project a bigger success.

You can do this by yourself as well, and you should do them after every project. From your 24-hour game jams to your three-year commercial games, your past work is one of your best learning tools. If you haven't made anything yet – even something small – you can lean on the postmortems from other developers, but as soon as you have tried anything at all, make sure you set aside time to reflect on your work.

If you have already dabbled in development or completed games, think about those projects before planning your next idea. You might uncover an opportunity for growth that is right under your nose.

Translation and Localization

One of the most overlooked scope considerations for indies is the need for translation and localization.

Translation is the process of adapting the literal meaning of your content into another language. Localization is the process of accounting for cultural and regional differences. A joke in one language might not make sense in another. A harmless gesture in one region of the world could be incredibly offensive in another. Even world maps can be problematic because of border disputes. Using the wrong version of a country's borders in that country's version of your game could upset players and even inspire government sanctions against your work.

Indies rarely manage translations and localizations internally because of the volume of talent needed to adapt a game into multiple languages. A publisher often helps here, but third-party translation teams are common as well if you intend to self-publish.

Not all games warrant a full international push, but today's gaming communities are largely borderless. Everyone in the world plays games, so choosing not to translate and localize your game can shut the door on thousands of potential players. Just as a multi-platform release helps you maximize your revenue, so too does making your game available in multiple languages.

Most major indie publishers will release a game in 10+ languages, but that is not universally true. Before we dive into the nuances of how to pick languages for your title, here's the big list of languages to consider:

- Arabic
- Chinese (Simplified)
- Chinese (Traditional)
- Dutch
- Filipino (Tagalog)
- French (European)
- German
- Hindi
- Indonesian
- Italian
- Japanese
- Korean
- Norwegian
- Polish
- Portuguese (Brazilian)
- Spanish
- Russian
- Swedish
- Thai
- Turkish

- Ukrainian

- Vietnamese

There are more languages in the world, of course, but these are most common for game developers. At this point, we should note that international markets for games are always changing. Once upon a time, the Brazilian games scene – and really, South America as a whole – was an afterthought for most game launch campaigns, but now it has become one of the strongest markets for indie games. Part of that is because gaming continues to grow in popularity, but the other part is the reality that Brazil has had a vibrant gaming scene since the 1990s but too few developers took the time to serve that scene with translated games.

Nimdzi analyzed 34,815 games on Steam to determine the top languages:

1. English
2. German
3. French
4. Russian
5. Spanish
6. Chinese (Simplified)
7. Italian
8. Japanese
9. Portuguese (Brazilian)
10. Korean

We encourage you to check current trends as you plan because this top 10 shifted from 2019 to 2020. Russian and Simplified Chinese increased their market share, and Korean knocked Polish out of the top 10.

The languages you choose for your game should be a balance of sales potential and budget management. Like the rest of your development decisions, the money you invest in this aspect of your game should lead to a net profit. If your genre of game is not popular in a particular region, you can delay releasing in that language and revisit the opportunity post-release.

For your planning, scope directly impacts translation and localization costs. The bigger your game, the more content that needs to be reworked. Fortunately, engines like Unity and Unreal have tools and systems to radically simplify this process so that you aren't manually replacing every word in your game, but volume still matters.

Translation rates vary by language and by vendor, but on average, you can expect to pay roughly $0.15 to $0.20 per word per language.

If your game has 1,000 words and you translate to 10 languages, the math is 1,000 × $0.30 × 10, which equals $3,000.

That budget is relatively manageable, but it is also incredibly optimistic. For context, a written novel usually has about 100,000 words. *The Witcher 3: The Wild Hunt* has 450,000 words. *Disco Elysium*, a breakout indie RPG hit, reportedly has over 1 million words in its script. With those numbers, $0.30 a word is a significant budget item.

Amazingly, *Disco Elysium* is available in nine languages on Steam at the time of this writing (with English as the only full audio option). Speaking of audio, localized voice-over is significantly more expensive than translated text.

As you work to estimate the scope of your game, account for your international release efforts as well. Use your comparable titles as a reference point for estimating word count, and use your market research to identify languages that are especially relevant for the kind of game you want to make. Next, don't forget that you should translate and localize your Steam page as well, and you should incorporate the translation and localization process into your development timeline as well.

Developers often use the term "code freeze," which means that code can no longer be modified. In gaming, this stage usually occurs at the start of console certification as a change in your game can trigger a new round of certifications if you want to change the version available in the store.

Similarly, you should consider a "word freeze." Once you start investing in translations, making changes to your game's script or story will require you to also reflect those changes in every other language version of the game. That can get expensive in addition to being difficult to quality control.

Remember, starting lean is okay. If you can only afford to make your game in English to start, you could reinvest later profits or gamble on fan translations to make your game available to more players. Even if you can't personally fund a full translation and localization push for your game, you should still take the time to identify worthwhile target languages as a publisher or investor may be interested in helping on that front.

Assessing Additional Development Needs

A classic indie game planning mistake is to not plan for development time that is not directly tied to finishing the game. For example, accounting for the time you need to make good demos might make you realize that you actually need two more months of development or more staff to carry the extra work. At the other end of the timeline, many indies budget for resources up to launch but don't consider needing a budget to fix post-launch bugs (which can take months) or what will be necessary to keep the game working and playable well into the future.

Some genres are more demanding of post-launch development than others. Multiplayer games often require ongoing tweaks, content updates, and community activations to keep servers active and healthy. Your narrative platformer might have less of a need for that volume of development and maintenance, but every game will need these kinds of resources to some degree.

When we mean every game, we mean EVERY GAME.

In games, surprises lurk around every corner, but here are the most common pitfalls we see wrecking indie development plans:

- Demo development – You need a demo to get new publishers and players excited. Can your current development afford a four-week demo-building sprint right before PAX East?

- Pre-launch quality assurance and fixes – Good QA takes time, so are you giving your team enough time to identify and fix issues prior to release?

- Post-launch bug fixes – The days immediately following a release can be critical to securing sales momentum. Are you ready to rapidly address player concerns and bugs as quickly as possible?

- DLC development – Fanatical players want more of what they love. Does DLC make sense for your game, and if so, what would you need to bring it to life?

- Porting processes – Testing your game's performance is often a fundamental part of the quality assurance process, but are you also planning for the length of a console approval process as well as potential time to fix new issues?

- Marketing – The quality of your game doesn't matter if no one knows it exists. Even if you work with a publisher with a great marketing track record, have you addressed the budget and time you need to promote your game as well as expenses for events or advertising?

- Platform or software fees – You might need a license for your game engine or special software to make your art. Do you have money set aside for these costs?

The good news is that these project costs can also be the most malleable parts of your budget. If funds are exceptionally limited, you might stagger your porting schedule, rely on a publisher for marketing execution, and set a sales goal that justifies moving forward with making DLC.

Malleable, however, does not mean free, so saying, "I am going to have a publisher do my marketing" does not erase your need to consider how much marketing budget is appropriate for your project. Knowing that number allows you to judge how that task can be most effective and if a publisher is allocating a proper amount to market your title.

That being said, most publishers require a recoupment of marketing costs via sales before releasing royalties to your studio. If you agree on a $25,000 marketing budget, you need to be aware that is $25,000 more that needs to be recouped on top of the other costs. Additionally, it's in your best interest to understand the breakdown of that budget in order to ensure the amount matches the execution

If you jump into indie development after a career in consumer marketing, you can make the argument that you and your team can spend $25,000 more effectively than a publisher in some areas, so you keep more of that budget in-house.

If you decide that your team does not have the expertise or the bandwidth to do all of the marketing in-house, you could instead view an additional $25,000 in publisher marketing recoup as a strategic advance, saving you in costs today while also giving you access to professional games marketers.

Remember, if a piece is crucial to making and releasing your game, your budget should account for both its scope and value, even if a partner ends up taking on the execution for you. Otherwise, you can never really know if you are making the smart business choice possible.

The Business Perspective on Engine Selection

A game engine is a development foundation that addresses the core building blocks needed to make a game, potentially carving years off of a development timeline relative to having to make every system and process completely from scratch. By building on top of an engine such as Unity or Unreal, painful but critical pieces of your project are already complete. Beyond efficiency-boosting tools including basic file and scene managements, game engines also address basic physics, graphic rendering, and lighting. A competent developer could build all of this, but usually the time and resources it would take to do so are better spent on developing the game itself.

Very few indie games warrant using a custom engine, and a publisher or investor might actually see a custom engine as a reason not to invest in your project.

An established engine has the following advantages that a custom engine does not:

- Experienced developers – Though every game is built a little bit differently, working within a well-known engine makes it easier for you to add team members to your project: If you are using Unity, another Unity developer can likely join with a reasonable amount of onboarding.

- Porting efficiency – Making your game available on multiple platforms is a great way to access new players, but it also requires additional development time: Many engines have built-in tools for streamlining this process, shaving big dollars off of already lean budgets.

- Assets, extensions, and plugins – Prominent game engines sprout entire creator ecosystems, which means you can shortcut major development hurdles with premade content: For example, you can get a plugin to handle your graphical user interface (GUI) for less than $100 instead of making it all from scratch.

- Support – If you encounter a problem you can't solve, using an established game engine means you can ask experts for help, either from the engine staff themselves or from the communities that actively discuss game development in one of dozens of online forums, chats, Discords, or Slack channels.

Speaking broadly, an indie developer should almost always be working with a reputable engine, especially if you are less experienced and have a limited budget. The time you save, the resources you can allocate elsewhere, and the access to help make it the smarter move.

Engines You Should Know

As we unpack the importance of engine selection, a brief primer on today's major players may be helpful:

Construct 3

The visual scripting of Construct 3 makes it an incredibly accessible 2D engine. A Construct developer can often build games quickly, but the emphasis on visual scripting might make Construct less attractive for games with more complex systems.

A few notable examples are as follows:

- *Cyber Shadow*, developed by Mechanical Head Studios and published by Yacht Club Games
- *Hypnospace Outlaw*, developed by Tendershoot, Michael Lasch, and ThatWhichIs Media and published by No More Robots

GameMaker Studio

Often referred to as just GameMaker, this engine is also strong for 2D titles. While more complex than Construct, GameMaker also relies heavily on drag-and-drop-style workflows but has room for deeper customization as well.

A few notable examples are as follows:

- *Undertale*, developed and published by tobyfox
- *Hotline Miami*, developed by Dennaton Games and published by Devolver Digital
- *Hyper Light Drifter*, developed and published by Heart Machine

Godot

Completely free and open-source, Godot is known for its accessibility, flexibility, and versatility. It can be used for 2D games as well as 3D games, and the indie community often recommends it for newer developers and for smaller projects. It's node-based format and visual editor are user friendly, and it has a ton of pre-built functionality.

A few notable examples are as follows:

- *Cruelty Squad*, developed and published by Consumer Softproducts
- *ΔV: Rings of Saturn*, developed by Kodera Software and published by Kodera Software and Kurki.games
- *Rogue State Revolution*, developed by LRDGames, Inc. and published by Modern Wolf

Unity

With perhaps the largest library of assets and plugins, Unity is capable of making virtually any kind of game. Though sometimes more complicated than GameMaker, Unity is also relatively accessible for new indies but also has a deep potential for additional custom development if you're willing to learn the C# programming language.

A few notable examples are as follows:

- *My Friend Pedro*, developed by DeadToast Entertainment and published by Devolver Digital
- *Pathologic 2*, developed by Ice-Pick Lodge and published by tinyBuild
- *Risk of Rain 2*, developed by Hopoo Games and published by Gearbox Publishing

Unreal

A powerhouse of a 3D engine, this Epic Games offering powers indie and AAA titles alike but is often used for large, graphically intense games. While the current version of Unreal has a slew of drag-and-drop tools, the underlying C++ structure can make it especially challenging for newer developers.

A few notable examples are as follows:

- *A Hat in Time*, developed and published by Gears for Breakfast
- *Outlast*, developed and published by Red Barrels
- *The Sinking City*, developed by Frogwares and published by Nacon

CryEngine

Often compared to Unreal for its rendering ability, CryEngine is also more commonly used for large 3D games rather than small indie projects. Like Unreal, CryEngine can be daunting for solo developers or for small teams because of its sheer scope, but that challenge comes with the reward of visually stunning games.

A few notable examples:

- *War of Rights*, developed and published by Campfire Games
- *Wolcen: Lords of Mayhem*, developed and published by WOLCEN Studio
- *Miscreated*, developed and published by Entrada Interactive LLC

Open 3D Engine (Formerly Amazon's Lumberyard)

Lumberyard is based on CryEngine, so a lot of the same power available in CryEngine is available in Lumberyard with the added benefits of a more seamless integration with Amazon Web Services (AWS) as well as baked-in Twitch integrations. In 2021,

Amazon pivoted Lumberyard to an open-source format, and it's too early to tell what impact this engine will have on indie development.

Other Game Engines

Your options for potential game engines extend far beyond the condensed list we have provided here, and our focus on PC and console games has kept us from exploring the multitude of mobile-focused engines available to developers as well. If an engine is not listed here, do not interpret its absence as a form of judgment. If you find an engine not covered in this book that fits all of your project goals, by all means, use it. The framework for all of the business considerations to make with regards to engine selection still apply.

That said, be cautious when using less mainstream game engines. Earlier, we said that using a custom engine can be problematic for integrating outside support (like the team a publisher provides) as well as for integrating internal support (a new development hire might struggle to understand the project structure). Use the same caution when selecting an engine that is more niche.

As you evaluate a potential engine, ask the following questions:

- Do you have training with this particular engine, or is it easy to learn?
- Can you make your game visually unique?
- What is the process for porting to other platforms?
- What is the license, fee, and/or royalty structure?
- Is the codebase maintained and actively supported?
- How active is the development community around the engine?

A platform like RPG Maker can be an amazing development tool for building a pixel art JRPG because of its RPG-specific design tools. The drawbacks, however, are that the same ease of use that makes RPG Maker attractive for newer indie developers can also lead to many games built in RPG Maker looking similar, to the point that a savvy eye can pick out an RPG Maker with relative ease.

Additionally, porting your game to other platforms with these kinds of hobbyist engines can range from being difficult to outright impossible.

Before you choose an engine, explore the full range of implications to save yourself the pain of having to rebuild your project in a new engine because the one you started in is missing an essential piece of functionality.

Publisher Preference

Engine selection is mostly thought of as a technical choice, but savvy indies also recognize it as a strategic business choice, which you should already be starting to imagine if you think of how much time you save customizing a GUI plugin over building your own system, but the ramifications of engine selection run even deeper.

While this is not universally true for every game from a publisher, most publishers tend to prefer working with games built in specific engines. If a publisher contributes technical resources and support – porting or localization – their internal team will likely be more familiar with a particular engine.

If a publisher always works with Unity, they can more rapidly assess and execute on the needs of a project. That efficiency reduces development timelines and lowers overall project costs. The potential complexity of porting a game to consoles, for example, is a major driver of why many publishers specialize in porting. Marketing to a select console audience has a high degree of nuance, but having a team that intimately understands the certification process for the Nintendo Switch and has also ported several dozen Unity projects to the Switch is a significant competitive advantage.

What this team can do in a few weeks could take a first-time developer a few months and several failed certifications. Additionally, the seasoned team is more likely to deliver a better experience for players because the console hardware will be better utilized and the game will have fewer porting-related bugs.

Again, publishers don't necessarily refuse to work in other engines, but because it is a business consideration for them, the engine you choose becomes a business consideration for you as well.

Genre Trends

In a vein similar to publisher preference, some types of games are better suited for particular engines. The lines are fuzzy here, but the raw power of engines like Unreal or CryEngine make them the go-to choice for FPS developers. Unity is also a capable FPS engine, but the flexibility of the Unity platform also makes it a common engine for RPGs or 2D platformers. GameMaker and Construct, meanwhile, are used almost exclusively for 2D games.

Because engine preference is a hotly debated topic among developers, we want to be careful here and make it clear that we don't have a preference (or any additional interests) for one engine over another.

As an indie, however, you need to understand how your engine choice can be perceived.

If you are making a retro 2D platformer, few publishers or investors would be surprised to hear that you chose Unity or GameMaker for development. If you revealed that you are working in Unreal, a few eyebrows in the room might go up, especially if you are relatively new to game development.

That does not mean that Unreal is the wrong choice, but since Unreal is perceived as having a more demanding development curve, you should be prepared to justify your choice to use Unreal. Perhaps you spent a decade working on AAA games in Unreal, so it was faster for you and your team to keep working in Unreal rather than learn a new engine. Perhaps you want to use a certain game mechanic or graphical effect that is easier to do in Unreal. Perhaps you won an Unreal-specific grant or contest to fund the first development sprint for your project.

Several reasons can justify your choice in later conversations, but you should think carefully about the best engine for your target genre before you begin development. Thinking about this now can save you development time and prepare you for the big business conversations that come later.

Licensing Fees and Other Terms of Use

Access to game development tools has never been more open than it is now. Any indie can download a major game engine and start developing, often with no upfront costs. At the time of this writing, Unity and Unreal are both available for free, which is remarkable because we remember the era where 3D engines could cost developers several thousands of dollars in fees to even get started.

Few engines are truly free, though. The major engines that offer no-cost downloads typically have royalty-sharing structures or subscription costs for key features. The Personal plan for Unity is currently free, but the fine print on the financial eligibility clause says the following:

"Eligible if revenue or funding is less than $100K in the last 12 months."

Once your funding or revenue goes beyond $100,000, the Unity terms of service require you to upgrade to the Plus plan, which is $399 per year per seat. As your revenue grows, that $399 becomes $1,800 and so on. Unreal follows a similar structure but leans more into royalty-sharing for non-enterprise users, taking a 5 percent royalty on gross revenues over $1 million.

Overall, these terms are incredibly fair, but they cannot be ignored. If you are developing Unity and pitch for a $200,000 publishing deal, the terms of your Unity license have now changed and you have to account for the potential costs of multiple seats for your Unity Plus license.

If you have four developers using Unity on your team, your budget should account for $1,596 in Unity fees.

$1,596 is not a lot of money as far as game development costs are concerned, but "a lot" is relative. For an indie, $1,596 can easily be the difference between making payroll for your team or having to fire someone, so understanding the full ramifications of costs from the start is important.

Platform Incentives

Industry stakeholders often incentivize developers to use their tools and tech to drive developer adoption or to bring more products under their umbrellas. These incentives can take a variety of forms, such as:

- Project funding – A platform gives you budget if you agree to use their tools
- Credits – The platform provides a set amount of access to their tools at no cost
- Early access – Your team gets access to tech before other developers do
- Placement and marketing – The platform agrees to promote your game in specific ways

We have already talked about how the Epic Games Store has used minimum guarantees to secure titles for its storefront, but the minimum guarantee idea can play a part early, as well as late, in a game's development.

In 2017, Oculus' Jason Rubin told *Shacknews* that Oculus (owned by Facebook), was on track to spend $500 million on funding for financing new Oculus titles. We worked with a few games who benefitted from this funding, and their terms were relatively simple: Facebook provided funding to bring more games to Oculus, sometimes in a minimum guarantee format akin to the Epic Games Store and sometimes to bring new and novel ideas to life.

Oculus is not a game engine, but the Oculus story should make it easier to see how a new competitor in engine development might offer benefits to attract new users.

Amazon's Lumberyard converted *Star Citizen* into a major title for its engine. Chris Roberts, the head of Cloud Imperium Games, is quoted as saying, "We made this choice as Amazon's and our focus is aligned in building massively online games that utilize the power of cloud computing to deliver a richer online experience than would be possible with an old fashioned single server architecture."

If you were also making a massively multiplayer game at a time when Lumberyard was making a serious push to compete with Unreal and Unity, the engine's default integration with Amazon Web Services and no subscription fees or royalties might be the collection of incentives to justify your choice to use that engine. That agreement in addition to the stack of AWS credits you got from a salesperson at a convention mixed in with the royalty structure could make Lumberyard a business win for your team.

Beyond the engine itself, the way other potential partners tether themselves to game development could impact your engine.

Currently, CORSAIR, a major player in gaming hardware and peripheral space, offers partnership to developers who agree to use iCUE in their games. If you're not familiar, iCUE enables developers to sync gameplay to RGB lighting effects.

If you're a gamer who loves RGB, your multicolored tower, keyboard, mouse, and monitor can become a part of the game experience. Those RGB lights might flash in sync with in-game gunfire or flicker red when you are damaged by fire. In exchange for expanding the impact of their products, CORSAIR offers partners "marketing support, free products, loaner hardware, and more!" according to their site.

In the future, CORSAIR could release a new Unity-specific plugin that makes iCUE easier to integrate, so easy that part of your choice to use Unity could be because you plan to later leverage a potential partnership with CORSAIR.

That's a hypothetical, of course, but these kinds of scenarios are common in the industry and are worth looking for.

Final Words of Caution

Developers often pivot mid-development to address shortfalls in budget or time. Major features (like a co-op mode), huge swaths of content (like fully realized endings), and DLC plans can get scrapped for the sake of actually finishing the project. Beyond the creative pain of having to cut great ideas, major mid-development plan changes can have business consequences as well.

The product itself could be weaker as a result, which you probably guessed, but that means more than losing a few sales. If you have done any marketing at all, the content you cut could mean breaking a promise you made to players. Where they might have been completely happy with your game otherwise, the very knowledge that your game was *supposed* to have something like a map editor can sour the experience.

If you landed investors or publishers, a plan change could mean breaking promises to them as well. These partners entrusted you with their success by betting on your ability to deliver, so having to break the news that you can't do what you agreed to do can hurt relationships, disrupt the livelihood of your collaborators, and trigger contractual ramifications.

Total scope perfection is probably impossible, but every ounce of effort you devote to doing it right pays off in pounds later.

Timelines, Budgets,
and Project Management

Brainstorming new gameplay mechanics and sketching character art are the exciting parts of game development. They are childhood dreams come true, and furious waves of creativity are a blast to surf.

Even for indies who have great ideas and the development skills to match, the boring back-office tasks of project and budget management are major failure points. For a full time team of seven, one additional month of development can mean needing another four weeks of payroll for seven people, a potentially catastrophic blow to your budget. For part-time developers who have the financial stability of a day job, budgets and timelines can be even more critical because these indies need to be so organized that they can succeed at having two jobs.

If you hate the idea of recording receipts, juggling spreadsheets, and mediating team member disputes, we are sorry. Few feelings are more painful than following the joy of building your dream game with the experience of watching the office lights click off one by one as each team member leaves to find rent money. You need to learn this now if you want to grow to the point of having the resources to hire someone to help.

Your process will look like this:

1. Initial project scope to a development time estimate

2. Account for notorious time traps in your timelines

3. Use best practices to pick a launch window

4. Estimate what resources and people you need for the timeline

5. Reevaluate your budget using your timeline and revise as needed

6. Assess the timeline fit and revise as needed

7. Build the team you need to follow the timeline

DOI: 10.1201/9781003215264-10

Mapping Scope to Time Estimates

Being an indie developer means you are perpetually asking, "How long will it take us to make this thing?"

How long will it take you to draw a character? How will it take you to animate one character? How about 10? How long will it take you to fix the physics glitch? How long will it take you to finish a demo?

You and your team have to string together the answers to this question for every component of your GDD to estimate a development timeline, and then you will have to course-correct on the fly as development needs shift.

Last chapter, we recommended you use prototypes and game jams to form a basis for how long a development task might take. While AAA developers and artists may need to produce a certain volume of work each week to stay employed, new indies typically come with a mix of experience and knowledge. Some are making a change in their programming careers. Others are booting up GameMaker for the first time, but brimming with ambition.

For indies, the industry average time for a task is not relevant. What is relevant is how long it will take *you* to do that task. That question encompasses an individual's performance as well as the collective performance of the team as they collaborate and exchange feedback. If you have to estimate a timeline with a group you have never worked with before, either practice on some prototypes to learn your dynamic or do your best to pad timelines to give you room to adjust.

Next, review your timeline to be sure it addresses the most common time-sucks in an indie development schedule:

- Demo creation and development
- Development time lost due to event attendance
- Quality assurance during and after development
- Translation and localization
- The porting and certification process
- Development time for post-release bug fixes
- Ongoing market support for post-launch activations

Most of these considerations are still development related, but a few may require working with an outside vendor. In those cases, ask that potential vendor how you should estimate their execution time or ask another indie to share their experience.

Though it may not change the total scope of your project or the length of your timeline, break your project into phases, milestones, and sprints.

Phases are broad periods of time representing major stages of development. Broadly, the industry thinks of these phases as pre-production, game design doc development, prototyping, production, gold (ready for release), release, and post-release.Contained within those phases are smaller development periods divided by milestones. Technically, a milestone can be any significant development moment. A freelance artist might be paid according to milestones that are based on the completing batches of sprites. A programmer's milestones could be based on feature completion. And so on. Outside of the development team, a publisher might structure funding according to milestones such as completing a prototype, completing a vertical slice, reaching pre-alpha, reaching alpha, entering beta, and reaching gold.

If milestones are fence posts, sprints are the rails, the tasks that need to be completed to move the project from one milestone to the next.

Having these degrees of resolution for your timeline – the ability to zoom in or out – make the management of day to day and week to week tasks more efficient because you can see both what needs to be accomplished in the near future and how any change in developing timing (like a delay) ripples through the rest of the timeline. If you see that your lobby management system took longer to complete than anticipated, you can look at the months ahead to find opportunities to recover time.

How that is accomplished will vary. You may have budgeted for unexpected delays, padding your schedule with "to be determined" development. If you did not have that luxury, you could trim scope elsewhere or hire a freelancer to help you catch up.

While this ties into the leadership and management material we cover toward the end of this chapter, sprints and milestones can also be highly motivating for your team. In a space where a product may not be complete for several years, ending a sprint or hitting a milestone can give your team a sense of accomplishment. They didn't complete the ultimate goal, but they got to hit a goal nonetheless. And that feels good.

Once you have a timeline, you need to see if it fits your release window.

Picking a Release Window

When to release your game is part development choice and part marketing choice. The realities of your project scope can influence when you release and the competition of the industry can influence it as well. You simply can't get it done sooner nor can you continue developing after a certain timeframe. You absolutely do not want to launch in the same month as a highly anticipated AAA title or you may have a unique promotional opportunity that you can only activate at a certain time of year.

You're trying to balance on a knife blade.

Many factors can play a role, but use the following best practices to get started.

Avoid Q4 and Major Holidays

Fourth quarter is AAA launch season and unless you want to compete with huge titles from major publishers, it's best to avoid this timeframe. Holidays can also be difficult because media and streamers have limited availability during this time, and that availability may also affect your partner relationships. If you need to pass lotcheck (console certification), you can expect a holiday to put a pause on that progress as employees take time off also. In addition, advertising channels will be in higher demand for every retail business, not just gaming.

Be Aware of Other Game Releases

The easiest way to avoid competing against other indie titles or against AAA marketing budgets is to research their launch dates. Many media sites compile and maintain a running calendar of confirmed releases (we often use *Game Informer*), and then share your potential launch date with your relevant platform representatives. They will not be able to tell you what games are launching if they have not been publicly announced, but they will usually give you an indication if your day you picked could be problematic. Continue to monitor gaming news and evaluate your options if a competing title plans to release around your launch timeframe.

Release in the "Slow" Season

The video game industry doesn't really have a slow season, but there are months that are better than others to release an indie title. These include the following:

• Q1 – Few AAA titles launch during this time and media/streamers generally have more free time to cover indie games: Consumers also potentially have leftover holiday money and gift cards to spend

• April and May – You might have a little more competition, but these months are still great for launch

• August – Avoid major sales such as the Steam Summer Sale and you'll be releasing when there's little noise to compete with: Additionally, families are often back for the new school year, so you don't have to worry about a summer lull

Consider the Good and the Bad of Tradeshow Launches

Launching just before or during a tradeshow may sound like a great idea, especially if you're attending the event, but it can also be a death sentence. Here are tips on how to launch around a tradeshow:

• Launch at least a week prior to the show

• Have codes available to sell

• Don't launch around major events such as E3. You may think some exposure there will help, but most people are focused on the AAA titles

• Be aware that media will have limited bandwidth

Launch One Month Later Than You Think.

You might think you'll release on the day you want, but the reality is no game launches on its initially scheduled launch date. Delays happen, and they will happen to you. No one gets through lotcheck or certification on the first try and if you do, thank your lucky stars. In order to line up marketing and store efforts, as well as ensure you'll actually hit your release date, make sure you add a one-month buffer from when your game hits gold and you plan to launch.

Weigh Potential Exceptions to Our Advice

These tips will help you select the perfect launch date but there can be exceptions. Releasing with major platform marketing support, for example, could yield wonderful results, so confirm that you are receiving major support such as feature store placement and promotional support, and not a simple retweet of your post before moving to a more competitive date. Speaking of competitive dates, holiday releases can also make sense, such as if you're making a horror game (Halloween) or a dating game (Valentine's Day).

Assess the Timeline Gap or Overage

When you drop your timeline on to your release date you will either have too much time (a few extra months of unneeded development before launch) or not enough time (your game will not be done in time). In either scenario, you face a budget challenge. Can you afford the extra development time to fill the gap without firing team members? Or, can you hire more team members to accomplish the same volume of work in less time?

If the answer to either question is, "I can't afford or justify an increase in my budget," your path is clear:

- If you have too long to finish the game, where can you move the release date with the least amount of marketing risk?
- If you do not have enough time to finish the game, what content can you cut to bring your budget back into balance?

This timeline exercise is worth repeating after you double check your budget estimates for overlooked expenses.

Budget Best Practices

Small businesses of any type are fragile. A new venture can be making respectable progress month over month, but since the business is young and capital is limited, a large surprise expense can end the journey. Something critical could break. You might need a license or have to pay a fee you did not anticipate. You could make a mistake and have to discard a bunch of inventory. Well-run small businesses collapse every day because they got blindsided by an expense they didn't know to even look out for.

For an indie video game studio, expenses usually break down into the following buckets:

- Development
  - Team members
  - Quality assurance testing
  - Translation and localization
  - Audio design
  - Console porting

- Hardware, software, and licensing
  - Development kits
  - Software subscriptions
  - Middleware licensing
  - Online server costs

- Marketing and public relations
  - Trailer and marketing asset production
  - Social campaigns
  - Ad spend
  - Community manager
  - PR specialist
  - Conventions/events

- Studio overhead
  - Office lease
  - Insurance
  - Utilities
  - Legal fees

This list should help you anticipate your potential budget needs, and you can use it as a framework for adjusting pieces of your business so that your projected costs (covered next) align with your budget.

Choosing what to cut in order to save budget is difficult, but many indies look to marketing and studio overhead to reduce expenses. If they borrow a family member's attic for a year and do all of the marketing in-house, they may not need to remove content or cut features. We fully support saving money on a lease, but if the answer to a budget obstacle is to cut part or all of the marketing budget, reconsider.

Your game will need marketing, so look to balance marketing and development cuts. Slicing too deeply in either area can compromise your profitability.

Important Budget Terms and Concepts

Learning the language of budgeting has two purposes. First, you have more productive conversations with business partners and publishers because you understand the shorthand and vocabulary. Second, you become more aware of important business ideas and are, therefore, more likely to apply them.

Projected Costs vs. Actual Costs

When you first read these definitions, you will not be impressed: a projected cost is what you predict you will spend on a budget item, and actual costs are the real amount you spend on that budget item.

Applying both of these ideas, however, is more useful than their self-explanatory definitions might imply. Projected costs are designed to help you right-size your initial budget (and what will become your "ask," or the amount you request from investors and publishers) before you start spending money. By tracking your expenses as they happen, you can identify shifts in budget needs more rapidly.

If you notice, for instance, that your art budget is running over by $200 every month, you can calculate what that means for potential cost overages. Small costs can add up quickly, so the $200 extra a month becomes a total of $3,600 in additional budget if the trend continues throughout 18 months of development. For some gaming budgets, a few thousand dollars is inconsequential, but for many indies, that's a lot of money. In either case, if you're responsible for using your funds wisely and doing so in a way that keeps your promises to investors, you should be able to quickly identify when you are spending more than you planned.

Burn Rate

When a business is not generating positive cash flow, which is to say more money is going out to cover expenses than is being made in profit, the business is "burning" capital. To continue operating, money from the company savings is used to cover overhead, keeping operations running long enough for the business to turn a profit. That savings could be the money you personally contributed to the project or the funding a publisher provided, and any expense can eat away at it.

Your projected costs give you an estimate of how long the business can continue operating based on the operating costs you anticipate. You will burn capital no matter what, but if that burn gets your rocket to its destination, that is capital well-spent.

Your actual costs let you see if your ship is on course or if you are in danger of running out of fuel too early. Every extra cost increases your burn rate, which will mean the business running out of capital and falling short of its goals.

A burn rate problem can be solved by reigning in costs or by adding funding, so you will revisit the budget outline above and adjust accordingly.

The Long Tail

A long tail is a type of data distribution where the volume and frequency of data points (such as game sales) are front-loaded at the beginning – or head – of a timeline. Then, the frequency drops suddenly and continues at a much slower descent over a long period of time. For many products, the time during and immediately after launch has the most sales density, but that can be misleading in terms of where your profits actually come from.

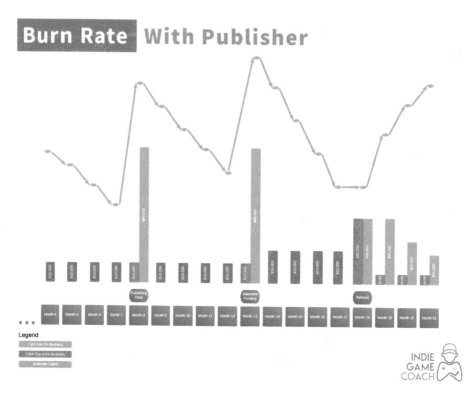

Burn Rate Without Publisher

Legend
Cash Into the Business
Cash Out of the Business
Available Capital

INDIE GAME COACH

Fans of *Borderlands* are excited for *Borderlands 4,* so they show up on launch day to be one of the first people to get a copy. The same thing that happens in games happens for movie openings or for the release of a new iPhone. After that first flurry, though, sales rates may decline rapidly, but they don't stop. Those early adopters tell their friends how much fun they are having and convince a friend to play with them. A promotional discount convinces some hesitant players to try the game, and when they end up liking it, they too recommend it to others.

The upfront spike of sales often gets the most attention because a launch is fun and big checks are exciting, but the 12 months that follow a launch could generate a total number of sales that is equal to or greater than the first spike. On any given day, sales numbers may not be notable, but if your long-tail revenue is equal to your launch revenue, you *doubled* your profit.

The longstanding game publishers thrive on long-tail revenue. A large back catalog of games can become a consistent and predictable stream of profit with a smart strategy and good marketing. An indie studio has a similar opportunity, but it is realized much more slowly. In the time an indie studio completes one game, a publisher can launch eight, so their back catalog sales volume will naturally grow more quickly.

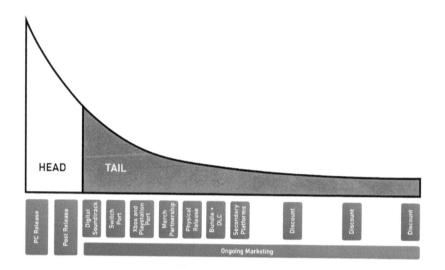

Start with a Budget Template

Every indie studio is different, but budget needs are common enough that we built a template to get you started. The spreadsheet accounts for typical costs, gives you a framework for organizing them, and helps you to track totals and trends in projected costs and actual costs. We recommend dividing your budget into months because months and quarters are common for production calendars, making it easier for you to compare your burn rate to your deadlines and future capital injections.

Go to indiegamecoach.com/resources/to download the template.

Building and Managing a Team

If your project requires more than just you to complete, you should also learn how to hire, how to delegate, how to manage, and how to lead. Human resources and project management are two other topics that have a false reputation of being boring or of having less importance than the creative side of the business. We don't think that's true.

If the unending wave of unsavory business practices and mistreatment of coworkers and employees in the games industry has not made it clear, allow us to: Culture matters. Some of the most prominent games companies in the world were undone not because they botched a marketing campaign but because they failed to take care of their people. They left toxic problems to fester, and the companies started to rot from the inside out. The same can happen with small indie teams when personalities clash. We've seen firsthand how a developer can make a highly successful game only for the team to break up afterward.

Even if you are a pure and respectful human being, poor management can frustrate good people and drive them away. While you may not have directly or intentionally hurt them, failing to give them an environment where they could do their best work is still a disservice. On top of that, having to recruit, hire, and onboard a new team member will require additional time and budget.

You might feel silly at first, but leadership and management are skills to hone with practice. Read books on those topics. Get advice. Maybe even work with an executive coach when your company gets big enough. Any progress you make on these fronts will lead to exponential returns over the course of your career.

Types of Team Member Relationships

Large studios, in terms of business structure, function similarly to large corporations. The organizational chart is clear, and most of the team is comprised of full time employees. For indies, the wild ranges of budget constraints and team sizes can lead to more startup-style approaches to operations.

Where the large studio has salaried artists, an indie studio might have one art director who doubles as the lead pixel artists but then outsources backgrounds and key art only as needed.

Where the large studio can segment executive duties into several specialized roles, one indie may need to be the CEO, CMO, CFO, COO, *and* creative director all at once.

Where a large studio typically pays a salary and may offer bonuses based on sales performance, an indie team might agree to work from their own savings or to take a lower pay rate in exchange for equity (a percent of ownership) in the game or in the studio as a whole.

We are not attorneys, so check your local and national employment laws before following our advice to the letter, but broadly speaking, working relationships fall into three categories:

- Full time – The employee receives a set hourly wage, is expected to be with the company for the indefinite future, and qualifies for benefits in the U.S. (30 hours per week or 130 hours per month, according to the Affordable Care Act).

- Contractor – A team member who either does not meet the hourly requirements to be considered full time or is a temporary hire with a set end date.

- Partner – A partner is a team member with an equity stake in the business who may elect or negotiate an alternative payment arrangement.

These distinctions matter because how you manage a team member could change your legal obligations under your employment laws. In the U.S., if you hire someone as a contractor but manage them like a full-time employee – setting their work hours, requiring their presence in the office, or tasking them with full time hours indefinitely – they may be eligible for the rights of a full-time employee. They could be entitled to health insurance, you could be required to manage payroll tax, and you may be obligated to pay unemployment in the event you terminate them.

Do not take shortcuts on this front. Do it properly.

Be Cautious with Agreements and Equity

Since many indies begin under loose arrangements, such as a few college friends building games for fun in their free time, they risk falling out of compliance on very important rules and regulations. The resulting fines, attorney fees, and potential settlements can be disastrous. The casual format of everyone chasing the same dream can quickly unravel if one team member exits under poor terms. If you didn't think carefully about how to manage that relationship, their memory of promises and verbal business arrangements can embroil your project in a lengthy dispute as you fight over ownership and revenue shares.

In all cases, if you work with someone and have any intentions of profiting from their contributions, you should have an agreement in place. In the U.S., that means an employment contract for full time or salaried employees, a work-for-hire agreement for contractors, or a partnership agreement for any member claiming a portion of ownership in the studio. All of these should transfer ownership of work product to the business so that no one can argue that the studio lacked the proper permissions to use an asset.

Clarifying the terms of your working relationship is good for everyone. A mutual confirmation of expectations and boundaries can prevent later misunderstandings, protect both parties from liability, and define a path for terminating the relationship in a way that is fair to both parties.

The same is true for partnership agreements, though compensation structures and dispute-resolution procedures can be much more complex. Because a partner is a team member who owns part of the studio, they might forego all or part of their salary early on so that the business can be more profitable later. They may also be entitled to voting rights and decision-making privileges, and they probably have a dilution clause, which is a part of the agreement that defines how ownership shares are redistributed in the event that the business needs to make more equity available.

For example, if Marshal and Alex own a business together, Marshal may own 30% while Alex owns 70%. Since Alex owns the majority of the shares, he has full decision-making control, but in the future, they might decide to invite a third partner, at which point either Marshal or Alex (or both) has to forfeit a percentage of equity to make room for the third partner.

Marshal's rights in this scenario should be defined in the partnership agreement so that the studio can continue to grow and take on investors if necessary while still respecting the value of Marshal's contributions and his ongoing role in the business.

Employment and partnership disputes are always difficult because conflict can be painful, but if you cut corners on something as important as studio ownership, a partner with a sizable portion of equity could quit working but still retain their ownership. Technically, that's the point of equity, but your intention was likely that they would see the project through to the end thereby earning their share. If your agreement does not define that, you might never get the equity back and the ownership of the studio's assets fall into dispute.

You should be deliberate with how you manage equity from the founding of the business.

When you're two best friends at the start of an indie journey, it may feel logical to split the studio ownership in half. After all, 100% divided by 2 is 50% for each person, but that's not how business ownership should work. Shares should not be divided equally by virtue only of how many people are present at the founding. Instead, shares should be reflective of initial and ongoing contributions to the business.

If Alex mortgages his house to fund the development of the demo and gives Marshal a monthly stipend to cover expenses, Alex is within his rights to command a larger share of the ownership. He took on more risk. He invested more resources. And he might not be drawing a salary for himself so that the business can fund more development.

If earning more equity was important to Marshal, they could negotiate an arrangement where Marshal agrees to a lower monthly salary in exchange for an ownership stake that grows (or "vests") for as long as he is employed, eventually reaching a predetermined cap. That way, Marshal can earn more equity by continuing to contribute, and the gradual increase in equity protects Alex as well.

No matter where you fall in a partnership, please talk to an attorney before signing anything.

Recruiting and Hiring

Finding the best team members for your project is a balance of finding the appropriate technical ability at a compensation rate that fits your budget and is completed in a way that the rest of the team is able to thrive in their work as well.

If any of these pieces is missing, your project is on course for serious problems from the moment that hire begins. If they don't have the competency to do the work you have assigned, your project will fall behind or suffer in quality. If the team member's rates are too costly for your budget, you will run out of money before the game is finished. If they are not a team player – either because their work-style does not match or they are actively creating interpersonal problems – you may alienate key talent while slowing development progress.

Recruiting is difficult because you have to find these traits in a person but also be able to identify those traits from relatively brief interactions with the candidate.

Before you commit to an agreement (full time, contract, or partner), take the following steps:

- **Evaluate the candidate's portfolio.** Does their past experience and work product meet your standards, style, and needs? What other skills does the candidate have that could also be valuable to the team?

- **Use paid test assignments or trial periods.** Before committing to an official working relationship, give the candidate a task that broadly reflects the kind of work they would be doing with your team. How long does it take them? What is it like sharing feedback with them? Is the work a match for your vision?

- **Lean on milestone payment structures.** Many indies use contractor relationships to reduce overhead, but they lose budget and time with poor management. Instead of giving contractors large lump payments for promised work, break their assignments into sprints and give yourself the option to terminate or continue at each sprint. This pay structure can motivate contractors to be more timely with their tasks while giving you an out if the contractor is too slow or not delivering quality work.

These tips assume that the rate and the culture-fit of the candidate is a match. With our intense focus on budgets and projections, the rate concerns are likely clear to you, but we should clarify what we really mean by culture-fit.

Team dynamics can be unspoken invisible forces that are difficult to define on paper, but you can feel when synergy is present and when it is absent. Some approaches to development mesh more readily with others, so equally talented sets of creators can have far different outputs. Though fit is important, the danger is equating "culture-fit" to "just like me."

Even well-meaning leaders make this mistake without realizing, and it is part of the reason why the games industry (and corporate cultures in general) has a diversity problem. The straight white guys hire other straight white guys who hire more straight white guys and on and on.

Culture-fit should be about mutual values, shared goals, and collaboration styles. When you prioritize those characteristics, you can build a productive team with diverse backgrounds, which should be a major goal for your business. The moral reasons you have heard before (and they still matter), but there are business benefits as well.

A collaborative and diverse team is more likely to see unique opportunities because of their varied life experiences and cultural groundings. That's a boon for creative potential, giving you far more places to find ideas that you can then mix and match and blend to create even more new ideas.

The human side of building a game, coordinating the symphony of skill sets that come together in an indie studio, can be a monumental challenge, but it's worth every bit of effort to get it right.

People and Project Management

The advantage of solo indie development is that you never have to explain your thinking to another team member. You don't have to show them where you save the art files, and you don't have to teach them how to use the custom level editor you built. You can spend every day focusing exclusively on your vision.

Coordinating a team, even if it is just one other person, introduces a significant amount of complexity to your project. When that complexity is mismanaged, you lose valuable time and budget rectifying your mistakes. Deeper project management training is worth pursuing as your business scales, but for now, you should know the major management oversights that often hinder indies.

Backups

In 2011, *Project Zomboid* was a highly anticipated indie release. Early footage of the isometric survival game showcased the litany of interesting choices a player could make to keep a zombie horde at bay, and gamers were excited to experience it for themselves.

Then, in October 2011, burglars broke into the shared home of the developers, stealing their two laptops. Though the team had regularly alternated making physical backups between the two machines, they rarely made cloud or off-site backups.

They lost months of work.

Ten years later, indies are still making the same mistakes. Fortunately, modern development tools are now largely cloud-based so you can configure automated cloud backups in addition to your physical backups. IT professionals often encourage three forms of backups. At least one should be offsite, and they should use different types of storage media in the event that one physical backup is compromised.

Do not skip this step. Make backups, and do so with regularity.

Version Control

Game development is highly iterative. Every file and every system could have potentially dozens of variations between the start and end of production. Managing versions, especially between multiple team members, is a priceless boost in efficiency and communication. Developers have lost hours, and sometimes days of development time, chasing the source of a bug only to discover they were using an outdated build when the rest of the team had moved onto newer, improved builds.

Even if you work independently, adopt a consistent approach to version control so that the most recent versions of every piece of your game is clearly identifiable. Then, back all of those versions up as you may someday need to "roll back" a series of changes to correct a problem.

Organization and Communication

An orderly approach to development may not come naturally, but it too produces significant rewards. When your team members can find what they need, when they need it, you avoid the development engine stalling because Naomi the programmer is waiting for Sim the artist to send her the next batch of characters to implement, but Sim is offline in a different timezone and may not log in for several hours.

Similarly, to avoid delays, your sprints and their associated tasks should be coordinated and synchronized. If you misalign a handoff of files, where one team member needs another team member to complete their part before they can begin theirs, at least one person is sitting idle, waiting for something to do. This is especially costly with full time employees, but even with contractors where you may not have to pay them extra for waiting an additional day, you still lost that day.

Cloud-based systems help here, but your team has to use them, so implement a standard "end of day" routine where your team uploads all of their recently completed work to a shared drive or server, using consistent version control practices, and updates the rest of the time. A remote indie team can run pretty far on this front with Slack for communication, Google Drive for file storage and backups, and GitHub for code.

More products exist, of course, for assigning and managing tasks (like Asana or Trello), and you can invest in more feature-rich tools for every part of your development process, but you may not need them at first. If you start to find that team members are struggling to communicate or after chasing down the location of files, you may need to fix your process or invest in better tools.

Most importantly, make sure you have systems in place so people know where to properly store files and find files. This makes it easier for everyone and avoids a delay if someone is out sick for a day.

Ongoing Course Corrections

In Chapter 5, we encouraged you to think of your business plan as a "living" document, and that advice applies to budgets, timelines, and project management as well. Your plan will undoubtedly be flawed in some way for a reason you did not anticipate, despite your best efforts, so you should continuously check in to see if your actual trajectory matches the path in your plan.

When it does, continue on. When it doesn't, correct course to put you back on track to your destination. Like driving a car, you can't hit the gas on a project, aim it where you want to go, and expect it to arrive safely. Driving is a constant process of assessment and adjustment to stay between the lines and to navigate around obstacles. Nudge and nudge your business plan in the same way. If not daily, do so at least weekly.

You don't want to be in a position of checking your estimated time of arrival only to discover you had drifted 300 miles off-course.

PART 3

Pitches and Publishing Deals

DOI: 10.1201/9781003215264-11

SIDE QUEST

Dodge Roll and *Enter the Gungeon*

A Compelling Prototype with a Bold Pitch

—

When EA announced the shuttering of EA Mythic, Dave Crooks and a few of his then co-workers chose to pursue indie development. In *Gamesindustry.biz*'s recounting of the story, EA Mythic closed on May 29, and the newly formed Dodge Roll team wanted to have a pitch ready for E3 2014.

E3 started on June 10.

Dodge Roll was not new to game development, but even for grizzled veterans, the prototype for *Enter the Gungeon* was built remarkably quickly. In a few days, Crooks was on his way to E3. He had a prototype, but he didn't have a badge and he had not booked any meetings with publishers. He knew that Devolver Digital could be a fit for *Enter the Gungeon*, and the publisher was hosting a space off-site but near to the convention center where E3 was held.

Since 2014, Devolver has made a habit of setting up an anti-convention of sorts in parallel with E3, hosting a "Big Fancy Press Conference" of their own that was heavy on parody and entertainment. A classically Devolver marketing move for the publisher was an opportunity for Crooks. He could crash a major industry event, meet with a decision maker for his preferred publisher, and pitch his game.

All without a badge.

Nigel Lowrie, Chief Marketing Office for Devolver Digital, played into Crooks' plan and heard his pitch. A mere week later, Dodge Roll had an offer.

Crooks certainly began his indie career with a few advantages. He had worked in games and had a team who also worked in games, so while the speed of Dodge Roll's prototyping process is likely an impossibility for less experienced indies, their chutzpah is not. They knew that if they wanted funding to come quickly, their pitch process had to follow suit. To maximize that speed, they skipped over weeks of attempts with cold emails and put themselves directly in front of a business opportunity.

And they had a pitch and game vision as well as a prototype on hand to showcase their ability. All of that could be done remotely, but Crooks' enthusiasm and tenacity likely persuaded Lowrie to give the indie a few minutes of his time. That emotional element is hard to replicate in emails and even video calls, and it gave him an opening just big enough for him to stick the landing.

https://www.gamesindustry.biz/articles/2016-05-09-dodge-rolls-speedrun-to-indie-success

Pitch Deck Perfection

A well-crafted pitch deck can put an indie developer on the path to a successful game launch, and all of the work you have put into planning, research, and development up until this point will better equip you to succeed in this stage.

In 2019, SteamSpy reported that 8,142 games launched on Steam. That's almost 160 new games a week vying for attention, not only competing against other new releases but also the momentum of established juggernauts in the gaming world. And each week there's a whole new batch. That new batch of 160 games will target the same press, land on the same storefronts, and post to the same social media channels.

Cutting through the noise of the modern games industry is a colossal challenge for indie developers, so many turn to a publisher for help for all of the reasons we have discussed already. The right publisher can open the door to funding, relationships with major platform stakeholders, and marketing resources that help a game stand out in a turbulent sea of new releases and big PR budgets.

Here's the problem: Hundreds of fantastic games never get their chance to shine, not because of the quality of the game, but because of an indie developer's ability (or inability) to pitch to publishers. If your pitch and your deck can't capture what is special about your project, publishers will move on to the next opportunity.

You can eliminate that hurdle.

In this section, we cover the following:

- How to create the perfect pitch deck for your game
- How and where to use your pitch deck
- What publishers want to see and learn about your game
- How to format your deck for maximum impact
- What details and information capture the vision for your project
- How to avoid common pitfalls and mistakes
- How to use our pitch deck template and checklist

DOI: 10.1201/9781003215264-12

As you work through the pitch deck chapters, you may come back to these resources and guides repeatedly, so here they are upfront:

- A downloadable pitch deck template
- A downloadable pitch checklist

(all free to download at indiegamecoach.com/resources)

Up until this point in the book, we have been leading you through an idealistic and sequential process for managing the business side of your indie game project. Though you may already be making your game, we structured these chapters in a step-by-step format. Unfortunately, that perfect sequential format starts to blur as you enter the chaos of development.

In Chapter 1, we mentioned that investors and publishers often have varying preferences around when they engage indie developers. Some prefer to invest as early as possible so that they can be an active part of the development process while others prefer to work with near-complete titles–and there are publishers and investors who prefer every stage in between.

Your pitch deck, as a result, can begin to come to life soon after you have begun development. Even if there is not much to actually play, you can string together early art assets and project plans to sell the vision of your game. Some indies start the pitching process soon after development begins, but the indies who find success with that approach typically have a back catalogue of successful titles to demonstrate that they can, in fact, deliver the game they describe in their pitch.

New or first-time indies should likely wait to actively pitch publishers until they at least have a reasonably polished demo as that demo can be a tool for eliminating publisher skepticism. Without it, your ambitious project can sound a bit too much like another video game dream with no real substance behind it.

With that in mind, think of your pitch deck as a living document, just like your business plan. Regardless of when you intend to formally begin pursuing investors or publishers, drafting your deck early can help you to refine your ideas over time as you gather feedback from everyone in your orbit. Additionally, having a deck at least partially complete can enable you to capitalize on a serendipitous moment with someone in the industry.

If you meet a publisher by chance at a convention, you could find yourself describing your game. If the publisher likes it, they may request a deck, and few things are as agonizing as trying to scramble together a pitch deck at midnight in your hotel room. With a deck ready, you can make the necessary updates and tweaks and fire it off with much less stress.

Pitch Deck Basics

A pitch deck is not a pointless formality. Your pitch is often your first – and perhaps only – chance to get the attention of a publisher. With a well-crafted pitch deck, you can better communicate the uniqueness of your game to publishers, addressing their common questions so that you can get to the next stage of the process: reviewing your demo and discussing deal terms.

Publishers are inundated with pitches and proposals to the point that giving every game a thorough analysis is logistically impossible. Their email inboxes are flooded. Their calendars are full. And at events, they are often booked for back-to-back meetings.

In fairness, this is their job. It's what they signed up for when they chose to work in publishing. For you as the developer, however, you need to acknowledge these realities and recognize that a pitch deck is your opportunity to cut to the front of the line by being more prepared and more polished than the other indies vying for a spot on a publisher's launch calendar.

Your deck should demonstrate the following for you and for your game:

- You are professional, organized, and prepared
- You understand the market for your game
- You have a grasp of the economics of your project
- You understand what needs to be done to complete and launch your game
- You recognize where you need the help of a publisher
- The polish of your deck reflects the quality of your game

That last point is worth emphasizing. Think of your pitch deck as the preview for your game demo. The goal of a game demo is to set the hook for a player to make them want to buy the full game. Your pitch deck serves a similar purpose: It should generate enough interest that a publisher is willing to sit down and play your demo.

That means you should be as thoughtful and deliberate with your pitch deck as you are with the game you are making. But you're a game developer, not a salesperson, so that can seem like a strange challenge.

We'll go into each of these in more depth shortly, but for now, here's a big list of what your pitch deck should include the following:

- Product details
  - Game concept
  - Launch timing
  - Game length
  - Game price
  - Platforms
  - Engine
  - DLC, if any
  - Target audience and similar games

- Marketing assets
  - Trailer
  - Screenshots
  - GIFs
  - Key art

- Launch roadmap
  - Market analysis
  - Ask
  - Budget breakdown
  - Marketing plan (if relevant)
  - Basic production roadmap

- Team makeup
  - Team lead bios and special skills
  - Accolades or major coverage for team and/or game
  - Previous games released

- Game demo and Game Design Document (GDD)

Our downloadable template offers a suggested structure for organizing these pieces and our standalone checklist should make it easier to fill that in, but your unique situation may make it worthwhile to place more emphasis on certain points. Generally, though, these are the ingredients for a knockout pitch deck.

As you lay those ingredients out, user experience matters. Remember that you may use this same deck in multiple scenarios, such as:

- In-person at an investor meeting
- In a virtual presentation or call
- On the floor of a gaming convention
- In a direct email to a publisher
- An indirect way (where someone reshares the deck without your direct input)

Designing a deck that meets all of those use-cases is not easy, but if you keep these principles in mind, it will be much less daunting:

1. Your deck should communicate all essential information with or without your being present to talk about it.
2. Rely on digestible bulleted lists instead of big, blocky paragraphs.

3. Use visual elements from your game to make your presentation compelling, differentiating it from other decks and also drawing publishers into your game experience.

4. Rich media, such as GIFs and embedded videos, are a powerful way to bring more life to your deck and to start to introduce gameplay.

5. As you incorporate graphics, make sure that all text is legible on mobile and desktop devices.

6. Make your contact information clear and easy to find.

Lastly, there is one final point for you to consider: where you build your deck.

Microsoft PowerPoint has been the software leader for deck creation of any kind, and the games industry is no different. Recently, however, we are seeing more developers use Google Slides because it is free, is easily shareable via the cloud (a big advantage if you load your presentation with GIFs), and can be dynamically edited. If you notice a typo in slide 7, you can edit the master version of the deck without having to send a new copy to every publisher you've told about your game.

Which software you use is less important than the content, but we want you to feel prepared.

Next, let's dive into the components of your deck.

Deck Content: Product Details

Every piece of information we highlighted on your deck construction checklist is critical, but the crown jewel of your presentation is your game. Naturally, the first thing a publisher typically wants to learn about is the game itself. The material that follows your game is part of the diligence behind making a deal. In other words, if they like what they see about the game, they use the rest of the deck to vet the idea and the team behind it.

Once you sell a publisher on the concept, you have to convince them that you or your team has the ability to bring it to life. Much of that happens in how you present your game, and the content that we cover later will build on that foundation.

For the game-specific content, your deck should include the following:

- Game concept
- Launch timing
- Game length
- Game price
- Platforms
- Engine
- Any planned DLC

Let's break those down, one by one, and explore why these points matter to a publisher and what you can do to address them as effectively as possible.

Game Concept

In this section, you quickly and succinctly establish the premise and hook for your game. It can be difficult to condense the full vision of your game into a few sentences, and it may take some practice to get it right. Fortunately, you have completed a great deal of market research ahead of making the pitch deck, so you should have a significant amount of material to draw from.

For this portion of the deck, here's what you should keep in mind as you flesh out the concept:

- Be brief, keeping your concept to one or two sentences.
- Articulate what the player does in the game.
- Communicate the personality and tone of the game.
- Avoid tying your concept to a mega-trend or a mega-successful game.

That's a lot to cover in a brief summary of your game. Here's an example of how the team at Mega Cat Studios handled this for their game, *Bite the Bullet*:

> *"Run, Gun and Eat your way through this roguelite RPG shooter. In a world where every enemy is edible, what you eat and how much you eat drives everything from your waistline to branching skill trees to weapon crafting. Shoot fast. Eat big. Satisfy your appetite for destruction."*

In a few lines, Mega Cat establishes the core gameplay (run & gun), teases the twist (eating), hints at the depth of the gameplay (roguelite + skill trees + crafting), and wraps all of that into vivid, descriptive sentences that drip with personality.

Again, this is a special challenge in its own right. For now, here's the big test for your game concept description: remove your game title from the description. Is it still unique or could what you wrote apply to several games because it is too general, broad, or generic? Too often, indie game descriptions sound like every other indie game description, so publishers don't see what makes your project special and players will eventually have the same difficulty as well.

Pulling from your comparable title research, you can compare your game summary to other successful titles in the space, helping you to balance the points that will draw in fans of the genre with description that clearly sets your game apart.

In the slides that follow your game summary, you can call out specific features in more detail, but each of those slides should feel like an elaboration of your first, strong hook.

Launch Timing

The release of a game is a significant strategic choice. While a potential publisher does not expect an exact date in a pitch deck, they do expect you to have considered:

- A realistic production timeline that takes into account Q&A, localization, and porting.
- Best practices in terms of timing an indie game release (e.g., avoiding AAA game launch season).
- Various deal scenarios, such as how the launch timing changes with funding support.
- Any relevant marketing considerations, such as timing your horror game to release for Halloween.

Not all of these points need to be articulated in great detail within the deck, but you should be prepared to speak to them in a thoughtful way. Also, keep in mind that your publisher will have their own launch calendar and strategic priorities to navigate, so your actual launch date could change when the relationship kicks off.

Fortunately, this part of your deck should also be easier because of the work we did in the previous chapter. If you're not sure when to release your game or how to estimate a launch window, revisit Chapter 8.

Game Length and Game Price

Any time you pitch, you may have the temptation to exaggerate or inflate what you promise for your game, and one of the most common areas we see that inflation is in estimates of game length. We also see the opposite: developers underestimating the length of their game because they play through it much more quickly than an average player. Have a fresh playtester give you their total playtime to be sure your estimate is grounded in reality.

If your game is not complete, do your best to benchmark the gameplay length based on the content you have already completed with planned features and how that compares to similar games in your genre. HowLongtoBeat.com can provide you with estimates of game length for released games, which might be helpful as well. One thing to remember when determining a game length, it isn't how long it takes you and your team to get through a game, but how long it would take a person picking up the title for the first time.

It's okay if your game is a brief experience, and it's okay if your game is an epic adventure that will occupy a player for days. What matters is communicating an accurate expectation to the publisher so that they can make an informed decision on whether or not your game is a fit for their portfolio.

When you talk about game length, consider defining two major metrics:

- Estimated gameplay length for a casual playthrough.
- Estimated gameplay length for a completionist playthrough (where every side quest is collected and every item is completed).

Yes, some players will move more quickly than others, but your rough assessment should be broadly accurate to the average player.

Speaking of comparisons, this is also a point where you will propose a price point for the game. Like all things in your deck, this is subject to publisher input, but at this stage, you should be able to demonstrate that you understand what players are likely to spend for a gameplay experience like yours, which means taking into account current gaming trends and the pricing strategies of your competitors.

If you want to retail your game for $59.99 when the most successful indie game in your genre is longer and retails at $19.99, that will make a publisher suspicious of your qualifications and your ability to make thoughtful, informed decisions about your game. Your earlier research into comparable titles will equip you to estimate a reasonable price point as well as to justify your reasoning during publisher negotiations.

Platforms

Various publishers approach platform relationships differently. As a developer, you need to know that some publishers have preferences over the types of games they publish. One publisher might exclusively prefer PC gaming experiences while another aims to publish games that can be readily ported across PC, console, and perhaps even mobile platforms.

When you say that you intend to make your game available for PC, Xbox, Playstation, and Switch, a publisher does not necessarily expect you to have the ability to handle porting your game in-house (although preferred), but they do want to see that you considered how your gameplay translates from PC to console (for example) as well as the preferences of those audiences.

Leaning into Switch porting for a retro platformer is a clear win, but for a complex, competitive RTS, porting to consoles might not make sense. That may not be your exact situation, but the potential pitfall should be clear: blindly assuming that your game is a fit for all platformers can undermine your credibility with a publisher. Sometimes, having a good justification for what you *won't* do can be a big signal to a potential partner.

Again, publisher input can change many of these decisions, but your deck is your opportunity to prove that you understand your game and the players you're targeting.

Engine

As we discussed previously, the tools you choose to use for game development can make you a better fit for certain publishers and less of a fit for others. As an indie, your best choice is generally to work with the tools where you have the most experience and the most comfort. Ultimately, your game's larger success hinges on the quality of the game. However, publishers sometimes look at the engine you're using to make decisions around the following:

- Porting – Publishers often provide porting services to indie developers and their porting team may have a preferred engine: If you are using a different engine (particularly a custom engine), that could mean a greater cost to the publisher.
- Efficiency – One of the benefits of working within an established engine is access to additional resources, such as plugins or additional talent to augment your team.
- Scope – GameMaker is a great tool, but if the game you are building does not match the strengths of GameMaker, that can be a red flag to a publisher.

For your deck, simply naming the engine you're working in is sufficient, but be prepared to answer follow-up questions about why you made that choice. Chapter 7 is worth revisiting if you need more ammunition here.

With all of the product details addressed, your next task is to bring that content to life with highly engaging marketing assets.

Deck Content: Marketing Assets

A game is a highly visual, highly interactive piece of art. Comparatively, slide decks are often bland, boring, and unremarkable. Your pitch to a publisher needs to suck a publisher in to make them interested in your game while also effectively communicating key information. For our part, we often see decks on the extremes. We will see decks that are super basic Google Slide templates with default backgrounds and fonts and very few visuals related to the game. And we also see decks that are so over-designed and flooded with visuals that they are unreadable.

Strike a balance. Use a clean design that captures the personality and content of your game without sacrificing readability or clarity. Downloading our pitch examples will help you to see what that advice looks like in execution, but you should also get feedback from peers and mentors you trust. If someone has trouble understanding your game or your ideas, you may need to revise your deck. While that criticism can be painful at first, you are far better off hearing it early instead of from your dream publisher in the only meeting you'll ever get with them.

With a basic discussion of user experience out of the way, we can talk about the fun stuff: your marketing assets.

Game Trailers

While publishers have differing preferences for where in a game's development, they like to begin a relationship, few publishers expect to see a finished product in a pitch. They do, however, want to get an idea of what the final product will look like and how it will be presented to players. A trailer for your game is one of your biggest opportunities to sell your game and to stoke the interest for your demo.

Generally, there are two types of trailers:

1. Gameplay – A gameplay trailer focuses exclusively on gameplay, and this is where most indie devs start.
2. Cinematic – A cinematic trailer might add animation or live-action elements to put a stronger marketing spin on the gameplay. Sometimes these trailers do not show any gameplay.

For a pitch deck, a gameplay trailer is typically the most impactful and cost-effective route to take. Unless you have some additional video production talent you'd like to flex (and that might be worth demonstrating), a solid gameplay trailer is probably your best choice. It demonstrates your competency as a developer. It reinforces your deck's description of the game concept. And it gives a publisher the chance to see firsthand what makes your project compelling.

For a gameplay trailer, here are some rough guidelines:

- Aim for a length of 60–90 seconds.
- Use high-resolution footage.
- Show breadth and variety.
- Use as many "wow" moments as you can.
- Use text to callout major features if necessary.

As you cut your trailer, remember that the goal is to capture the vision for your game in a brief window. Publishers are ultimately savvy players, so lean on creating something that would also get players excited. Players want to see the variety of the levels in the game. They want an idea of what action to expect. They want to know what makes this entry in the genre different from the rest. Publishers are the same.

Trailers, like many aspects of this book, are a deeply nuanced art form in their own right, so don't be afraid to ask for help from a seasoned video editor if this is not your strong suit. If you don't have the budget to seek help from an outside editor, return your comparable title research and analyze their gameplay trailers. Try to understand the structure of these trailers. Look at what they show and when they show it. Look at how long they hold on a clip before transitioning to the other. Consider how they use text, music, and other visual effects.

Like a pitch deck, trailers can easily become "over-designed." Your gameplay is the ultimate focus, so focus your efforts on clearly demonstrating the features and breadth of your game with the footage you choose.

Screenshots and GIFs

There will be opportunities throughout your deck to incorporate visuals from your game. While using assets such as logos, concept art, and character art all have their own place and can be worthwhile, screenshots and GIFs will go the farthest in your goal to generate publisher interest in your game because they show the actual game the publisher is supporting.

As simple as capturing screenshots or GIFs might sound, doing these visuals well can be an unexpected obstacle to many developers. Take your time. Be highly critical of your selection. These screenshots could be the only thing a publisher ever sees of your game, so make them count if you want to get to the next conversation.

When we talk to developers about this part of the process, whether it's for a pitch or for building out store pages, we give the same advice. That advice is to remember the following:

- Focus on action: Publishers want to see your game coming to life on the slide.

- Variety is critical: If you shoot all of your assets in the same level, the impact of those screenshots rapidly diminishes from slide to slide.

- Showcase the variety of features in your game: Use your assets as another opportunity to show off everything that's interesting about your concept.

- Take advantage of in-engine camera positioning and posing options: Setting a scene for a screen capture is time-consuming, but it's beneficial if your content is hard to grab on the fly.

- Use GIFs liberally, as long as they are high-quality and well produced: A good GIF is worth a thousand pictures, so be deliberate about where you cut and loop a GIF in addition to what you capture.

- If you need to explain what's happening in a screenshot or GIF, that might be problematic: Use captions if a quick sentence can make the reader understand what they are seeing.

- File compression may become a necessity: As you add assets to your presentation, pay attention to file sizes and resolutions; if you need to attach a presentation to an email, a large file can make it harder to get to a publisher and if you need the presentation to load from the cloud at a convention, excessively large files can obstruct your deck.

Like your trailer, screenshots and GIFs are pivotal parts of whether a publisher asks to learn more or politely passes on your project. Treat this process with that level of seriousness and don't hesitate to redo a screenshot if it's less than perfect. If you aren't sure what kind of screenshots are effective, again, go back to your comparable titles research and see what other successful indies have done with games in your same genre.

Other Key Art

Since we are speaking broadly about pitching indie publishers, we cannot dive too deeply into any specific genre or platform considerations, but that doesn't mean that those factors are any less important. As you think about what a publisher should see to fully understand your game, work through areas of your game that are especially important and capture those art assets for your pitch.

Here are some examples of genre-specific art that might be relevant to your presentation:

- Big-picture view of levels if you are building a platformer or metroidvania.

- A variety of character illustrations if your game is story or character heavy, such as a visual novel or an RPG.

- Menus, gumps, and other interface elements if your game requires complex decision-making such as in a resource management game.

- Teaser material from incomplete aspects of your game, such as level, weapon, or character concepts.

Like the other materials we have covered thus far, the goal here is to show a publisher that you are delivering on fundamental genre expectations while also doing something (or several things) that are new and interesting. To go back to our Metroidvania example, a title like *Ori and the Blind Forest* has the sprawling and varied level design that excites fans of the genre, but the art direction and character design is different from other standout titles in the genre. It's eye-catching, and when you dig in even more, you find more twists on the classic Metroidvania experience.

Since we are working in generalities and hypotheticals for this section, here are some questions to ask yourself as you consider what art might be relevant to include for your game:

- What do players of games in my genre care about? How can I show them that I care about those things too with game art?

- What did I do in my game that deliberately departs from the norm and does something new or unexpected?

- Is there a particular strength in the art direction for my game that I can bring more attention to?

- Is there enough diversity in the gameplay that will keep players engaged? How do I scale the difficulty and the acquisition of new abilities/items?

- When a game is done poorly in this genre, where are those mistakes often made? How can I demonstrate that my game is not making those mistakes?

With content about your game collected and polished, we can turn our attention to the high-level conversation that comes after a publisher expresses interest in your game, swinging us back into the in-depth business considerations we have been preparing for throughout this book.

Deck Content: Roadmap to Launch

Up until this point in the deck, most of our focus has been on the game itself. While that will always be the most important part of your pitch, a large portion of how you present your game also reveals much about you and what it might be like to work with you. Publishers recognize that signing a publishing deal is not entirely unlike a marriage. That deal tethers your fates together, and you will spend a significant amount of the next year or more collaborating on your game.

And then, if your game is a success, that relationship could extend into another game.

With that in mind, publishers want to work with developers who have a grasp on the business of games and who have expectations and goals that align with their own. As the developer, you need to convince the publisher that they can trust you to execute on your promises and that you will spend their money judiciously and effectively.

That conversation will happen indirectly through all of the material we have covered thus far, but the meat of the business conversation comes out in the next two sections, your market analysis and your ask. A market analysis is the pitch deck form of the research we explored in previous chapters, and the ask is what kind of terms you want for your relationship, which usually encompasses funding, intellectual property rights, revenue sharing, and so on.

Market Analysis

Your game does not launch in a vacuum. It enters a landscape full of fresh competitors as well as legendary titles that have defined the genre. If a publisher helps you to bring a game to market, the publisher wants to see that you understand the players you aim to capture and that their investment in your work will turn a profit.

For a pitch deck, the work you put into a market analysis will mostly be limited to a single slide, but having that knowledge ready for reference in a conversation will be useful even if you can't fit it all into your deck. In practice, a deck is the basis for a deeper discussion, so just because you don't get to show all of your knowledge right away does not mean it won't be relevant later.

Here are the basic points you should bear in mind as you build a market analysis for your deck:

- Choose games that are relatively recent to make your deck timely
- Choose games that have some of the same ingredients as yours to demonstrate the overlap in player interest
- Choose games that have a scope similar to yours (don't just pick games that have sold millions of copies)
- Use actual sales numbers wherever possible even if those metrics are incomplete based on sales data limitations
- Highlight any major market trends, but be careful to show that you are positioning your game ahead of the trend instead of making a copycat

There is not an exact science to what is best to include on market analysis slides, but we can say from our direct publishing work and our larger work in the games industry what hurts a publisher's enthusiasm for your game: Unrealistic expectations. Your analysis should be a projection of how your game could reasonably perform in the market if it is done well.

Yes, *Fortnite* is a major success, but if you're a two-person team working on a pixel art battle royale title, comparing your project to *Fortnite* makes you look naive or delusional. Instead, work from numbers for games that are more squarely your competitors or indicators of how a game like yours could perform. You heard this advice before – because we said it in previous chapters – but we feel we have to emphasize it again because enthusiastic creators who are inexperienced with pitching or with sales can be prone to hyperbole.

Most publishers will find a frank business analysis refreshing. Publishers will still want you to shoot for the stars, but they also don't want to work with a developer who has their heads in the clouds. So to speak.

The Ask and Budget Breakdown

Next, your pitch deck should address your ask as well as your budget and budget breakdown. If you haven't already, you might want to check out our indie game budget template (Chapter 8) as well as the accompanying video tutorial that will walk you through how to use the template (indiegamecoach.com/budget) because having that material will make this portion of your deck much easier to complete.

The "ask" is what you want from the publisher. Typically, that's a dollar amount, but it can also include support for localization, console porting, Q&A, and marketing. Fair warning: Every publisher is different and takes their own approach to what they provide developers, but showing a publisher that you are thinking ahead on these variables builds your credibility. If your ask is not a precise fit for a publisher but is close enough, you can often negotiate the rest of the terms to find a mutual win.

As you formulate the dollar amount for your ask, your math and budget breakdown should focus on total costs involved to develop and launch your game, including the following:

- Your burn rate, how much capital you use each month to complete your project – This is a useful metric for milestone-based budget agreements: And you should consider if this will involve taking your current team full time if you are currently working on this project on the side.

- Outsourcing/contractors – This would be any outside companies or contractors that you may need to hire to complete the game, including artists, music composers, programmers, etc.

- Porting – If you're not handling all the porting internally, make sure you include any potential porting costs you may incur.

- Hardware/software costs – Be sure to include any costs for software licenses, dev kits, tools or resources that you need to complete the game.

- QA/localization - This one is often overlooked, but you want to include any estimated costs for QA testing and localization, which you can get quotes on from various QA and localization vendors.

- Marketing – This one is often overlooked and actually really difficult for most developers to determine. It's ok to leave this marked as TBD so you can discuss with the publisher, but if you want to include it, then a good rule of thumb is to estimate about 10-15 percent of your total game budget

- Post-launch costs – this is often overlooked and an ask that may not apply to every developer, but if you are planning DLC or other major content, how much it would cost to produce your DLC if the game hasn't recouped.

- What you have invested in the project to date (in actual dollars, sweat equity does not count.

As you work out this math, resist the urge to use anything but the real numbers. Don't inflate or deflate your budgets. If you are talking to an established publisher, they have a wealth of experience in their own right and a team of experts to vet your ask. If you try to manipulate anything to get more than you need or if you are truly not informed in your ask, a publisher can tell. Additionally, don't try to get the publisher to cover your business costs, such as office space, lawyers, and so forth. This is your cost of doing business. Smart developers will factor these costs into their burn rate, and if you're going to ask for these costs, make sure you go this route.

Our advice from Chapter 8 applies here as well: Use market rates and actual estimates at all times. You should still plan for the worst-case scenario and be realistic about what it will take to complete the game, but work with real numbers. If you aren't sure what those should be, do some research and talk to other developers to better budget for your project before taking it to a publisher.

From this point, a publisher will let you know if your project fits within their typical budgets. Negotiating with a publisher is a big topic in its own right, so we devote much of Part 4 to the nature of publishing deals and how to advocate for your interests in those conversations.

The last piece to cover before setting up your game demo is how you present your team, which is a topic intertwined with both your vision for the game you want to build and the people you may need to hire to bring that vision to life.

Deck Content: Team Information

Throughout this chapter, we have emphasized the idea of building a publisher's trust in you and your ability to execute on your promises. Up until this point in the deck, all of that has been accomplished by being professional, prepared, and polished. You've shown it rather than communicated directly.

This section is your chance to present your team and, perhaps, to brag a bit.

Here is what you might include for the team portion of your slide:

- Brief bios of each core team member with headshots.
- Total team number.
- Unique or special skills that your team members bring to the project.
- Previous accolades or notable accomplishments for your team (game relevant and/or specific to the project at hand).
- If you have a worthwhile social media following, share your numbers.
- If the game is live on Steam, share your current Wishlist numbers if they are notable.
- Highlight previous game launches if you have them.

Before you panic, every person in an indie publishing conversation understands that many indie developers are on their first game and, therefore, may not have a wealth of previous industry experience to point to. If that's you, that's okay. Try some of the following tips:

- Highlight industry-relevant skills like previous programming, writing, art, business, or marketing experience.
- Mention previous projects, even if they are small game jams.
- Find and showcase project allies, such as advisors/mentors or notable industry partners who have agreed to promote your project when it is completed.
- Highlight any accolades from competitions or small shows where you may have shown your game.

Effort matters here, so do your best. Every developer starts at the beginning, and you may need to have a few conversations to find the right publisher for a first-time developer if that's the situation you're in. That's okay as long as you continue to do your best to present yourself professionally and continue to try and grow your industry experience between publisher conversations.

If you recall our story about *Turnip Boy Commits Tax Evasion*, the team at Snoozy Kazoo had never released a full game when we met them at PAX East, but they could still show us a well-rounded team that encompassed the major development needs for the project (programming, art, and music), and they could point to their traction on social media as well as previous events to show that this team's talent was already capturing the curiosity of players.

Other unproven indies we have worked with have been college professors–a sign of technical ability and broad development knowledge – or entrepreneurs who were investing profits from other successful ventures into their game studio – a sign of business acumen and of an ability to bring products to market. Your resume may not be incredibly long to start, but there is likely more about you to share than you might initially realize. And, as you continue your indie journey, you can expand that resume.

If everything has gone well with your deck up until this point, the final phase for the deck is the publisher trying your demo and reviewing your GDD.

Deck Content: Demo and GDD

These last items will likely occupy the least real estate in the deck itself but are no less important. Following a great deck with a great demo is the ideal one-two punch for opening up a publishing deal, and having the GDD on hand is a quick way for a publisher to confirm that you have thought your project through and the scope of your project matches the scope of your promises.

Game demos and GDDs are another part of this process that are beyond the focus of this particular book. For our purposes, here are some quick pointers:

- Share a vertical slice demo that is reasonably polished. It's okay if there are minor bugs.
- Clearly communicate what inputs (keyboard and mouse vs. controller) are ideal for the game.
- Communicate within the demo when the demo has come to an end.
- Use a service like Google Drive to host your demo so that you can update the demo with fixes without having to distribute a new link.
- Link to your GDD or note that it is available on request (but make sure it is readily available).
- Consider creating an executive summary form of your GDD to capture scope and production roadmaps without giving away every detail of your plan.

Remember, any publisher having a conversation understands that they are not receiving a complete game, but there should be enough remarkable content to leave that publisher wanting more, just like a player would want more. That's a significant challenge for a product that's in active development, so think about how proud of your demo you are. If you don't think your demo truly captures where your project is going, wait to talk to a publisher and put more time into development.

Also, assume that your demo will be shared to other people beyond your direct contact. Any legitimate publisher will honor the sanctity of your project (so don't worry about your demo ending up on Twitter), but most of the representatives you meet at events or at investor summits are the tip of the spear. They scout for titles, and if a game catches their attention, they bring it back to a larger team that then evaluates the game as well.

Like your pitch deck, you have to account for the fact that you may never meet the people evaluating your game, so you won't be in the room to explain what to do or where to go or what button to push. Your demo has to succeed entirely independent of outside input from you or one of your team members. Make sure you have sufficient tutorial information and that you get to interesting content as quickly as you can with your demo.

Taking this thinking even farther, since your demo could be shared to others without your knowing, make sure that pertinent details about you, your studio, and your game are readily accessible from the demo. Use your team's branding. Include a website. And link to the Steam page if it is live.

How to Present Your Pitch

At the start of this book, we argued that business is a skill that can be developed and honed, just like great art or great music or great game design. Some people are born with natural talent, but any of these can also be learned.

Salesmanship is one of these skills, but the industry stereotype of the solo, introverted indie developer can discourage indies from seeing the value of sales technique or pitching technique. You aren't hocking penny stocks, but you are convincing a stranger to invest potentially thousands of dollars into your project. That's a big bet at any scale, and persuasion matters.

If two pitches are equal on every front, a publisher or investor is most likely to choose the presentation that was most compelling. Like being prepared or being professional, a refined pitch inspires confidence and helps to convince a publisher that you and your team can actually make your game and would be pleasant to work with.

We spend more time on the back and forth of a sales conversation in the next chapter, so for now think of your pitch as a form of public speaking with a question-and-answer component built in. You will probably need to think quickly to address a query you had not considered, but, for the most part, all of the material we have covered thus far will prepare you to speak intelligently about your game and how you plan to build it.

The good news is that indie publishers and investors do not expect indie developers to be slick-talking salespeople. They know the space well enough that they can spot a charlatan, and they are savvy enough to forgive nervousness and the occasional stumble.

Even if you have no sales experience whatsoever, if you take these steps you can deliver a knockout pitch:

Account for Time Constraints

If you have a 30-minute meeting booked with a publisher, you should be able to comfortably pitch your game in that time while also leaving room for some introductory banter and a few questions throughout. Running out of time when you still have half your deck to cover is a big missed opportunity, so cover as much critical information as you can and use what you did not cover as an incentive for the publisher to book a second meeting with you. The actual amount of time you get will vary by situation – from a 30-second "elevator pitch" on a show floor to a 5-minute networking pitch to a 60-minute deep-dive on a Zoom call – so be prepared.

Rehearse Your Pitch

Your first time delivering your pitch should not be when you are sitting across the table from your dream publisher. As goofy as it can feel, practice your pitch in the mirror. Ask teammates and colleagues to listen to your pitch. Critique yourself and get feedback. You don't need to memorize a script, but you should be able to hit your key points in a way that seems natural and articulate.

Prepare Your Own Questions

A pitch can initially feel like a one-way interaction–you convincing a publisher to work with you – but a great pitch is often more like a mutual interview. You can learn a great deal about a publisher in your research before a meeting, but you should also probe with your own questions. For example, you should ask about the publisher's preferred deal structure, if their future lineup has any significant deviations from what they have published historically, at what point in a game's development they prefer to invest, and so on. If you can get a sense for what your audience cares most about, you can adjust your presentation accordingly.

Pitch Delivery

The above three components should add up to a strong delivery for your pitch. A strong delivery means:

- Communicating clearly – Your ideas and your intention are easy to understand.
- Communicating concisely – You can get to the point without burning a lot of time or rambling.
- Communicating with confidence – Your posture and tone show that you believe in your project and your ask.
- Adjusting to the scenario – Your ability to understand what a particular context or audience cares about matters.
- Improving over time – You use each pitch as an opportunity to make the next pitch better.

Communicating clearly, concisely, and with confidence largely comes down to practice, but planning matters here too. If you find that you often stumble on the elevator pitch, maybe it needs to be reworked. If you find yourself afraid to discuss a certain feature, that might be a sign that you need to put more thought into how that feature works or how you explain it. To do all of that with poise, though, will take time.

During that time, practice pitching to your team. Then practice pitching to family and friends. If you have a business or industry mentor, give them the pitch too. And then don't be afraid to roleplay through answering questions about your project and your ask. All of this can feel silly when you do it – trying to convince your mom to buy your game in her living room is goofy no matter how you look at it – but it helps more than you realize.

Whether you are practicing pitches or pitching for real, give yourself time to debrief after each pitch. Where did you struggle? Where did your audience seem confused? What didn't come out quite right? Did the audience share a nugget that you could use to your advantage in the future?

We've seen really talented indie devs adjust their pitch on the fly. Sitting at a table at a GamesIndustry.biz Investment Summit, you get to see a lot of pitches, and great indies sometimes learn that one aspect of their game is much more interesting than they realized. Maybe the art style is in line with a game that is just recently getting a lot of attention, so publishers are interested in exploring titles like that. We've sat at a table with a developer where we were the ones that mentioned the similarity and why that's exciting only to hear that become a part of the pitch when they move to the table next to us.

You don't always need to be that nimble, but that should give you an idea of how much you can learn from a publisher conversation, even when it's short. Unfortunately, pitching your game typically means facing a great deal of failure.

As painful at that can be, you can make it productive and learn even if you don't get the deal.

When a Pitch Fails

The nature of pitching any kind of product is that no matter how talented you are and how good your product is, you will always hear "no thanks" more often than you hear "yes." If you attend a GamesIndustry.biz Investment Summit, for example, you could pitch to 10 or more publishers in a single morning. You can typically only work with one publisher for your game, and a publisher can only support so many games in a year. As a result, the simple math says that the majority of these conversations will not lead to a publishing deal or an investment.

While rejection can be painful, few publishers or investors in this industry are outright malicious when they decline a game. Some are blunt, sure, but rarely will someone attack you or your work just for the sake of making you feel badly about your efforts.

One failed pitch is not the end of your project, nor are a dozen failed pitches. Rejection can be an opportunity to improve your deck, your ability to pitch, and the game you're pitching. If you reflect on your pitch experience, learn from it, and apply those lessons moving forward, you can get better at the business of games.

The caveat, though, is that the conclusions you can draw from a rejection are not always immediately clear. Here are reasons that a publisher could reject your pitch that have nothing to do with the quality of your idea or the quality of your pitch:

- The publisher's schedule is full.
- Your budget or ask is not a fit for the publisher.
- The publisher's budget is spoken for.
- Your title does not align with a new but not publicly disclosed business direction for the publisher
- Your game would compete against another title they have not yet announced.
- The publisher is focused on signing titles that will release in the next 12 months, while your release date is farther away.

That said, assuming that your pitch and your game cannot be improved is also a mistake. Hubris often masquerades as self-confidence, and neither a pitch nor an idea for a game is likely to be perfect in its early outings. If you did not get an offer from a publisher, seize the opportunity to find ways to get better.

Try the following if the conversation does not feel like it is moving toward a direct "yes" or a clear next step:

- If your contact is not clear about their stance on your game, directly ask, "Does this feel like the kind of game you would publish?" (or something to that effect)

- Politely ask if they would take a few minutes to share feedback on your pitch
- Probe to better understand their process for selecting games, such as target budgets, deal structures, and pitch content so you can be better prepared to pitch them in the future
- Request their permission to pitch them on your next project if it aligns with what they say they are looking for in a game
- Ask if they have a recommendation of another publisher who might be a better fit

This approach is much easier to execute in person or in a virtual meeting than it is in an email, so be mindful of the social context you're operating under. If you have limited time – or word count, in the case of an e-mail – be selective about how much you ask for and do your best to assess the publisher's appetite for giving you more help. If a publisher has declined to work with you and does not seem overly friendly, pressing for more could sour future conversations, but if they seem friendly and engaged, asking their advice is worthwhile.

Lastly, not all advice is good advice. Or, perhaps to frame it more fairly, not all advice is *the right advice for you*. The games industry is full of passionate and highly opinionated people, and part of your job as an indie is to decide when you should make changes and when you should stick to your vision.

If you make every change suggested to you, your game will devolve into a confusing quagmire of half-baked ideas.

If you ignore every change suggested to you, you will continue to stumble on the same obstacles again and again.

But how can you tell what feedback to take and what feedback to ignore? That's part of the art of business. No one really has the answers, and it's up to you to figure out.

These reflection questions can help:

- Is their criticism valid? If so, what can you do to address it?
- What could invalidate their criticism? Could you pre-empt that objection in your pitch?
- Can you identify any patterns in pitch reactions, feedback, or questions?
- What questions did they ask that you weren't prepared for?
- What did they react positively to?
- What did they react negatively to?
- Where did they seem confused or what did they misunderstand?
- Did they make any assumptions that you were not prepared to address?
- If you ranked how much you wanted to work with this person, how would that influence the importance of their perspective?
- When you share the criticism you received with your team and/or with your mentors, do they agree with it? Why or why not?

When you are newer to the industry, recovering from a failed pitch might take some effort. Once you get accustomed to taking meetings with decision makers, you will find that they get easier over time and that rejection feels less like failure and more like networking. As long as you are professional and courteous, every connection is a seed planted for the future.

In our own work, we ended up working with developers and partners whom we had met months or years prior, at a time when it just didn't make sense for us to collaborate. But, in our meetings, we learned more about each other's goals and recognized that even if the project on the table today wasn't the right starting point, we would be very open to working with this person or team in the future.

You are likely to have the same experience in the long term, but we recognize that thinking that way can be hard when your goal is to bring your game to life today. We hope, though, that you are at the beginning of a decades-long journey and that every small step matters later.

If your pitching goes well, your next step will be to negotiate a deal with your new partner.

How to Negotiate with a Publisher

Reaching the point of negotiating a publishing deal for your game is momentous. It speaks to the level of effort you've put into your game, pitch deck, and publisher outreach. Getting here confirms that you've made the right choices with your project so far.

But don't lose sight of your true goal: Finding the right publisher fit to successfully launch your game.

As an indie developer, especially if you haven't been at the negotiation table before, the idea of pushing back on an offer from a publisher can feel like a threat to everything you've worked for. What if something goes wrong? What if the publisher walks away? What if you lose the deal? These are normal feelings, and they are also why many indie developers end up with bad deals.

You have to stand up for your interests because no one else will, and no reputable publisher will take offense to a good faith negotiation. The games industry is built on compromise and collaboration, so as long as you make the conversation constructive, the act of negotiating should not eliminate the potential deal. If it does, then the deal probably wasn't right for you in the first place.

Before we explore the indie game deal structure and discuss strategies and tactics for negotiating, we should review the major goals of negotiation, which are as follows:

- Find the right publisher fit for your game and for your business goals.
- Arrive at terms that are fair with regards to compensation and support for your game.
- Structure your relationship for the short- and long-term potential of your game.
- Avoid the common pitfalls that hinder indie developers.

With our experience as game publishers as well as our work in marketing and PR where we work directly with developers, we can give you a well-rounded perspective on what both sides of the negotiating table might expect and might want.

DOI: 10.1201/9781003215264-13

This chapter continues to build on the ideas, concepts, and material we have explored thus far, but these are the major takeaways for our focus on negotiations in this section:

- The role your pitch deck plays in negotiating a deal.
- The typical steps of reaching a deal with a publisher.
- Common deal structures and vocabulary.
- Tips and suggestions for managing the conversations around your deal.
- How to vet a deal to ensure it's fair.

By the end of this chapter, you should have the education you need to have a worthwhile conversation with a publisher. You will know what questions to ask, you will know what the answers mean, and that knowledge will make it easier to speak with confidence about your project. Landing a publishing deal is always tough, whether it's your first or tenth game, but it's even harder when you know nothing about the process and have no context for how a deal should work.

Negotiation Overview

Just as no two games are exactly the same, no two publishing deals are exactly the same. Each publisher will have its own process, its own preferences, and its own priorities. Depending on the circumstances, some publishers may be ready to write you a check at your booth while others will have an intense diligence process before inking an agreement.

We highlight these points about variation so that you can stay flexible and agile.

In general, though, the major elements of an indie game negotiation are similar from conversation to conversation, even if they are sometimes out of order or blend into each other.

Those stages are as follows:

1. The discovery call – In this stage, you pitch your game and confirm your ask.
2. Publisher review – The publisher reviews your materials internally with their business teams and gathers market research regarding your title: During this phase, you may have additional calls with a publisher, as well as back-and-forth e-mails.
3. Publisher offer – Intrigued by your pitch and your materials, the publisher offers you terms for publishing your game and follows with a letter of intent (LOI).
4. Agreement – both parties agree to and sign a publishing agreement.

How and where these steps occur can change the exact execution of each stage. For example, if your "Discovery Call" begins on the floor of a gaming convention, which is common for our industry, you may need to repeat the Discovery Call in a more formal meeting setting with the full publishing team. If your pitch starts at an Investor Summit – think speed-dating but for indie developers and game publishers – your pitch may need to be radically truncated to fit the format and some material review could take place before you leave the table for your next session. Again, you will likely need to repeat part or all of your pitch for a more formal meeting with the full publishing team.

The framework, however, is valuable because it gives you a roadmap for moving your game closer to a deal.

We're going to look at each stage in-depth later in this chapter, but first we should give you the background information that goes into making any detail.

Key Background Insights

First-time home buyers often make a slew of mistakes when they purchase a home. They might not know what to look for in a home inspection. They may place too much trust in the realtor. They might know what interest rates are fair. They might not know what kind of mortgage to pursue. They might not know how much to expect for a down payment or what to anticipate for a monthly payment, especially with taxes and homeowners' insurance in the mix.

Even if everyone involved in the process is honest and has the first-time home buyer's interests in mind, that individual can still make several costly mistakes.

That's the nature of making big choices with limited experience and even more limited knowledge. If you don't have a mentor to guide you through the process of buying a home, it's easy to get off track. Publishing your first game is no different. You can easily make mistakes simply because you don't know what to ask or what to look for.

This section will give you the footing you need to launch a successful negotiation. We cover the following:

- What an advance is and what it's for.
- Common revenue sharing models.
- What a recoup is and how it affects revenue sharing.
- Other post-launch financials.
- IP considerations for things such as media and merchandising rights.

Beyond the textbook knowledge, we will also explore some basic sales techniques. The idea here isn't to *Boiler Room* your way into a publishing deal but rather to help you represent yourself in a professional, respectable way. This could be a book in its own right as sales is a deep topic, but for our purposes, we are expanding key ideas that we started in the last chapter with these additions:

- Why rapport matters.
- How to adjust your pitch based on the meeting context.
- How to deliver your pitch deck.
- How to run and participate in a sales meeting.
- How to use your agenda to confirm expectations and set up next steps.

All of this will take practice, of course, but even just reading the rest of this chapter will give you a big advantage over the other first-time indie developers vying for a slot with your publisher of choice.

Basic Indie Publisher Deal Structure

As we covered in the introduction, no two publishing deals are exactly the same. From budgets to IP rights to porting to revenue sharing, every publisher brings a unique focus and a unique approach to the deal table. You can't look at the final figure in a deal to say whether it's good or not, so you need to understand the components of the deal so that you can decide whether or not it fits your goals.

Now a big chunk of this comes down to your ask, which we covered in your pitch deck and built from your thorough planning process, so revisit Part 1 and Part 2 if you aren't sure what you or your project really needs.

The five biggest terms you will hear in a deal conversation are milestones, advance, recoup, revenue share, and intellectual property rights.

Here's what those mean:

- Milestone schedule – An agreed upon schedule where you as the developer must hit development milestones in order to receive payment for your work: Generally, milestones occur every month.
- Recoup – The idea that the publisher gets their initial investment back in game sales, either partially or in full before beginning to share profits with the developer.
- Revenue share – How the publisher and the developer split game profits when the recoup period is over.
- Advance – Money given to a developer at launch to keep the developer afloat during the recoup period: This is an advance payment of your future royalties.
- Intellectual property rights – The permissions granted for how the "world" associated with a game can or cannot be used in other contexts, such as a television adaptation.

And, as you may have guessed, there are more nuances to each of these beyond their simple definitions.

Milestone Schedule

A milestone schedule will be familiar to anyone with development experience. Milestones break a large production schedule into stages so that a studio can unlock funding for achieving set goals. Publishers like milestone schedules because they incentivize key deliverables and encourage efficiency. Since you're only getting funding when you reach certain deliverables, you're motivated to use your time and resources wisely.

As the developer, a milestone schedule should not scare you, but you should analyze it closely before signing an agreement. The idea of milestone-based funding is to incentivize developers to stick to timelines and to carefully manage budgets since they can't unlock the next payment until the current stage is complete, protecting the publisher's investment and helping to keep a game on schedule for release.

If you don't review the schedule carefully, however, you might end up critically underfunded at a key stage in your game's development. You may find that your current burn rate puts you one month short of funding if you adopted the publisher's milestone schedule, which is a long time to not have a budget for paying your people. That situation will be even worse if you are behind schedule by a few days, let alone a few weeks

If you find that a milestone schedule is not practical, you should talk to the publisher about revising it. As long as you come to the table with a fair alternative and sound reasoning for your position, adjusting the milestone schedule should not be a significant challenge and is often an expected step of the process.

Fortunately, you should have your budgets and timelines clearly mapped from the work we did in Chapter 8, and that work will help this conversation to go even more smoothly.

Recoup

If you recall the sales analysis math we did in Part 1, right-sizing your budget to your sales projections is a critical part of making your game profitable, and the size and structure of an advance should align with that math. That said, we have also seen deals where post-launch advances are not a part of the recoup, so read the terms of your offer carefully before you start to negotiate.

A publisher is also likely to consider other activities part of an advance even if payments do not go directly to you as the developer. Publishers may consider marketing activities and porting as part of the advance, for example, making your understanding of what's covered by your deal even more important. If you miss the fact that porting costs are part of an advance, you may not budget appropriately and find yourself behind on bills even when your game is for sale and doing well–all because you didn't factor in the extra money that went into porting.

The delivery of an advance can sometimes be complex. Since publishing games is a high-risk endeavor, many publishers will use milestone formats or other funding structures to break a total advance into smaller pieces, like we discussed earlier. If any part of that is confusing or unclear for you, talk with the publisher before signing to get clarity and to make the adjustments you might need.

If the size of the advance is roughly in line with your ask, though, you're on the right track.

The concept of a recoup, on paper, is simple. If a publisher funds your game for $100,000, then your game needs to make $100,000 in profit before you start to see royalty checks. In practice, however, a recoup may not be as simple.

Just as there might be more to an advance than what a publisher gives to a developer, a recoup may not be a straight line from game profits to paying back an advance. Here are three major variations of recoup that you might encounter:

- Simple recoup – The publisher funds the project, and is reimbursed that exact sum with profits from game sales.

- Staggered recoup – The publisher begins partial revenue sharing at a certain point in the recoup even though they have not been completely reimbursed.

- Incomplete recoup – A publisher might not expect a recoup on all dollars invested; for example, some publishers might not recoup on certain kinds of marketing or perhaps on games porting: This is rare and typically only occurs if a publisher thinks there will be significant games sales to offset these costs.

None of these recoup models is necessarily better than the other. What is good or bad is largely dependent on the project and the people involved, but understanding what's in your agreement will give you the power to negotiate. For example, asking for a larger funding amount with a staggered recoup might be more sustainable for your business than if you took the same funding with a simple recoup because you could, in theory, have revenue coming into your studio much sooner.

The incomplete recoup can look like it's always a good thing, and it often is, but you should dig a bit to see if there are any tradeoffs or concessions you make to get that benefit. One publisher might have an exclusive relationship with a specific platform, so they bake-in a set amount of ad credits on that platform. That relationship, however, could limit your access to audiences on other platforms, which may or may not be a problem for your project.

Comparing your original plan to the publisher's terms is helpful here, but being willing to adjust your strategy to capture new opportunities is important. You may not have planned to make your game a platform exclusive, but if a publisher's connections make that possible and the minimum guarantee is a business match, pivoting could be a good idea.

Emphasis on *could*.

Be willing to adapt and adjust. It may not always be the best option to do so, but passionate creators can sometimes be inflexible and miss out on big wins as a result. So, at the very least, be open minded.

Advances

As you might have guessed – or maybe already learned from preliminary conversations with publishers – the size of the advance from publisher to publisher will vary dramatically if they do one at all. Some publishers don't provide advances and some have minimums. Others have maximums. Others scale the advance according to certain aspects of a game, sometimes even going as far as to plan for post-launch advances in scenarios where a game is designed to be a long-term revenue driver, which can be relevant for multiplayer games or games with extensive seasonal content.

This is important: An advance is not profit for you as a developer. An advance is a very specific type of loan. Typically, you have to pay it back later with game sales, which is why sizing your ask to the exact needs of your budget is important. The bigger the advance, the more sales you need to make before your game reaches true profitability.

Revenue Share

Revenue share, or "rev share" as it is often called in the industry, is the point at which a publisher and a developer start to split the proceeds of game sales. This stage usually occurs after the recoup is complete and can come in varying ratios such as 80/20, 60/40, 50/50, and every variation in between.

If a developer offers you an 80/20 revenue share "in the publisher's favor," that means that 80% of the profits after the recoup period go to the publisher and 20% of the profits go to the developer.

Again, there is no right or wrong answer here. Your initial reaction might be to assume that the deal where the largest share goes to you is the best revenue share relationship, but in practice, a deal is not that simple. The publisher offering a higher revenue share might not have a track record for reaching a large volume of game sales, so you might get the larger revenue share but have far fewer overall sales.

With the right math, 80/20 in the publisher's favor can be more profitable for you than a 60/40 revenue share in your favor. That said, be critical here. An 80/20 rev share *could* also be predatory, so do your research on the publisher's track record and calculate how many units you will need to move to reach your revenue goals when you put the advance, the recoup terms, and the revenue share together.

Though this is less common, we should note here that just as recoups are sometimes staggered, revenue share can also be rolled out in tiers. Early stages might favor one party over another, but as certain revenue goals are met, the ratio shifts. The revenue share relationship may start at 80/20, but after $20,000 in sales it shifts to 70/30, and then to 60/40.

In addition to being generous, this approach can be another way to reduce the initial revenue obstacle that a recoup can present by making it possible for the developer to begin collecting revenue earlier. It might also be a carrot to incentivize ongoing development post-launch because the developer stands to earn much more overall if the game has a longer shelf life.

It's important to understand the relationship between revenue share and recoup because it can help you better understand offers. As we previously noted, an incomplete recoup might sound like the best option, but often, the revenue share in this scenario is highly in the publisher's favor (80/20 or 90/10).

Coupling this knowledge with the research and planning processes we have covered thus far will put you in a good position to assess a deal. Without that prework, judging the fit for an offer becomes much more dangerous because you are gambling with your future.

Intellectual Property Terms

Intellectual property, or "IP" as you will typically hear it called, is the ownership you have over your game and the assets related to your game. *Star Wars* is an IP, and the value it has comes from more than just the films that make up the core of the property. The *Star Wars* IP also includes streaming revenue, merchandise revenue (from t-shirts to toys and everything in between), book adaptations, comic book adaptations, television adaptations, and a litany of sequels and spinoffs.

Star Wars might sound like an impossible comparison point for indie games, but savvy indies have a history of leveraging the full potential of their games. For example, Supergiant Games, the studio behind *Bastion* and *Hades* are masters of channeling fan passion into merchandise. As we discussed earlier, they have a hugely successful line of vinyl soundtracks. They sell posters. They sell t-shirts. All of that is possible because of how they managed their IP.

When you sign a publishing deal, you grant a range of permissions related to your IP and in some cases outright transfer ownership of certain portions of the IP. There are a variety of rights related to a game IP, but the most common ones negotiated beyond the IP of the game itself are the following:

- Sequel rights – Who has the permission to create and profit from a sequel to the game tied to the agreement.

- Media rights – Who has permission to create and profit from a film, television and other media adaptations of your game.

- Merchandise rights – Who has permission to create and sell products related to your game, including t-shirts or pins.

We say your game in these definitions, but it's also possible that your publishing agreement outright transfers the ownership of your game to the publisher. This is not common in the indie space, but it does happen. Like everything else we have talked about so far, there are no right or wrong answers here.

Yes, it might be a red flag if a publisher takes full ownership of your IP, but it could also be a really big opportunity if the terms are right. If a publisher gives you $10,000 and owns your game, that's not a great offer, but if the publisher is providing a substantial sum and also multi-year salaries and stock options for your core team, well, that might be a deal worth taking.

And that line of thinking will play out with any rights you share or transfer to a publisher. Sometimes the deal is good. Sometimes the deal is bad. The context and the potential tradeoffs matter.

As you weigh those options, ask yourself these questions:

- What would I do if I kept those rights?
- Does the publisher have a track record of success with those rights?
- Does the potential compensation make transferring those rights worthwhile?

To return to our Supergiant Games example, they have done really well with an internal merchandise team. At the same time, producing and fulfilling that much product is a substantial risk for an indie developer. It is capital intensive and requires a great deal of work hours to manage on a day-to-day basis.

If you don't have merchandise experience and encounter a publisher who does have that track record – they have plushies and t-shirts and pins and every event they attend they sell out and they have retailer partnerships across the industry – you may be better off letting them run with their strengths. The revenue share might look small on something like this, but if you get an idea of sales volume, the actual money you could make is substantial.

The same thinking applies to media rights. If your publisher spins out television or film tie-ins on a regular basis, that's worth paying attention to. Generally, this is rare for indie games, but with more media companies entering the gaming space – such as Crunchyroll and Netflix – media rights are likely to become more relevant for indies in the future.

Sequel rights, on the other hand, can be more complicated. Very rarely should an indie dev outright transfer ownership of sequel rights because that means getting cut out of the long-term potential (and revenue) of your game. We've seen it happen, and it's painful to watch let alone experience firsthand.

Most publishers will not ask for ownership of sequel rights, but you may encounter a "right of first refusal" clause, which means that if you decide to do a sequel to your game, your publisher has the right to automatically take the deal before you offer it to anyone else. Typically, there is language attached here around what those terms might look like, and they might scale based on sales performance of the first title. Generally, though, the terms for the sequel are often similar to the original title, but can be negotiated based on how the game performs.

Signing over any manner of sequel rights can feel like a big commitment, because it is, but it's also a sign that your publisher is thinking about working with you long-term. If you find success together with the first game, the logic of working together for the sequel is sound and is often good business.

You don't need to know exactly how you want to handle these rights prior to talking with a publisher, but you should discuss these points with your team so that you have a general idea of how you plan to handle these aspects of your business. That will make it easier for you to recognize the right deal when it comes along.

And that's a good point to revisit your pitch deck as well.

The Negotiation Process

Now that you have a foundational understanding of key terms and negotiation points, we can start to unpack the actual negotiation process. Process is an important idea here because any creative process is not strictly linear. We can predict the major points your negotiation is likely to hit, but some negotiations will be more formal than others, and you may need to repeat a particular stage several times to reach a compromise that is acceptable to both you and the publisher.

Like your initial pitch, few publishers expect an indie developer to be a master salesperson or a legal expert, but having a process to follow will eliminate difficult surprises and boost your credibility.

Revisiting Your Pitch Deck

Yes, we just spent a full chapter on your pitch deck, but as you talk with publishers, you should revisit and re-familiarize yourself with your pitch deck on a regular basis. Here's why:

- Consistency matters – If you say one thing and your pitch deck says another, that's a red flag for a publisher.
- Structure is helpful – The structure of a good pitch deck can make it easier to keep your thoughts organized during a stressful meeting, even if you aren't formally presenting the deck.
- Things change – Part of publishing is gathering information: You might learn something in a meeting that changes how you think about your pitch, prompting a revision.

You don't need to memorize your deck, but some items are worth knowing inside and out:

- Budget – How you arrived at this total and the nuances of the numbers that add up to the total.
- Development Timeline – How do you intend to spend your development time and how that timeline might shift if you had more budget or additional resources.
- Ask – What kind of deal you are pursuing and why.

We have come back again and again to the idea that there are no clear right or wrong answers when you're negotiating a publishing deal. There are exceptions and contextual details that will change from conversation to conversation, so as much as we would like to issue our own commandments for indie publishing deals, we can't.

Your budget could be completely accurate, making your ask reasonable and fair as a result, but if you learn that a publisher includes porting as part of the relationship and has generous terms around how porting budget is addressed in the recoup, your budget and ask might change. In this situation, your ask could go down and your timeline could shorten because your publisher is taking on the burden of porting your game to consoles.

That's a big detail, and you should be able to roughly work out those numbers on the fly, at least enough that the conversation can continue without you having to call three different people on your team before you can tell a publisher how that changes your ask.

These are the moments where negotiations really begin, and you won't be equipped to negotiate if you don't come to the meeting with a solid grasp of your pitch deck and all of the factors that go into building that pitch deck.

From there, you can start to be more creative about all of the variables of your project. If you want to keep the same ask even if some of your workload is decreased by the publisher, maybe you can pitch investing that budget into expanding content or into building an additional feature or into extra resources that can be used to accelerate your development timeline.

Thinking on your feet in these kinds of situations takes practice, and that's why sales and business development are competitive professions, but your pitch deck and your preparation should help you to feel more confident as you build these industry relationships.

Pitch Context and Rapport

The games industry is on track to see $100 billion in annual worldwide revenue. For how big this space is, many deals in the games industry are driven by relationships and are made behind the scenes, in-person, at industry events. If you've worked in sales in any capacity, this may not surprise you, but we find that many indie developers aren't prepared for this reality.

If you want this to be your career, you need to build business relationships and you need to learn to ask the right questions in a sales conversation.

Relationships are built on rapport, which is why you will hear rapport talked about in nearly every sales guide and course you can find. Relationship Selling is an entire sales system built on the premise that people do business with people they like, so this approach turns being likeable into a multi-faceted system of sales techniques. We aren't aware of a sales system built specifically for games, so we are not recommending any specific format or style, but we can draw on our own experiences in sales and with the industry to give you practical sales principles.

Rapport begins with your first impression and is affected by choices that might be largely invisible to you. These tips are a good starting point:

- Stand up straight and smile – Your body language communicates a great deal about how you feel.

- Speak with confidence – Roleplay pitches with teammates, practice public speaking, and fake it until you believe it.

- Be presentable – You don't need to wear a suit, but a t-shirt that's at least clean and not wrinkled helps.

- Learn about the person – A relationship is not just about what you get; you should try to connect personally with the people you meet in the industry.

- Remember what people tell you – Take notes when you're talking business and also don't be afraid to jot down memorable details about conversations as well.

This part of being an indie dev can be excruciatingly difficult for introverts. The good news is that you can learn these skills with practice–a bonus benefit to being a regular at gaming conventions where you have to talk to industry types and also work a booth where you pitch players all day. You always have the option to ask one of your teammates to take on this role, but we encourage you to put the effort into these skills, especially if you are investing your own money.

Remember, publishers are more human than you might think they are. They are often direct in their conversations but are also friendly. No one is out to embarrass you, and publishers know that pitching is hard, so don't be quick to give up.

Meeting Context

We already mentioned that even though publishing talks typically follow a predictable series of steps, the line is not always a straight one. To review, publishing talks usually proceed in this order:

- The discovery call – In this stage, you pitch your game and confirm your ask.

- Publisher review – The publisher reviews your materials internally with their business teams and gathers market research regarding your title with their playtesters: During this phase, you may also have additional calls with a publisher, as well as back-and-forth e-mails.

- Publisher offer – Intrigued by your pitch and your materials, the publisher offers you verbal terms for publishing your game and follows with an LOI.

- Agreement – Both parties agree to and sign a publishing agreement.

How and where meetings happen can influence how these talks play out.

If you meet a publisher at your booth at an event, you might have time to pitch the concept and get a controller in their hands, but you may not have the time (and it may not be appropriate) to take a deep dive into the backend of your project. Moreover, you might not immediately recall that publisher's catalogue, making it harder for you to assess the situation and to ask thoughtful questions.

In this case, get a card and try to book your next meeting – a call – before that person leaves. If you're not able to set up a call, which is most likely, follow up with an e-mail that includes your pitch deck and any other pertinent information the week after the event. Then you can pick up where you left off the next time you connect.

If your first meeting comes out of an e-mail, that first meeting will be very different from a booth interaction. You will have more time to discuss your project, but the publisher's initial curiosity may not be as strong as if they approached your booth organically. A cold e-mail is a legitimate way to begin the pitch process, to be clear, but the initial enthusiasm of the first meeting will not be as strong as if the publisher saw your banner from across a show floor and was drawn in by the gameplay on your demo monitors. Moreover, it's possible that the publisher already reviewed your deck via e-mail and doesn't need a full presentation for you when the meeting does happen.

Lastly, the expectations that precede a meeting also matter. If you're doing a speed-dating format at an investment summit kind of event, the expectation is that you will be able to quickly pitch your game and ask the right questions in a truncated manner. If our hypothetical booth meeting scenario was real, your expectation is to give an in-depth look into your game–because the game is right there and playable–and you might have time to discuss the trajectory of your project and business.

The scenarios we describe here might feel obvious in this format, but we often know that inexperienced salespeople can underestimate the importance of context, which leads to having the wrong kinds of conversations at the wrong times. This is largely due to nerves, but as you expand your knowledge and perhaps read books on sales and maybe even work with a sales coach, the temptation to always follow a prescriptive, step-by-step path will be strong when in practice you should be assessing the situation and adapting accordingly.

General Sales Tips

No matter how or where a meeting starts, ending a meeting with clearly defined next steps is a good best practice. Again, that sounds simple, but in the excitement of talking to a publisher at your booth, you can forget to ask for the next meeting, leaving you to chase them down via e-mail later when you could have confirmed a calendar time and sent an invite right then and there. Because this sales misstep is so common, some sales gurus repeat mantras like "book a meeting from a meeting" to drive the point home.

In this way, knowing where you want a meeting to end is a major part of knowing where to begin.

The end goal of a meeting is not necessarily a sale. If you're in a discovery call, for example, the goal is to find out if the publisher has enough interest in your game to conduct a deeper review, and to ensure that this publisher is right for you. Otherwise, you will burn time in unproductive meetings and with follow-up that won't actually go anywhere.

We're going to explore each stage more deeply in upcoming sections, but speaking broadly, here's how to make all of your meetings more effective:

- Confirm the agenda and length of the meeting at the start.
- Determine expectations and outcomes for the meeting at the start.
- Practice your pitch and plan your questions.
- Research the publisher so that you can skip questions that can be answered by a Google search.
- Use both the agenda and the goal for the meeting as tools for keeping the discussion on track.
- Confirm next steps before you end the meeting, and book the next call if you can.

A good discussion has a natural back-and-forth dynamic, but new indie devs can often get railroaded in a meeting because they lack experience and confidence. No meeting is one-sided, and it's up to you to advocate for yourself and to steer the meeting in a direction that's productive for you.

A discovery call just isn't a discovery call for the publisher. It's an opportunity for you to learn if the publisher meets your criteria for your ask and project vision. If you go into a discovery call without that in mind or make the mistake of not confirming how long the meeting is – assuming you have an hour when the publisher actually only has 30 minutes – you might find the meeting ending without you ever having addressed the points that were important to you.

The newbie mistake here is to assume that you asking questions or confirming an agenda somehow reflects poorly on you. In reality, a good publisher loves a developer who is organized and who asks thoughtful questions as those are big indicators of what it might be like to work with that developer.

Sales is a big topic. If you plan to be the front person for your studio, you should consider practicing your public speaking skills anytime you can, and you should consider studying-up on sales techniques. The idea isn't to turn you into a fast-talking salesperson, but rather to help you go toe-to-toe with industry veterans and to have them come away feeling like you are a true professional.

Next up, we dive into the discovery call stage, one of the meatiest parts of negotiating a deal for your game.

In fact, make it a part of your process to confirm next steps before you end any meeting. That will give you clear expectations for the next meeting.

The Stages of a Publishing Deal

At the top of the chapter, we outlined the general direction of a sales process in games. As we have said repeatedly, the conversation won't be a straight line, but if you find that a discussion with a publisher has skipped major steps, stages, or points, it may be worthwhile to call for a pause and to confirm that those topics are sufficiently addressed on both sides. You may uncover that someone along the way made an assumption about the relationship that may not be accurate, so taking the time to be thorough and eliminate potential surprises is worthwhile.

Let's break down each stage.

Discovery Call

We've talked already about how what we define as a "Discovery Call" can take a few different forms. Your first encounter with a publisher could be on a convention floor, or at an investment summit, or in a Zoom meeting that you booked from a cold e-mail. The pieces, overall, are the same.

Here is a high-level view of the discovery call:

- Pitch your game as a fit for the publisher.
- The publisher asks you questions about your project.
- You ask the publisher questions about their process.
- Both parties lay the foundation for a negotiation.
- Confirm next steps.

Before that first call ever happens, though, you should do your homework.

General Preparation

As it is with all aspects of business, preparation is important. What you do before a discovery call can have a big impact on your success and whether or not the potential of your game actually gets to shine. To prepare for a discovery call, you should:

- Practice your pitch – If the first time you verbalize what's in your deck is in front of a publisher, you're doing it wrong: Get your pitch down and smooth it out before a meeting ever happens.
- Know your numbers and ask – We have hammered this before, but the point is still crucial: Know the specifics of your budget and your ask inside and out.
- Research the publisher – Know what kind of games the publisher has released in the past and dig into what they've shared publicly about their approach and philosophy.

- Prepare your answers – Thanks to resources like this book, you can enter a meeting with a reasonable prediction of what a publisher wants to know: Have that material ready.

- Outline your questions – You don't need to read a script, but knowing what questions you need to get answers for will save you awkward follow-up e-mails.

Taking notes is recommended, and referencing notes is perfectly acceptable, but you should be able to give the elevator pitch for your game to anyone, anywhere, and you shouldn't have to pause a meeting for several minutes to dig up an answer about your budget. If you don't know the answer off the top of your head, tell the publisher that you would be happy to follow up with it in a future call. For our work as publishers, several of our titles came from spotting a great demo at an event such as PAX and striking up a conversation with the developer right there. We never expect anyone to be a robot, but you can clearly tell when an indie is serious about finding a publisher because you can see that they came to an event or a meeting prepared.

Preparing for Specific Publishers

We've already talked at length about how every publisher is different, but we need to repeat it again because how you angle a pitch should be at least partially (if not largely) driven by the publisher you're speaking with. If you are given the chance to prepare for the meeting, you should be able to get a good idea of the following publisher details:

- Publisher focal points (genre, platform, monetization model, etc.)
- Their back catalogue of games
- Recent news related to the publisher
- Connections you have in common (LinkedIn)

The part of this preparation that comes from Googling a publisher will come naturally to most people reading this book, so let us emphasize the last point on this list: looking over your mutual connections. LinkedIn as a business tool is sometimes overblown and sometimes misunderstood, but if you know you are meeting with Alex Josef and you see that one of your indie developer colleagues is already connected with him, reach out to that person to find out how deep that connection is. You might learn that we just swapped business cards and never really talked, or you might learn that they pitched Alex at one point and have a ton of intel on how he runs meetings and what kind of questions he asks.

That's knowledge you'll never get from a search engine, but don't forget that the easily available information matters too.

If you know that a publisher is known for their free-to-play games, you will be able to tell pretty quickly how well your game fits that focus. That said, don't disqualify yourself immediately because you may not be aware of the publisher's future strategy. Instead of assuming your game is not a fit, ask a thoughtful question:

"I know that you typically publish free-to-play games and our project is laser-focused on being a great premium experience with ongoing DLC. Is publishing a premium title too far outside of your strategy or is there room for that kind of title to fit in your portfolio?"

Naturally, the answer to this question could be a flat rejection, but you might also learn this publisher recently brought in a new investor and now has the capital to expand their operation into different types of games. With that one question you can demonstrate that you did your homework, that you understand that monetization models are an important factor, and that you are being critical about who publishes your game.

If your game is clearly not a fit, that's okay too. Again, context matters. If you were clearly not a fit and came in through a cold e-mail, you might be wasting the publisher's time by insisting on a meeting (or having even pitched something so far outside of their specialty in the first place). If the publisher came to you at an event or booked you for a slot at an investment summit, you can still make the meeting productive.

Ask the publisher who they would recommend you speak to. Ask the publisher what they look for in their preferred style of game if they would mind you following up in the future if you work on that kind of project. Ask the publisher where they see opportunity in the space or what mistakes people often make pitching them.

All of that might only be in 5 minutes before they leave your booth or before the buzzer rings, but because you knew something about the publisher ahead of time, you positioned yourself to learn a lot and still leave a positive impression.

Preparing to Answer Questions

Publishers will always want to know more than what you share in a pitch. Part of this is truly exploratory in that the publisher wants to know more about your project and is genuinely curious. Part of this is also diagnostic. Publishers have seen several gaming projects come and go by the time they talk to you, so they know where to look for problem areas and have their own list of red flags they may try to identify before going deeper into talks with an indie developer.

The most common questions fall into these four categories:

- Budget: What and why?
- Timeline: What and why?
- Engine selection: What and why?
- Market fit: How and why?

If you followed our recommendations around planning, building a budget, and building a pitch deck, most of this work is already complete, but there are some nuances and wrinkles that can trip you up.

Budget and Timeline Questions

When a publisher probes you about your budget, they are trying to determine if they can afford to fund your game and how much they can trust you with their money. One side of that equation is learning if you put actual math into your budget or just guessed, and trust us, publishers can tell which is which. The other side of the equation is the publisher seeing opportunities where they can have an impact on your project if they decide to work with you.

For example, if your ask includes $100,000 to finish the art for your game, how did you arrive at the number? How much have you spent on art so far and how does that proportionally align with what has yet to be completed? If the publisher offered you less than your ask for the art budget, is that a deal-breaker or do you have options for making a smaller budget amount work? Conversely, what would you do with more art budget if you had it?

If a publisher thinks your estimate is high, you can provide additional context. Maybe you used this specific art style at a previous company and you learned that it works best with this extra polish, so you budgeted accordingly. The reality may also be that your publisher has access to an art team that fits the style of your game, and they know that they could give you the high-quality assets you need but for half the cost.

And the tricky part is that these layers of nuanced questions apply to virtually every part of your budget, from the engine you chose to your console porting to translation and localization. The expectation here is that you can justify your budget and potentially have a conversation about adjusting it. If you followed our advice in previous chapters, you should be well equipped for this challenge but may need to refresh yourself on your research and organize major points so that you can find them quickly.

Whatever part of your project the publisher is inquiring about–from budgets to timelines–you should be prepared for the following types of questions:

- How did you reach this conclusion?
- Can you show the math and justify your assumptions?
- Where are there opportunities to save money or accelerate timelines?
- If you had to cut something to reduce the scope of the project, what would it be? Would it be detrimental to the game?
- If you had more budget or more resources than you asked for, where would it go?
- What tools, services, or resources are you using to complete the project?
- What parts of your project are in-house and what parts do you need external resources for?
- What are you doing that isn't budgeted (such as your own personal expertise that you bring to the project)?
- What parts of your project are squarely in your wheelhouse and where are you inexperienced or uncomfortable?

You won't get all of these questions in every meeting, and they won't be phrased in these exact ways, but if you prepare for these kinds of angles, you will be in a much stronger position to fight for your project.

Engine Selection and Market Fit

As we discussed in Chapter 7, the engine you choose to use for your game can make your project more attractive to specific publishers and less attractive to others. Beyond using a reputable engine with an established industry reputation, choosing an engine based on a target publisher rather than on the basis of your team's strengths is probably unwise, but when you reach the point of talking to a publisher you should understand how your chosen engine might sway their interest.

In many ways, this can tie into market fit as well because an engine can sometimes be an indicator of how well you understand your target genre and the expectations players have for games in that category. For example, GameMaker is a fantastic engine, but it is definitely better for 2D experiences and the scripting language might limit your access to external resources.

Our goal here is not to get you to switch to a different engine for the sake of getting a publisher, but you should be prepared to answer questions around your engine while also demonstrating your big-picture view of where your game fits in the market.

If a publisher asks you, "Why did you choose GameMaker?" an answer that talks about your previous experience in the engine and your team's comfort with the tool is a solid response. At the same time, you can take that answer a step further and discuss why the engine is a great fit for your specific project. You might consider covering the following points:

- How the strengths of the engine align with your project.
- What you perceive as the engine's weaknesses and how you are accounting for them.
- How your engine choice positively impacts your budgets and timelines.
- How the engine aligns with your long-term vision (such as porting to consoles).

You could extend your answer to talk about how your platformer fits among other GameMaker greats such as *Spelunky* or *Katana Zero* to show that you are paying attention to what's happening in your space.

Things get a little trickier when you have a custom engine. Most likely you won't, but if you do, there will be many questions regarding its liability, porting ability, and so on.

Ultimately, all of this diligence is an effort to determine market fit, the careful alignment of game concept, development scope, developer ability, and publisher expertise. You'll end up having the market fit conversation directly anyway, so you might as well start to address it early and connect diligence questions like what engine you're using to how that ripples into impacting the viability of the game at launch and beyond.

When publishers lean into the market fit topic, however, prepare to answer questions like the following:

- What are the core gameplay loops?
- What existing titles do you feel are your biggest competitors?
- What were your major inspirations?
- What does your game do that's different for this genre?
- This looks like a ripoff of _____. Is that accurate?
- What are your sales projections and what are those numbers based on?
- How do you know players will be interested in this project?
- What's the game's story and how will it resonate with players?

The difficulty of market fit is that no one really knows what games will be mega hits, so publishers use a discovery call to uncover interesting hooks and opportunities within your game and within your team while also probing for landmines that they know could cripple a project.

The negotiation for your deal starts with the very first meeting, and how you answer questions will play a big role in how much potential a publisher sees in your game. This isn't easy. Your answers have to convey confidence and competence while also selling the publisher on the idea that players will turn out in droves to buy what you create.

That means that you need to balance being objective and realistic with convincing aspirations around what your game could be or could do. Prepare ahead of time, and then listen carefully in these discussions. A publisher could give you very big hints and unspoken feedback that shows you how to answer these questions more effectively in your next meeting.

Asking Your Own Questions

A discussion should never be a one-sided conversation. Yes, you are at the disadvantage because you are the one asking for money and also the one who may be less experienced, but no one is going to stick up for you but you. Finding the right deal for your game requires an understanding of how a potential publishing partner operates and how they approach their terms. Don't wait to read the agreement to figure out these factors. Get them out into the open early so that you know what pieces are on the board.

Your questions for a publisher should help you learn the following:

- How a publisher approaches porting – Is porting a standard part of their deals? What platforms do they prioritize? What timeline do they use for porting (and how does that fit into your timeline)? Is porting a speciality? How are porting costs addressed in the recoup? Can your studio port the game or do you have to use the publisher's porting studio?

- How a publisher approaches translation & localization – Is translation and localization a standard part of their deals? Which languages are typically included? How does the publisher handle that process? Are there specific regions that are a focus point for the publisher? How are these costs addressed in the recoup? Is the publisher willing to localize to a language that isn't typically included?

- What marketing support a publisher provides – What does a typical launch campaign look like? What are some examples of launch campaigns the publisher is particularly proud of? How does the publisher expect the developer to participate in marketing activities? Are there major areas of marketing the publisher does not address, and why is that? Where is the marketing money spent? How much say do I as the developer have in marketing decisions? Again, how are these costs calculated and how do they factor into the recoup?

- How recoup and revenue share works – What is the typical sweetspot budget for the projects the publisher signs? What terms are standard for the publisher? Does the publisher deviate from those terms, and if so, under what circumstances? On average, how long does it take their average project to recoup? Does the publisher do post-launch funding, and if so, under what circumstances?

- How milestones and payments work – How does the publisher typically structure payments? Is there flexibility in how milestones are defined? What happens if either party encounters delays (the publisher *or* the developer)?

- How your game might fit into their upcoming schedule – What games does the publisher have coming out soon that could impact your game? If a game ahead of yours is delayed, how does that impact your release date? Do certain games have a higher priority than others? If a game looks similar to yours, how will yours be marketed differently? What is the publisher's dedication to the game's long term success?

That's a lot of questions, and they likely won't come up in this exact order. During the discovery call, you should have opportunities to organically ask many of these questions during the natural flow of the conversation rather than rapid-firing through them in the last 10 minutes of the meeting. That said, make sure you get the information you need to assess the fit, and don't be shy about asking.

To take that even further, don't be afraid to admit when you need more clarification. Your first instinct might be to nod along to an answer as if you understand, but if you don't, ask the publisher to explain what they mean. The discomfort of admitting that you don't understand something is unpleasant in the moment, but it's far less painful than having to come back to it much later.

If you did your homework everywhere else, most publishers won't mind elaborating on a point of confusion. In addition to that professional courtesy, a publisher might simply handle a specific aspect of the process differently from other publishers. We've been doing this a long time, and we still encounter reputable publishers who have a unique twist on a deal or on a process that we haven't encountered before, and that can also come with unique lingo or a different take on terms.

If this happens to you, take control and say something to the effect of, "I'm sorry to interrupt but I don't want to lose the thread. I heard you say _____. Can you tell me more of what you mean by that and how that works?"

It's simple. It's polite. It's professional. Be brave and learn what you need to learn.

When the discovery call goes well and everyone has the chance to ask and answer questions, the next phase of your project is the publisher review process.

Publisher Review

The on-the-spot offer for an indie project is mostly a fairy tale. It can happen, but typically the person you talk to first about your project has several steps of diligence and vetting to work through before they can make you an offer. They have a team to answer to, and several decision-makers will likely need to weigh-in on the potential of your game before offering an LOI.

Unfortunately, much of this process will occur outside of any formal meeting with you, which is part of why we have emphasized preparation so heavily. The clarity of your answers turns into notes that your point of contact takes back to their team. In addition to those meeting notes, you will also likely hand over the following:

- Your pitch deck
- Your budget materials
- A prototype or demo (playable and/or video)
- A Game Design Document (GDD)

That last item, your GDD, is not typical for early meetings. However, if your first discovery call was incredibly in-depth and the publisher is keen on fast-tracking a deal, they may ask for your GDD right away. Tread carefully here as a GDD is a major piece of your project's competitive advantage, and you should only share it with a publisher who has verbally expressed a strong interest in your game.

If you aren't comfortable sharing your GDD at that stage, push back, saying, "How close to a deal does this feel for you? I'm more than happy to share a GDD, but I'd feel most comfortable if we had an LOI place. In the meantime, our pitch deck, budget, and demo are pretty thorough." Another option is to ask the publisher to sign an NDA, though you probably want to avoid putting that obstacle between you and your pitch.

How exactly you handle this will vary depending on how you read the situation. For most publishers, the first three items will provide plenty of material to assess whether the project should move into the LOI phase.

While this part of the negotiation process is mostly hands-off, happening outside of any formal meeting with you, you might still play an active role. When the discovery call ended, you should have confirmed next steps and gleaned an expectation for what a publisher's review timeline might look like. If they promise a week and it has been two with no word, send an e-mail to check in. Conversely, if they said four weeks and it has been two, be patient and respect their process.

In the meantime, be available for questions. The simple act of checking your e-mail and voic e-mail regularly can be a big factor. We have seen silly problems like a developer using a generic bulk account for their studio and not checking that e-mail regularly (or missing that a reply went to spam). If a publisher has follow-up questions and requests, you should be able to address those in a timely manner, so don't let a small technical misstep be the iceberg that sinks your pitch.

Depending on the publisher and the project, you may need to do different versions of the discovery call again for other members of the publishing team, or you may need to reconvene to address deeper questions or possibilities for your project, but when all of this goes well, you enter the next phase: an offer and the LOI.

Receiving an Offer or an LOI

By the time you reach the point of a publisher committing to an offer, a significant amount of the negotiation process should already be complete. There is more to negotiate, sure, but as you've asked your questions and as the publisher has asked theirs, both parties will have a pretty good sense of fit. If your ask was radically different from the publisher's target project budget, that would be known and, perhaps, addressed. The same is true of most major elements of the publishing agreement.

That said, while some offers are generally in the realm of your ask because you have had several conversations with the publisher already, a publisher may offer you more or less than your ask for perfectly valid reasons.

It's up to you to decide if an offer is fair or if you should continue negotiating.

If the Offer Matches the Ask

An offer rarely matches an ask exactly, but if a publisher commits to giving you close to the budget you requested under the terms that are important to you, you might be close to signing a deal. Before you do, though, you should pause and reassess. The excitement of getting a publishing deal, especially if it's your first, can blind you to opportunities as well as pitfalls.

Here's what you should do next:

- Review your project's fit with the publisher: Can you see yourself working with the publisher's team for a year or more? Can you see your game standing proudly in their portfolio? Do the publisher's strengths complement yours? Your offer could be great on paper, but if the wrong publishing team is behind it, the deal might not be that good after all.

- Consider the long-term potential of the relationship: Not only will you have to work directly with the publishing team for some time, you might also get to work with them again on a sequel or a new project; furthermore, the publisher should be just as committed to supporting the long-term success of the game as you are.

- Compare the offer to others. If you have other publishing offers available, how does this offer compare? What are you gaining and what are you losing? Is one publisher better suited for your project than another?

All of these factors orbit an offer but are not immediately apparent in the offer itself, which is why many indie developers end up signing with the wrong publisher. They see the dollar amount at the end of the agreement, and they trip over themselves to sign. As hard as it is to wait, step back and assess the big picture.

You might find that, while the offer is perfect, you've already found that your work style creates conflicts with the publisher's work style, or perhaps you see that the publisher is not experienced in promoting your type of game, or perhaps another offer on the table leans harder into an area that's important to you, such as merchandising or acting on media rights.

You might be thinking, "What if this is my only offer?" Well, that matters too, but it's not the dead end that it might feel like. Later in this chapter, we will look at how you can leverage one offer to get another. In the meantime, let's look at an additional potential scenario: Getting an offer that doesn't match your ask.

If the Offer Does Not Match Your Ask

When a publisher makes an offer that differs from your ask, all is not lost. In the previous section, we mentioned that seeing a big number at the end of an agreement can blind you to points you should consider, and that's true here as well. Just because a publisher does not offer you what you asked does not mean that the publisher is not the best fit for your game. Additionally, that gap between your ask and their offer gives you more room to negotiate and, therefore, improve the terms.

Before you choose your next move, make sure you understand what pieces are on the board. Consider doing the following:

- Ask the publisher how they arrived at their offer. If an offer is substantially different from your ask, the publisher likely has justifications for that. They may be using their resources to save costs on development, they may have done their own analysis and reached a different conclusion on total profit potential, or they may really want to work with you but simply don't have the full budget you're looking for. Whether or not you take the deal in the end, all of these points are great intel and are worth exploring.

- Look at the benefits the publisher provides. Just as a publisher might have resources that lower your overall budget needs, a shortfall in upfront capital could be compensated by perks elsewhere. For example, if your publisher commits to an aggressive calendar of promotional events and also intends to invest heavily in deploying a merchandising strategy tied to your game, those advantages might be worthwhile, depending on the specifics of the agreement.

- Look at the realities of your burn-rate relative to your profit potential. If an offer comes in under your ask, revisit your budget to see how much damage that does to your development. You may find the offer is not viable simply because you'll run out of money three months before the game is complete and won't be able to pay your team. That is potentially solvable, but you should do the math and know the numbers prior to responding to the publisher.

- Playout multiple scenarios. If an offer is low but still attractive, you might be able to adjust scope and timelines to make the budget work. That might mean cutting a feature or delaying content (like multiplayer support or a level editor) until after the game's release. Mapping out these options will give you valuable negotiation tools.

When you reconnect with the publisher to discuss how the terms might be adjusted, come prepared. By giving you an offer that differs from your ask, the publisher has already signalled that your full ask is likely off the table, so at this point you are working toward a compromise. Put another way, you are submitting a revised ask that is somewhere between your original ask and the publisher's first offer.

When you begin this conversation, you should already know the following:

- What that new ask is, how it differs from the offer, and your reasoning for requesting those adjustments.

- What aspects of your new ask are flexible and what aspects are non-negotiable.

- How flexible you're willing to be on each portion of your offer. You might be willing to negotiate a lower budget than your revised ask states, but how much lower? What revenue share are you willing to do? Where is the point of no return?

The exact nature of your new ask is going to be highly variable, so mapping out a template for you to follow at this stage is almost impossible. As we've discussed previously, you have several levers you can pull in an agreement. Using what we've covered so far, you should have an idea of what factors are critical for your project.

To review, when you come back with your revised ask you might request adjustments in the following areas:

- Terms for recoup and revenue share – If the offer is low, you might be in a position to ask for a higher revenue share to compensate.

- Sequel, merchandise, and media rights – If the publisher's offer has terms relating to these, you might ask for revisions that give you more control or allow you to retain complete ownership.

- Marketing activations – You could ask for increased marketing support or for more favorable terms around how these costs are tied to recoup.

- Development timelines – Depending on the offer, you might benefit from extending or reducing the timeline, perhaps releasing your game earlier so that you can start generating revenue as a means of making up for budget you didn't get in the ask.

- Porting, translation, and localization – You might request more support on these fronts or you might request to take these responsibilities back from the publisher: It may be that you have a more efficient pipeline for porting and can do it for less money than what the publisher has budgeted.

- Post-launch advances – If you delay content or have plans for DLC, asking the publisher to commit to a post-launch advance (perhaps unlocked by sales performance) can be an option.

Again, not all of these factors will apply to every negotiation, and our examples may not fit your project exactly, so think creatively about how you might structure a counter that is more appealing for you while not alienating the publisher.

How to Counter

Most publishers are savvy business people. They expect a developer to counter their offer with new terms if it doesn't match exactly what the developer wanted from the start. As scary as it can feel for you as an indie developer, this is not new territory for publishers. Asking to negotiate terms is not disrespectful or offensive. It's good business, and when it's done well, it can actually increase a publisher's confidence in you. Just as asking good questions and being able to have a productive conversation about your project in the discovery phase demonstrates your competence, so does a good negotiation.

This isn't some weird artificial test of your character, but remember there is no actual deal on the table yet. You may have an LOI in place, but there certainly isn't a signed agreement. Either party can still walk away.

To keep the publisher from walking away, your counter needs to be reasonable and presented in a manner that's collaborative, not adversarial.

Here are some tips:

- Avoid negotiating via e-mail: It may feel safer, but nuance and tone are too easily lost or misinterpreted in this medium: Schedule a call instead.

- Follow the sales and meetings tips we discussed earlier. Have an agenda, key points, and desired outcomes mapped out before the meeting begins.

- Lean on rapport: By now, you should have some rapport built with your points of contact at a publisher: Continue building that by being kind, gracious, and reasonable.

- Ask questions instead of making demands: In the spirit of being collaborative, avoid phrases like "I want this" and instead ask questions like "what if we did this?".

- Clearly and confidently explain your needs and how receiving less than your desired amount will result in a lower quality product.

The conclusion to your negotiation could very well be either party walking away, and that's okay. As you navigate your way to that conclusion, however, you should behave in such a way that you can feel perfectly comfortable picking up the phone to pitch this publisher on your next game because everyone parted on good terms.

As you present your counter, keep your audience in mind. If you have several points to discuss, outlining your offer in bullet form might be helpful, but if you have one or two big areas to address and everything else is fine, a simple conversation could suffice. You don't have to follow this script exactly, but this framework might help:

- Identify the point you'd like to address.
- Share your reasoning for the adjustment.
- Clearly present your revised ask.
- Be prepared to follow-up with additional questions.

In practice, that might look like:

> We'd like to talk about the development budget and the milestone structure. Our current timeline and budgets put us at needing more funding than you've allocated. Can we explore a post-launch advance and delay online co-op development until after the release? We picture those milestones and budgets looking like this under that approach.

You may need to follow this up with questions if the publisher flatly says that what you've proposed is not possible. Those questions might include:

- "Understood. Is this approach completely off the table or is there a way to revise it to make it viable for you?"
- "If we can't make up for the budget shortfall here, can we make up for it here instead?"
- "How do you suggest we adjust the scope or the agreement terms to compensate for the budget shortfall?"
- "What other options do we have for compromising on this point?"

As you can see, a "no" does not have to mean failure. If you poke at the problem from a few different angles, you might uncover a path that addresses your concerns. At the same time, using questions helps to make the process collaborative and also gives you access to the publisher's perspective as well as their industry expertise. You might find that the publisher has a better idea for a compromise than you do, but you'll never discover it if you aren't asking questions.

If you find the publisher unwilling to make concessions on key terms that matter to you, be honest and clear about how that impacts your appetite for the deal. You don't have to make threats about leaving the negotiating table, but if something is actually a dealbreaker, say so. If it's simply important, also say so, and share why, but don't get stuck.

Make your position clear and move on to the next variable you'd like to negotiate. What you accomplish in other areas of the deal might make the sting of that one variable easier to absorb. By the end of the meeting, you should have a pretty good idea of whether this is a deal you'd commit to or not, at which point you either walk away or start moving toward a signed contract.

Shopping Offers and Walking Away

A business negotiation is rarely a two-party affair. An offer from one publisher is a big bargaining chip to use in negotiations with another publisher. An offer could be the leverage you need to move a slow publisher to take action or to push for more favorable terms. At the same time, this process can make it even more clear when you should walk away from an offer completely because you have offers to compare.

Shopping an offer is a delicate process that can easily backfire, however. In our publishing work, we have made offers to indie developers we were excited to support, which makes getting an e-mail that says "This publisher offered me this. Can you beat it?" all the more disappointing, and at times, frustrating. Publishers expect an active indie to pitch several parties at once, so hearing that another offer is on the table is not necessarily the problem. In fact, sometimes it can be beneficial to be transparent with a publisher because honesty is key in this industry. How that conversation is presented is where the relationship can start to deteriorate.

If you've followed our advice this far into the process, you will have developed some level of rapport with the publisher, and they with you. That means a mutual respect and, perhaps, even the beginning of a professional friendship. With that lens in mind, think about how you'd like a potential business partner to approach you about an offer they've received from a competitor.

Approaching a Publisher Who Has Not Made an Offer

When approaching a publisher who hasn't yet given you an offer, that shopping process might begin with an e-mail like this:

Hi Alex,

I know we're still in the discovery process with our talks, but I feel I owe you the courtesy of letting you know that another publisher has made us an offer.

We aren't sure if it's the right fit for us, and part of that hesitation comes from how excited our team was by the prospect of working with you because of X and Y. Can we schedule a meeting to discuss? At the very least, I'd love to hear your perspective.

I'm flexible Wednesday afternoon if you are.

–Marshal

I'm sure you can already see how this approach lands differently than skipping over the humanity of the people involved to talk solely about getting your project more money. The e-mail is kind and respectful yet candid and direct. If this publisher was interested in your project but simply moving slowly, knowing that an offer is on the table might be the spark that accelerates the process.

Approaching a Publisher Who Has Made You an Offer

Shopping an offer to a publisher who has already made you an offer is a different beast. In this context, your goal is to use your new offer to motivate the publisher to give you better terms on their existing offer.

That difference matters because it brings back into focus all of the negotiation advice we shared with you earlier because in addition to your existing justifications for requesting better terms, you now have another offer that proves your project is competitive and may also be able to point to terms that are more in line with what you're requesting.

The sticky situation here is that you may have to reopen old wounds to get the terms you want. That's not comfortable for anyone, so you need to do it tactfully. That means reopening the negotiation in good faith, which is to say that you are sincerely pursuing a compromise out of a genuine interest in working with the publisher, not just trying to squeeze out more money or a higher revenue share.

If you're coming back to a publisher to share a competitor's offer, you should be able to clearly communicate what would make you pass on the competitor to take the offer this publisher has given you. Keep it succinct. Keep it simple. And stick to your word. Again, this isn't simply to get a bidding war. Only approach a publisher with a competitor's offer when you absolutely want to work with them. Playing one publisher against another in bad faith will ultimately hinder future relationships.

So, a meeting might sound like this:

We received an offer from another publisher. The offer is appealing, and they seem like a great team to work with, but we think your team is the ideal fit for our game because of X and Y. If we can adjust the funds and revenue share to match the scope or vice versa, it's an easy yes for us to turn that offer down and sign with you.

And if you say something like that, mean it and follow through. Don't ping pong offers back and forth between publishers. That's a great way to lose both offers.

Walking Away

Some offers are just wrong for your project. As we've talked through how to negotiate – knowing where you have flexibility and knowing where you have to stick to your guns – we have also armed you with a process for determining when a deal is simply not a fit. That might be obvious in the first offer because of how radically different the offer is from your ask, or that might come out later in negotiations if the publisher is unwilling to compromise on key terms.

Once you can clearly see that a deal is not right for you, the best thing you can do for your long-term career in the industry is to walk away respectfully in a timely manner. Some terms won't change no matter how much you argue (such as the size of the development funding the publisher offers), and fighting for that impossible change wastes time and can damage your reputation.

When you see that the negotiations are dead, call it. Thank the publisher for their interest, respectfully let them know why you're walking away, and ask them if you can share future projects with them that might be a better fit. That might sound like this:

> *"It looks like this project isn't a great fit for you. I understand that you cap advances at $50,000, and I fully respect why you do that. For us, we simply can't afford to go less than $100,000. You've been very kind through these talks, and we're still fans of what you do. Even though this game isn't right for you, we'd love to circle back to you in the future with a new project that might be a better fit."*

Don't burn the bridge. Don't waste more of the publisher's time. Exit gracefully and, in doing so, keep the door cracked for you to revisit the relationship in the future. We have seen indie developers pitch the same publishers on three different games over the course of several years before inking a deal, and that's because fit and rapport matter. Just because you decided to walk away today doesn't mean that the same publisher isn't perfect five years from now.

Letter of Intent

An LOI is a big step toward finalizing a publishing deal, but many indie developers misunderstand the purpose of an LOI, how it works, and what it can mean for your deal.

An LOI is a legally binding document that prevents you from pitching your project to other publishers while the publisher who offered the LOI completes their diligence and pre-deal process. The exclusivity period essentially takes your project off the market for a limited time, allowing the publisher to fully vet the project, to finalize availability of funds and work with you to come to a contract.

When you're the indie in this equation, an LOI is a great sign that you've almost reached a signed agreement, but it can also feel a bit anticlimactic. Since an LOI is not a final contract, the publisher could reach the end of the exclusivity window without making an offer or formally passing an offer. With your game on the line, that can feel a bit unfair, as each day the LOI is active as another day you can't pitch to other publishers.

For the publisher, the LOI is a way to start activating significant resources and conversations with big stakeholders without getting the project ripped away from them. Credible publishers use this exclusivity period to fully vet your company (reviewing financials in some cases, doing background research), to talk to legal counsel about potential friction points in the deal or related to your game, to talk to their investors, and to finalize terms with you. Writing a big check and signing a big contract comes with checks and balances.

Before you sign an LOI, you should do the following:

- Review your publisher discussions to see if other publishers are close to making an offer
- Make sure this publisher is the correct fit and that you can come to terms during contract negotiations
- Assess the exclusivity period and request changes if necessary
- Ask your attorney to review the LOI if the terms are unclear or if the LOI comes with commitments beyond an exclusivity period

Engaging a video game attorney is a big topic in its own right, so we talk about that in the next section. Prior to talking to your attorney, you should have a good sense of whether the exclusivity period is fair. Speaking broadly, a fair exclusivity period is typically between 7 and 30 days. Long exclusivity periods can cripple your ability to find the right publisher as they could take you off the market at critical moments in your development cycle or at critical moments of the year, as well as delay the start to development.

For example, a 90-day exclusivity period covers a ton of development time, and that's time you can't recover if another publisher in your pipeline requests a pivot. 90 days ago, that might have been possible, but now, that's a significant amount of budget to lose. Additionally, the end of an exclusivity period could create timing challenges. If you are targeting a Q1 release, you likely need a publisher to sign your game in Q1 or Q2 of the previous year. An exclusivity period can easily push you too deep into a year without a deal, and when you emerge to pitch again, you might find that publishers have set their calendars and are booking for the following year instead.

Like all of the variables in a publishing deal we have discussed, these situations are highly fluid and unique to each developer. When you get an LOI offer, be wary of long exclusivity periods, be critical of where you will be if you reach the end of an exclusivity period without an offer, and use the quality of your previous meetings with the publisher to assess whether those risks are worth the reward of the deal.

A big word of caution here: Honor the terms of your LOI. We have been in the unfortunate position of receiving pitches from indie developers who already committed to an LOI. Publishers will see this as a sign that you don't honor your agreements, and if you're willing to negotiate behind one publisher's back, they'll believe that you'll probably do it to them as well. That's a great way to destroy your industry reputation very quickly.

With any legal document or agreement, we always recommend talking to an expert in the field before signing. LOIs are usually brief documents, but legal language can be dense and you might not fully understand the commitment you're making.

Working With an Attorney

Always talk to an attorney before signing an agreement. Always.

Legal guidance is not cheap, and that can be painful for an indie development team who is already scraping by with a meager budget and a mountain of sweat equity. If you are going to cut costs, though, legal advice is not where to do it. One signature marries you to a publisher, and if you overlook or misunderstand a key part of the agreement, you might commit to terms that undercut your goals.

If you spend a long enough time in the games industry, you will hear a few horror stories about developers who didn't realize that they signed away sequel rights or committed to recoup terms that permanently kept profits out of their pockets. Reputable publishers aren't actively trying to deceive developers, but even a legal misunderstanding could put you in a bad position.

We can't give you the knowledge to be a video game attorney in a book like this, but we can help you find the right fit for your project.

Here's what to look for in a video game attorney:

- Proven industry experience
- Fair and clear rates
- Responsive and available
- Relevant regional credentials

You don't need the biggest and most expensive firm to represent your indie project, but if you meet these criteria, your project and future will be much safer than if you had gone it alone.

Proven Industry Experience

Video game publishing represents a unique intersection of several business considerations that attorneys outside of games may struggle to properly manage. The ideal option is to work with an attorney who regularly has game clients of all sizes and interests so that you benefit from a well-rounded perspective backed by plenty of in-the-trenches experiences.

Most attorneys in this space have active web presences. You can see notable clients on their websites, and you can read the articles they have published on gaming topics. Many of our favorite attorneys are regulars at gaming conventions and often volunteer to be on panels related to indie game law.

Not every attorney will have an active blog and a backlog of convention appearances, but you should do some digging to see if the attorney you're considering does.

Lastly, ask your network. They will likely know an attorney or two that can help out.

Fair and Clear Rates

An established attorney can charge upward of $200 or more per hour for their services. That's a big number for most indie developers, but it's also fair. Good attorneys command rates that clients are willing to pay, and higher rates can be a good sign in many cases.

But it's a bad sign for your budget.

A respectable games attorney will understand the plight of an indie developer and will be aware of your budget challenges. For this reason, we often see attorneys offering package deals and flat rates for standard developer needs, like setting up an LLC and creating work-for-hire agreements for contractors.

When you are negotiating a deal with a publisher, ask your attorney if they can review the agreement for a flat fee that includes at least one revision. Many attorneys will work with you on this front, and while it may not lower their hourly rate, it will at least cap costs and allow you to budget more effectively.

Responsive and Available

Attorneys are unlikely to share their calendar with you, but before committing to your pick of legal representation you should ask them to clarify what their availability is like and what response time to anticipate – questions posed professionally and with courtesy, of course.

If your attorney is deep in an IP dispute case and won't be able to review a publisher agreement for another two weeks, that could hinder your ability to negotiate effectively with a publisher and threaten the deal. You can't reasonably demand a 24-hour turnaround for a full agreement review, but you can get a sense for how often an attorney will reply to e-mail and how much time they will need to effectively represent you.

That clarity will make it easier for you to plan, and your potential publisher will appreciate that you told them ahead of time that your lawyer will need a week to review the agreement. That upfront communication builds your credibility and creates clear and comfortable expectations for everyone involved.

Relevant Regional Credentials

Where your attorney practices can matter. If your agreement commits you to Canadian laws because of your publisher's location but you are in the U.S., you should work with an attorney who is qualified to advise you. As the games industry continues to grow, many publishers are taking a borderless view for what developers they engage. They don't care where you're from; they just want to publish great games.

When it comes to the agreement, though, you should work with an attorney who is familiar with the laws you're agreeing to. That might mean finding an attorney local to that country or relying on your attorney's network of contacts to get the advice you need.

Finding an attorney is a big first step, but an attorney is ultimately another type of resource. You have to use that resource effectively to get the most for your game.

Managing the Client–Attorney Relationship

Your attorney's job is to safeguard your interests, but you still need to take an active role in their work. Even the best attorneys will not immediately understand the nuances of your exact needs, so you should stay engaged with the process of reviewing and vetting your agreement.

When you ask your attorney to review your agreement, you should also provide the following:

- A list of the terms your publisher verbally agreed to: Your attorney can use this as a guide to make sure everything is accounted for and matches your expectations.

- Your key points of concern: Emphasize major negotiation points that are important to you that you want to make sure are effectively addressed.

- Your own questions about the agreement: Read the document first and highlight areas that seem problematic or unclear to you.

- Request additional feedback: Most attorneys will flag points of interest without your asking, but it is still worthwhile to directly ask your attorney for their perspective on the terms so that you can benefit from their broader experience of having read dozens of agreements like yours.

From here, your attorney will mark-up the document and make recommendations for changes and for additions. Ask for clarity on points you don't understand, and professionally pushback on changes where you might not agree. Your attorney will have a justification for their reasoning, and you should weigh that alongside your judgment and talk it through more deeply if necessary.

At a certain point, however, you will have to trust the recommendations of your attorney, but you should always reach a point where you clearly understand the commitment you are making with the publisher.

Taking Changes to the Publisher

Do not be intimidated by the process of sharing your attorney's notes with the publisher. Lawyers are a completely normal part of the process, and no publisher will be surprised that you asked for an expert to review the offer before you signed. If you continue to be professional, courteous, and collaborative, the process of finalizing the agreement will often resolve itself over a few e-mail exchanges.

In the event that your attorney flags a major issue, proceed carefully. If the problem area is a contradiction of what you verbally discussed, share your memory and notes of the terms and offer a meeting if that point needs to be revisited in greater depth. It's unlikely that the publisher was deliberately trying to deceive you, but in these circumstances an e-mail exchange can start to feel accusatory. If it's a big item, a friendly meeting may be the better path to a resolution.

If there's an egregious issue, having your attorney present for that meeting may be the fastest path to a resolution. But remember, this could be expensive.

If the final points are a matter of a nuance but your major terms seem accounted for, a next best step for finalizing the agreement is for a call to see what the issues are and what correcting them look like. We have seen deals delayed by needing to change a single word.

For how significant an agreement is, our relaxed tone here might surprise you, but that's by design. Throughout this chapter, we have encouraged you to negotiate from your very first encounter with a publisher, which means that the hardest work for your deal should be done well before the agreement lands in your inbox. All of that effort of asking the right questions, picking the right publisher, and discussing potential terms will make this stage much easier to navigate.

Advocating for Yourself

While an effective relationship with an attorney requires trust–you have to let them do their job–you should not lose sight of the fact that no one has more at stake in this deal than you and your team. The publisher is taking a big risk with your project, but they are also betting on half a dozen other developers this year, and your attorney will have other clients to service when they finish working on your agreement.

You have your game, and that game could represent years of work and a big gamble for your future. If something doesn't feel right or a term in the agreement does not match your vision, push your attorney to remedy the issue or use them as a scapegoat to get the outcome that you think is fair for you and the publisher. Again, it's not about winning. It's about what is fair to everyone. If you go into a negotiation with a "I need to win mentality," the partnership is not going to work.

Giving you exact advice here is difficult because of how many variables are involved, but we feel it's important to encourage you to advocate for yourself. If your attorney continues to disagree with your position, take that opinion seriously. Your inexperience may be biasing you, but you could also talk to your network of peers to see how they would navigate your concern. You could find an alternate solution to your problem, or you might learn that you are overthinking something.

That's a delicate dance, but we hope that calling attention to it here helps you to be more thoughtful before committing to any particular decision.

Juggling Business Development with Game Development

Negotiating terms with a publisher will always be a challenge, but now you have an arsenal of tools and recommendations to help you along the way. As we've said before, negotiation is a skill. It will take practice to hone, so treat every meeting you take as an opportunity to learn more about the industry and to refine your craft. Whether you are a brand-new indie developer or an experienced veteran, negotiation will always be important, and you can always improve at them.

With a signed agreement in hand, you have reached a major milestone in your indie developer journey, but there is still much work to do. You have to finish your game while also positioning yourself for a successful launch, and you may have to do that while simultaneously pursuing a publishing deal.

PART 4

The Road to Release

DOI: 10.1201/9781003215264-14

SIDE QUEST

Hopoo Games and *Risk of Rain 2*

How Giving Away 50% of Launch Sales Created Bigger Profits

48 hours. That's all Hopoo Games needed.

They hopped into the indie dev scene in 2013 with their first game, *Risk of Rain*. It was a small indie title with 2D pixel art and rogue-like mechanics. Though not a runaway hit, it had its fan base and sold enough copies for the developer to continue developing games. After 6 years, *Risk of Rain 2* came to PC and later consoles to massive success. They went from making 2D titles to making a full-fledged 3D game with no prior experience to launching a game that would sell more than 4 million copies on Steam alone.

Duncan "Hopoo" Drummond and Paul "PaulTheGoat" Morse are self-taught developers. They started working on the first *Risk of Rain* back in college, in 2012. The title was ready in a year while both were attending school.

Risk of Rain was published by renowned studio and publisher, *Chucklefish*. Afterward, Hopoo Games self-published *Deadbolt*, a mix of stealth and action highly acclaimed by critics and players alike. With two games in their library, they sought to reach new heights with a 3D sequel to *Risk of Rain*. As they shifted gears, the three-person team found an ally in Gearbox Games.

In May 2017, after six months of development, Hopoo Games shared their first update on the sequel. In the blog post, they said "We think that 3D allows for much deeper design spaces and more possibilities for cool gameplay. Feelings of scale and atmosphere are also much stronger." They shared screenshots and gameplay clips, and fans were excited.

But *Risk of Rain 2* faced a few significant challenges. As an unorthodox sequel, it risked being overlooked by players who may assume they could not enjoy the second without first playing a sequel, and some of its greatest gameplay touches, such as online co-op support, meant that players needed friends who had the game to fully experience *Risk of Rain 2*.

If players were going to be hesitant and skeptical of the game, that did not bode well for the likelihood of players trying online co-op as they would likely not have a Steam friend who also had the game.

Two years later, on March 27, 2019, *Risk of Rain 2* released into Steam Early Access. They, alongside Gearbox Studios, made an interesting decision. For its first 48 hours, if you bought *Risk of Rain 2*, you received a second copy for free.

The decision could not have been easy for both Gearbox and Hopoo Games. As the promotion meant losing 50% of launch-driven sales, a potentially big financial blunder if the game underperformed in sales.

The gamble paid off. The 48-hour window used that pressure of missing an exclusive and great deal on a game with a clever incentive for two friends to connect for co-op. Armed with a free copy, early supporters for *Risk of Rain 2* could become ambassadors for the game by getting to be the cool friend that gives their buddy a game, just because.

Risk of Rain 2 crossed 1 million copies sold within its first month. The gamble on using free keys to grow sales paid off because it was woven into a smart marketing plan.

https://www.gamasutra.com/view/news/348375/How_moving_from_2D_to_3D_shaped_the_design_of_Risk_of_Rain_2.php

https://gamasutra.com/view/news/342011/Risk_of_Rain_2_crosses_1_million_sales_in_first_month.php

https://gamasutra.com/view/news/339667/Risk_of_Rain_2_is_running_a_buyonegetone_free_launch_promo.php

https://www.pcgamer.com/we-finally-get-our-first-look-at-risk-of-rain-2/

https://www.pcgamer.com/uk/risk-of-rain-2-devs-talk-hitting-500000-players-mod-support-and-whats-coming-next/

https://community.stadia.com/t5/Stadia-Community-Blog/Interview-with-Hopoo-Games-on-Risk-of-Rain-2-Arriving-Sept-29-on/ba-p/30595

https://www.pcinvasion.com/risk-of-rain-2-interview-paul-morse/

https://hopoogames.com/meet-our-team/

https://web.archive.org/web/20180118042945/http://hopooo.tumblr.com/post/160452455554/devblog-1-our-next-project-weve-been-working

https://store.steampowered.com/app/632360/Risk_of_Rain_2/

CHAPTER

ELEVEN

Quality Assurance

The creative process and the business process for the indie games industry are intertwined. While they can be addressed separately, we have spent the entirety of this book exploring how, in the right hands, business and creativity are directly connected. From the engine you choose to how you manage your team, a smart business decision can unlock new creative opportunities, and the opposite is also true.

Your path to release will vary, and you will likely have to navigate difficult development decisions while also navigating the business of your game. You may need to account for an unexpected expense, or you may need to negotiate with a publisher while simultaneously reviewing new level designs and editing character dialogue. That's the life of an indie, and that juggling act can be hard sometimes.

Moving forward on multiple fronts can be difficult to manage, but delaying key tasks can do a great deal of harm to your game's viability.

For example, planning for the release of your game can feel like a post-agreement activity. While you would release your game after making a publishing deal, which sounds obvious, many of the strategic choices you need to make may happen before or during the process of securing a relationship with a publisher.

If you pause development for the six months that it might take to pitch and negotiate, you would lose valuable momentum and may miss your ideal launch window. Though you may not have the full runway of funding you need to actually finish the full vision of your game, you should be following every best practice you can as though you were approaching release. That mindset will prevent serious (and potentially expensive) problems down the road, and your commitment to preparing for launch will better position you to adapt to a publisher's timeline. Additionally, it may open your eyes to the fact that you may not need a publisher because of what you've accomplished on your own.

Whether you have landed the deal or not, everything we cover in Part 4 matters, and you should incorporate the release mentality into your planning as soon as possible.

In this section, we discuss:

- Quality assurance – Commonly referred to as "QA" for short, this is the process of eliminating bugs and improving overall user experience through testing and feedback gathering.

- Translation and localization – As discussed in Chapter 7, this is the process of making your game available in other languages and adapting to other regions and cultures.

- Porting – This is the process of making your game available on other platforms, such as making the necessary changes for your PC title to run on the Nintendo Switch.

- Press Engagement – Talking with games journalists and content creators to garner media coverage for your game.

- Events – Promoting your game at conventions and expos to build player interest and to develop business relationships.

- Marketing – The major points to promote your game as well as common pitfalls to avoid.

For this section, we will cover these topics broadly with the intention of giving you the key best practices to apply almost immediately to your work. At the same time, though, we want to give you a strong enough introduction that you can delve into any of these topics more deeply in the future, whether that's picking up other books that focus on these subjects for their entirety, taking courses, or hiring an expert.

We begin with QA because practically speaking, your vigilance for eliminating bugs and improving user experience should start early, but philosophically, assuring quality for your release is a good frame of reference. Just as you should not wait until launch day to look for and address problems in your code, you should not wait for launch to prepare your game for launch.

Though we are covering this section later in the book, everything here should be a routine part of your process, a cyclical part of your development sprints that comes up again and again. Saving them for the end is often the most costly way to approach it, and by costly, we mean both in terms of literal budget and also in the impact it may have on your returns.

A poorly developed file save system could bloat the size of your game, a minor problem for PC users but a potential certification-breaker if you are porting to a console such as the Nintendo Switch. Now, to pass console certification for Nintendo, you have to fix the file save system, but if you don't get that fix in quick, your resubmission will delay your Switch release. That wouldn't be so bad, but you negotiated an exclusive promotional release window in the Nintendo eShop, but it was contingent on meeting a release date.

If your game gets delayed, you lose that promotional window. Sensing the importance, you rush to fix the save system, but when you troubleshoot the potential source of the issue, you discover that unraveling the problem would mean reworking several major systems.

You simply do not have enough development hours to make the fix, do it right, and pass console certification. You do what it takes to get the save system corrected, and you miss the promotional release window.

We have seen a version of this story play out with dozens of developers.

Rushed in the final hours of your launch efforts, a preventable issue like this hypothetical save system may mean paying overtime to your developers (a raw cost) and missing key moments with partners, such as exclusive marketing placement (a wasted opportunity). If you had noticed the problem sooner, you may have been able to fix it with a regular development schedule and not miss that critical deadline.

The Business Implications of QA

Continuing our save system example, if your team had identified that issue based on a piece of tester feedback months ahead of the Nintendo Switch release, you could have built a plan for addressing it. You may still have needed the same amount of overall development time, but if you were aware of the issue prior to entering certification, you could negotiate an exclusivity period that you could actually hit.

Part of the advantage of an effective QA process is giving you and your team that clarity. You might not always be able to solve a problem more quickly, but the earlier you are aware of the problem, the better equipped you are to navigate around it.

Furthermore, the business impact of an effective QA process ripples through the entirety of your development, launch, and post-launch process. We use the exclusive promotional window with the Nintendo eShop as our hypothetical because that value is likely obvious. That's a big loss for a game launch, but you should also keep in mind that small wins and small losses matter as well.

No game will ever truly be bug-free. That's a given. But the rewards of a strong QA process can be as follows:

- A more predictable and manageable development process overall as you proactively pursue and address problems.
- Early player experiences are of a higher quality, making them more likely to talk about your game to their friends and give positive user reviews.
- Preview showcases and first-look moments with press will be more productive as the lower bug count means more attention on what makes your game special.
- A clear QA process is comforting to potential partners, including publishers, because it demonstrates your professionalism as well as your reliability.
- Your player community will be more loyal because they see that you listen to their input and are devoted to improving the game.

- Launch-day reviews are more likely to focus on gameplay rather than bugs, a significant marketing advantage when a single game-breaking bug can taint your first 100 Steam reviews.

- Post-launch development time will still include bug fixes, but with major problems already eliminated you can focus your team on improving the product instead of putting out fires.

Publishers and players understand that early builds will not be perfect. When we load the demo attached to your pitch deck, we are not surprised to discover a bug or a broken feature. That's normal, and it happens, but we have also opened demos that look as though no one actually confirmed they were functional. Button inputs don't work. Scenes don't load. Loading times hang.

When those problems are big and so obvious, we start to question the reliability of the team behind the demo. In the worst cases, we pass on the project without ever getting to play the game simply because no version we receive from the developer works.

We have also seen indies coordinate a big piece of preview coverage with a major Twitch creator and the stream had to cut early because a boss battle failed to load, making it impossible for the streamer to continue. All of that effort to coordinate a stream, pay for the placement, and to promote the preview only for viewers to see 10 minutes of a broken game.

For all of these reasons and more, QA should not be thought of as solely a background technical process. QA directly impacts the revenue potential of your game, either bolstering or undermining all of the efforts you have made to ensure your success.

Managing QA for Indie Games

AAA studios have entire departments devoted to QA and often lean on outside QA firms as well. Yet, some of the world's most anticipated games have launched with infamous amounts of bugs. If the biggest, most highly funded projects can't win the war against bugs, what hope does an indie developer have?

The challenge is a big one, sure, but your advantage as an indie is that the scope of your project is likely more refined and your development team (whether that's you as a solo developer or a small team of individuals) are far closer to a project than many AAA developers. For you, the same person who watches a player experience the demo at a convention can be the person who is also responsible for implementing changes. Where an AAA level designer may focus exclusively on creating one level and one level only, your level designer probably worked on most, if not all, of the levels in your game.

You and your team are closer to every aspect of the project. Seeing the bigger picture can be easier for indies, and the feedback you use to improve your game likely comes directly to you and your team rather than through a layered management system of memos and task assignments.

If you have not managed a QA process before, here's how you can capitalize on your unique position as an indie:

- Be diligent about documentation: An independent developer may not feel the need to annotate their code or to make formal reference material for how their game is built, but some well-placed effort to identify major functions of your backend – especially if they are highly customized – can make it easier to track down problems and to add new team members later.

- Maintain change logs: Though you might never share these notes publicly in the way that large studios may formally share patch notes, keeping a list of updates and fixes can help you to retrace your steps if a fix in one place creates an unexpected problem in another.

- Use version control and backups: Tools like GitHub simplify the process of tracking multiple versions of your project and give you restore points if you ever need to "roll back" an update: Setting up separate cloud and physical backups of these files is also recommended.

- Track and prioritize bugs as you find them: Addressing every bug and edgecase as they happen is likely impractical, but if you keep a running list of those issues, you can triage what you address and when you address it based on severity: This approach enables you to have the full view of where problems are and will help you delegate resources for addressing those problems.

- Regularly gather feedback from testers: Even if the feedback process is informal and related to incomplete builds, cycling testers through your build can reveal blindspots and help you to identify problems as well as opportunities.

- Talk directly with players and content creators to gather feedback. Instead of relying on simple bug reports and written surveys, you can use a platform like Discord to actively engage with your target players to improve your game.

- Test the whole game: The danger of handing a player a fresh build is that most players will experience the first 10 to 15 minutes and not play the full game, which leads to having a huge amount of feedback for the first few levels and a dangerously low amount of testing on late-game content: Make sure testers play all of your content or break testers into groups to ensure coverage of all of your content.

- Use beta branches and beta keys: If you are working through Steam, take advantage of their beta testing tools so that you have more control over who plays what content: You can tie keys to certain "branches" of your build, and you can disable access when a testing period has concluded.

All of these recommendations are meant to help you address challengers earlier and position you to capitalize on the agility and community-driven aspects of the indie games industry. A major studio head will likely not watch a player struggle with a level at a convention demo station, fix the problem in their hotel room that night, and have a fresh build ready the next morning. But an indie can. You lose that advantage, however, when your process is scattershot and inconsistent.

To avoid the pitfalls of poor QA and to seize the rewards of good QA, you should aim to standardize and regiment your process. You may have noticed that many of the recommendations we made were organizational, focusing on recordkeeping and notetaking. That is intentional because disorganization is the most common root cause of QA woes for indies. In the flurry of building a game and juggling all of the responsibilities that come with it, forgetting that one menu glitch in the level 3 crafting challenge is easy to do. Then you remember it when a reviewer blasts your crafting mechanics in their frustrated Steam write-up.

Our suggestion if you're new to QA: Build it into your development schedule from the start, giving testing the same priority as your other development tasks. When you hit a milestone in development, build a QA stage into that plan so your team has budgeted time for it and so that no one forgets that step of the cycle.

Managing this stage of development – as well as development as a whole–is a deep topic, and there are whole consulting firms devoted to optimizing these kinds of processes. If you do not have formal development experience or are new to managing a team of developers, reading up on development methodologies and project management workflows might be worthwhile. Learning something such as a Scrum process, a framework from the popular agile development methodology, is not as sexy as designing a new video game villain, but that knowledge can save you thousands of dollars in budget and weeks of frustration by virtue of making your development process better.

For that process to be useful, though, you need testers, and that can also be a problem for a cash-strapped indie with limited industry connections.

Sourcing Game Testers

When we act as publishers, providing an additional QA pipeline is one of our value-adds. We recognize that indies often struggle with this aspect of their projects, so we bring in a producer-led team to regularly test builds, identify problems, and provide feedback. We get the extra assurance that the game we release will be of high quality, and the developer gets more hands on deck to help with the tedious process of playing and replaying content.

Whether or not a publisher is providing those additional resources for you, taking ownership of your product and facilitating your own QA is ideal. No publisher wants a game to do poorly, but if one title in their portfolio underperforms, they have several other titles that can make up the difference.

If you release a game that underperforms, however, you might not have the resources to make another, so this piece of the process is much more dire for the indie than it is for the publisher.

You need regular access to testers. No way around it. These are your options:

- Indie development communities – Indie developers of all kinds congregate in a variety of groups online, from Facebook to Reddit to Discord: A community like Reddit's r/playmygame is built specifically for the purpose of connecting developers to testers, so if you dig you can find communities that are helpful and the right fit for your game.

- Gaming events – Exhibiting at a gaming event, even a small one, will give you a steady stream of players for your project: While most of these gamers will only get to see the first few minutes of your game, they can be a great starting point for player feedback.

- Build your own – If you are thoughtful about creating, maintaining, and growing an e-mail list and a Discord community around your game, you can have a pool of dedicated testers available to you at all times, but be wary that intense fan bias can skew feedback for both better and for worse.

- Mentor feedback – Input from a highly experienced expert can be more productive than several testers, especially for design-level considerations: This kind of testing is great for major mechanics and presentation considerations but not ideal for deep bug testing.

- Twitch and YouTube creators – Streamers and content creators, especially the smaller ones, are often receptive to being testers for indie games: As community leaders, their feedback can be representative of a larger group, and if the testing is done live on stream, you can watch along or review a recording afterward.

- Outsource – Several companies offer QA as a service. For a fee, their testers play your game and provide bug reports as well as feedback: Though this can become costly, the rigorous and disciplined testing that a good QA team provides can be extremely helpful.

No singular QA pipeline is better than the rest. Great indies gather feedback from a range of sources to make more informed decisions about their development. Where one weekend they are at a local gaming convention talking to players, the next weekend they are posting in a #screenshotsaturday thread and asking Twitter viewers to vote on which character outfit they like better. Then, they direct all of that player interest to places where they can retain their testers: Steam Wishlists, e-mail lists, and Discord servers.

With that kind of approach, these indies take an investment (like having a booth at an event) and turn it into a long-term win (by inviting excited players to join their testing team in Discord). Over time, they get better at working on all fronts, resulting in a built-in fandom ready to test new games and a streamlined process for engaging QA testers via other channels.

We suspect that most indies will have limited budgets, so the most practical QA options will be to bootstrap your QA as much as possible to save on the costs of outsourcing or hiring QA testers.

Many of the developers we have worked with have taken this path, but it is hard work. Robi Studios, the team behind the 3D platformer *Blue Fire,* spent months diligently building a Discord community around their game. Blazing Stick, the developer of the synthwave parkour title *Cyber Hook,* did the same and later supplied their community with a level editor so that they could build their own content.

In both of these cases, the developers started with very little in the way of financial resources, but they made up for that disadvantage with work hours and consistency. Not only did they set up a Discord server, but they also made sure to stay active in gaming communities that shared their target audience. Even when their Discord communities were small, they treated every member with kindness and continued to make Discord a worthwhile place for those members to be by posting previews, sharing memes, asking for feedback, and genuinely building friendships with their players.

Even when we entered the relationships and brought our own QA process with us, these communities continued to be essential parts of testing builds. They were already loyal fans, so if something excited them or frustrated them, that was a big signal, but they also championed the game. Every time they got to test a build, they were thrilled to share their experience with others, which brought more users into the Discord and grew the community.

Building your own testing community is slow. Many indies expect players to flock to their Discord or to their e-mail lists, but in practice, these seeds take a great deal of care and nurturing before they bear fruit, so most indies give up far too early.

For every aspect of QA but especially for building your own testing group: Start early, be consistent, and be patient.

Gathering Feedback

The value of a formal QA process is that you can more effectively manage your time and resources while making forward progress on improvements. Just as your process for finding and engaging testers should be structured and organized, so should your approach for collecting feedback.

Opinions are easy to find, but what feedback do you trust? What do you incorporate into your game? What do you ignore? How do you weigh one respondent's feedback over another's?

The first step toward answering these questions is gathering good data. A thoughtful approach to collecting feedback can simplify your efforts to identify trends, determine meaningful or irrelevant outliers, and separate constructive insights from less useful criticism. In the marketing world, these best practices are commonplace for research surveys and product testing, and they are also useful in games. While major companies have dedicated marketing teams to manage this side of the business, most indies don't, so a basic primer on best practices will be very helpful for you.

The feedback you gather will likely be a mix of the following:

- Informal conversations – Casual feedback provided outside of a structured format, such as a player who tries your game at a convention or a publisher reacting to your elevator pitch.

- Observation – Though a player does not mention it directly, watching how someone plays your game can tell you a great deal about what is and is not working in your design.

- Gameplay footage – Also a form of observation, this approach captures recordings of gameplay for later review and analysis.

- Surveys – Usually delivered through a tool like Survey Monkey or a Google Form, this is a questionnaire that asks every tester the same set of questions about their gameplay experience.

- Focus groups – A member of your team leads a discussion about your game with a small group of players to gather feedback about the project.

- Formal interviews – A mix of scripted questions and open dialogue, a formal interview is a deep dive with a single player to more intimately understand their feedback as well as the context for their feedback.

- Analytics – Depending on the development tools you use, your build can automatically track data about player actions, play time, and crash reports for later analysis.

- Internal testing – Various internal team members test builds and provide feedback with the benefit of knowing what the game is *trying* to accomplish.

Every feedback mechanism has its own nuances, and certain formats feel more natural for some individuals. The most outgoing indies we have worked with shine when they are directly engaging players in person. For these indies, talking with someone who is actively playing the game feels the most natural. Therefore, they gravitate toward applying in-person feedback to their work because it is easier to get and is more comfortable to them.

More introverted indies rely on surveys and questionnaires to gather feedback. On the one hand, surveys are able to reach more users than one-on-one talks, so they are useful for identifying patterns or trends in user reactions. At the same time, though, they can be a shield, a way to hide from having to face a strong piece of criticism from someone in person.

You will likely have a personal preference as well, but tread carefully. You can bias yourself and your feedback if you do not pursue diverse sources of feedback, and that bias can negatively affect all of your QA efforts, limiting your ability to improve the overall experience by creating new blindspots for you and your team.

Get out of your comfort zone and use as many feedback sources as you can because the final product will be much better as a result.

Regardless of the exact feedback format, apply these best practices:

- Make it easy for testers – The more work you put between your players and them sharing their thoughts, the less feedback you will get, so streamline the steps as much as you can.

- Don't be defensive – You may have the instinctual reaction to defend your work if feedback is negative, but you should resist that urge: Even if you don't agree, seek to understand the basis for the feedback and still thank the tester for their input.

- Avoid leading questions – How you craft a question can bias the results, so aim to keep questions simple and direct: Having another team member review your questions for problematic or confusing points can also be helpful.

- Build context – Having some insight into the player providing feedback can help you to evaluate their responses: If you know that the player spends most of their time playing looter shooters, you may be less surprised to see that your RTS felt too complex for them, at which point, perhaps you disregard that feedback to focus on serving RTS fans.

- Reflect and look for patterns – After reviewing a large amount of feedback, step back and look for commonalities in responses: If players talk about how much they love the cute side kick in almost every reaction, that's notable; likewise, if 60% of players quit at the first boss, that is also notable.

- Ask follow-up questions – If a tester provided interesting notes and gave you permission to contact them again, connecting with that tester to learn more about their reaction can be valuable: We have seen this approach open the door to pivotal community relationships in addition to improving the game.

- Reward participants – Major corporations often use giftcards or discount codes to incentivize users to provide feedback, but for indies, small swag items (like a pin at a convention) or community recognition (like a profile badge or an exclusive Discord role) can make users feel valued and appreciated.

- Revisit the same testers – While fresh feedback is still important, many indies don't share new builds with previous testers, so they miss an opportunity to assess the impact of a fix or a change.

Your feedback efforts will improve with time and with practice, but if you take our advice and build multiple QA stages into your business and development plans, you can skip over many of the lessons that many indies learn through trial and error.

Implementing QA Feedback

In Part 3, we talked about how an unsuccessful pitch was still a valuable opportunity for gathering feedback on your pitch and on your game. We also cautioned that you should not incorporate all of the suggestions you receive because even the advice shared with the best of intentions from a reputable individual may not be the right fit for your project.

The same is true for player feedback.

Fortunately, some feedback is easy to assess. If a player's reaction is clearly based on a bug or a feature not functioning as expected, you can prioritize that fix and put it into your development queue. When you start to grapple with ideas such as how a game feels to play or how to scale difficulty, your analysis can spin you in circles because these concepts are incredibly subjective.

Revisiting testers to gather new reactions to previously problematic content is helpful, but no matter what, the choices around what to address and what to ignore are not scientific. This is part of the art of game design. You have to juggle your lofty ambitions as well as the hard realities of what players are telling you. That's difficult because if you ask a platforming fan what they want in a platforming experience, they won't articulate the GDD for *Shovel Knight*. Though that game is now a clear success, you have to be able to imagine a time where the concept of a shovel-wielding hero romping through a retro world may not have sounded like the best game idea of all time.

But how do you know when to stick to your vision and when to pivot?

You can't ever know for sure, but you can challenge your own ideas. The research and planning you have done thus far can help.

Take the following steps.

Recognize Your Own Biases and Limitations

In the section on building a team, we discussed how being aware of your own strengths and weaknesses was a guiding light for choosing people to work with. You can use that same exercise to identify where you should be more receptive to feedback. If you know that art is not one of your strong suits, you should be more willing to hear criticism of your game's art direction and be open to applying it.

As you do this, you should also be aware of how you typically respond to feedback. Indies often default to extremes, either being too receptive or too resistant. If you catch yourself assuming that your tester is always wrong because they just don't "get it," you need to be aware of that so that you can make an effort to be more objective. On the opposite side of that, if you find that you struggle to stand your ground, you should be conscious of that as well.

Revisit Your Comparable Title Research

Earlier, we talked about how meeting the expectations of a genre is a delicate dance. Players want a new experience, but fans of a genre also want a particular type of experience. If you are targeting Metroidvania fans but don't have a mechanic where the player progressively gains access to more of the map via items or abilities, that audience may not get excited about your game.

For feedback, if the majority of self-professed Metroidvania fans are raising similar concerns, you should pause and consider that. The goal of testing is to improve your game, which for our purposes, is to make the game more profitable as a result. Players telling you what they do and do not like can also be code for what they will and will not buy.

Going back to your comparable title research in these scenarios will help you to ground feedback in what you already know about your target player base and the titles that have already been successful. If you use that knowledge to put yourself more squarely in the perspective of players, do they have a point? Is there feedback valid? If you were a player, how would you want their concerns to be resolved?

Again, it's not a science, but if 90% of your ideal customers are saying the same thing, you should do your best to listen as that's a lot of unit sales to sacrifice for what could be hubris.

Seek to Understand the Root Issue

Player feedback, when it is not tied to what is obviously a bug or a mistake, is often more like gathering clues than reading a map. The issues testers directly raise is not necessarily an indication of what you should change.

Early in the development of *Blue Fire*, Robi Studios faced a strange conundrum: some players found the platforming to be too difficult, so they would give up on completing levels. Meanwhile, other players felt that the platforming was too easy, and they wanted the levels to be harder. This kind of feedback seems to contradict itself, so the Robi team initially thought they would have to choose between what players to keep and what players to lose.

But they revisited their inspirations for *Blue Fire* and realized that the problem was not that any one level was too hard or too easy but rather that players did not have any agency over the scope of the challenges they were willing to face. In *Mario 64*, the solution to this problem was to make many of the collectible stars purely optional. If a player found one star too difficult, they could move on to another and get the necessary stars to unlock more of the game.

For the players that relished a challenge, though, they could gather every star in every level, making the game more difficult by choice. *Blue Fire* used a similar philosophy in constructing rifts, optional levels designed for the hardcore platforming fans. These levels came with bigger rewards, but they could be skipped without making the core storyline impossible to complete.

That's not what players directly asked for, but it did help address the concerns of both sides. Great game design often comes out of this dynamic.

Run Tests

An A/B test is a process where you deliver two versions of the same experience but change one specific variable. In marketing, for example, testing subject lines by splitting your e-mail list in half and sending one version to one half and another version to the other gives you insight into what e-mail subjects your audience is most likely to open. If your tracking is robust enough, it could also start to reveal what subject lines make prospects more likely to buy products.

Game development is rarely that tidy, but creating different versions for players to compare is worthwhile. Asking a player if they like your main character is useful, but it is vague. If you ask a player to choose between two variations of a main character, you can start to hone in on a more clear understanding of *why* they prefer one to another. Your process for testing does not have to be as refined as a classic A/B marketing test, but the spirit of the approach is worthwhile. Over time, a series of tests can help you to effectively iterate in the most productive direction for your game.

Every developer will have moments where they deliberately disregard a player's feedback in service of the larger goal of the project.

QA as a Skill

Every aspect of game development, from the creative to the business to testing, is a skill that can be honed and improved. Your QA process will not be perfect the first or even the fifth time you make a game, so just as you work to get better at art or at leadership, you should do the same with QA. At major milestones where you assess your development progress, debriefing and reflecting on your QA efforts is worthwhile as well. With this approach, you can improve your processes for the long-term and proactively identify problems or opportunities in the short-term.

For example, a QA debrief can give your level designer time to point out that while players have thoroughly tested levels 1–5, they have seen very few players test levels 6 and 7, which is worrying because those levels introduce a new ability and the designer is unsure if players understand how it works. That small moment of discussion enables you to identify an issue you may have overlooked and to push testers through those levels immediately, which is far more practical and cost-effective than finding out two weeks before launch that players find the ability confusing and unfun.

Pay attention to what works well and what is inefficient throughout your development cycles. Identify the areas that are problematic, and get outside help if you don't see yourself or your team making progress. Your current project will benefit, and all of your future projects will benefit as well.

CHAPTER

TWELVE

Translation, Localization, and Porting

In Part 2, we covered translation and localization as well as porting through the lens of making budget and development planning choices. Whether you are self-funding or pitching to publishers, anticipating these costs and their related development tasks helps you to effectively budget, plan, and communicate your project needs to potential investors. When you move from planning and into development.

Once development is underway, you have to decide how to follow-through on these plans. Part of that is making smart preparations to make a task like porting a game more efficient and less costly, and the other part is being agile in how you assess what you do and do not do. When you start to approach the phase in which you translate or port your game, which is usually at the end of development, reassessing your budget and your market opportunities is a smart business decision as a great deal can change in the time that has passed since you first drafted your plan.

Best Practices for Preparation

When we first talked about translations and localizations in Chapter 7, we mentioned that engines like Unity have plugins and tools to make translating your content to other languages more manageable. With these kinds of tools, exporting all of the text in your game takes a few button presses, and when you get the translated text back, a few more button presses inject it back into your game.

Granted, we are oversimplifying the workflow a bit, but working with these tools is far easier than manually updating every line of text in your game.

If you don't think about that until the project is nearly complete, it may be too late to implement a time-saving solution. The task of actually translating and localizing a game may be one of the last development steps, but if you do not plan for it from day one, you could add weeks of work to your schedule.

Porting can pose similar obstacles. If you do not think about the console experience until your project is nearly complete, you may find that beyond struggling to

DOI: 10.1201/9781003215264-16

meet the technical requirements of console hardware that the experience of playing your game doesn't quite fit for console players. Menus can be hard to read. Controls can feel awkward. And whole stretches of content that feel immersive on a PC screen just don't translate well to a television screen. There are two major issues here, controller support and optimization. It might take longer than you expected to get the controller working properly and you can easily run into optimization issues where your game is not running at the proper framerate.

Those problems are expensive to solve when your game is already built. If you keep in mind that you intend to make your PC title available on consoles as well (and maybe even mobile), you can pre-empt those design challenges with more elegant solutions.

That will mean the following.

Get the Tools You Need

Research the translation and localization tools available for your engine of choice, and also explore their workflows for porting to other platforms. While you're doing that, begin the process of requesting a developer's kit from your target console platforms. Even if you outsource the actual porting, you will need a way to test builds on the appropriate hardware.

Routinely Assess Your Workflows

Just because you downloaded the translation plugin and have the Xbox dev kit on your desk does not mean that your development team is making the right choices. Check in periodically to make sure that the best practices you identified were crucial are being followed. If you are a solo indie, that means holding yourself accountable as well.

Flag Potential Obstacles

Just as you should keep a running log of bugs, you should also keep track of the content or components that could be problematic later. For example, if you have a story moment that is steeped in cultural nuances, perhaps relying on pop culture references that make sense to an American audience but might be confusing to a Japanese audience, note it so that you can revisit the text later with the help of your translators. If you know ahead of time that it is a potential issue, you are more likely to find an effective solution.

Porting often requires more technical considerations, but looking at your development with that end-goal at mind could help you see that the keycode puzzle is intuitive with a keyboard and mouse but is incredibly cumbersome for a controller.

Like our localization example, you don't necessarily need to address that obstacle right away, but being aware of it prevents more serious challenges later.

Test It Out

You don't have to start porting once your game is content complete. You can begin the process sooner to see how it performs, particularly for a console that has motion controls. If you notice issues, then you can revise the schedule to give yourself adequate time to correct the situation.

Plan for the Unexpected

You may never be able to anticipate every problem and roadblock, but you can make educated guesses about where you might find them. If you have never gone through Sony's console certification process, you can't know what might delay your project, but you can recognize that you are likely to make a few mistakes in your first attempt. So, in addition to doing some extra research on how to best prepare for that process, budget for extra time in your development to complete that process without impacting your release date.

When to Change Your Plans

Just because you identified seven target languages and two major consoles as opportunities for your game when you were in the planning phase, that does not mean those opportunities will be the same when you near launch. The indie video game industry can change quickly. A new hardware announcement or a shift in player trends could strengthen some opportunities while weakening others.

You may have decided that your initial launch focus would be PC, but because of a chance meeting with a publisher at GDC, your development roadmap now includes a Switch release. Your publisher has an in-house porting team, so the addition of that console release does not change your development timeline significantly. However, you notice that you did not originally plan to translate your game into Japanese.

Since your game will be on the Switch and the Switch is popular in Japan, you should consider adding budget to translate and localize your game in Japanese. If more budget is not an option, you could look at dropping a language on your list to make room for Japanese.

Or, you might be preparing for a PlayStation and PC release and happen upon a tweet from Martin Lindell, an Advisor for Embracer Group, that says:

> I can attest that Brazilian Portuguese was an important addition for Kingdom. Also worth point[ing] out that Turkish is great for PC games, and for the right game Arabic, if you're doing PlayStation (a bit like Japanese & Switch).

193

After some additional diligence, you discover that the comparable titles from your research tapped into these language trends as well and you have a sizable number of Steam wishlists to match, so you amend your gameplan to account for what could be a significant sales opportunity.

While the goal of a late-stage pivot is to seize new opportunities, remember that no pivot is without risk. If you are going to deviate from your original plan, give that deviation the same degree of thought and diligence as your initial plan. Assess the market opportunity. Estimate the budget and development you will need. And then compare your new potential profit against the costs of making the pivot.

When Chris Wright, the head of Fellow Traveler tells GameDiscoverCo that Chinese localization for Fellow Traveler titles moved the total units sold in China from 5% to 20% (or more), that's a clue that you should consider the option, but it is not a clear sign that it is the right choice. If that projected bump in unit sales does not come close to covering the costs of translating your text-heavy RPG into Simplified Chinese, it's probably not the best move.

Coming back again and again to the profit potential of a decision can sound unsexy to a team that values bold creativity, but remember that our goal here is to enable you to make several more games, so preventing you from spiraling into inescapable debt is critical. Ultimately, your pivot should be a careful consideration of risk and reward, both for your business and for your creative potential.

Opening New Porting Opportunities

In Chapter 2, we explored a breakdown of the major platforms relevant for indie developers, so by this point you have likely put some thought into what platforms are most relevant for the game you intend to make. Barring a major change in the platform landscape, your original assessment will likely remain accurate up through the release of your game, but you should be open to new opportunities that may arise.

When the news of Apple Arcade hit the games industry, it came with a landrush of developers and publishers pitching to Apple, hoping to secure minimum guarantees and exclusive promotion for their titles. For their part, Apple seemed to be investing significant budget into securing high-quality exclusive titles that would attract new users to Apple Arcade.

In 2018, a year before the announcement of Apple Arcade, an indie was unlikely to think about Apple as anything more than a mobile platform, but if you're a year into development and have a chance to talk to an Apple Arcade scout at a convention, you should be willing to listen to what might be possible. As you might recall from earlier in the book, Supergiant had a similar experience with Xbox in the early days of developing *Bastion*, and that chance meeting opened several new doors for the fledgling indie studio.

You can never fully anticipate the creation of new platforms such as Apple Arcade or Google Stadia, and there is no way to ensure that the right gaming executive bumps into you at Starbucks. You can, however, mentally consider what would make a change in porting plans worthwhile for you.

If you didn't intend to target the PlayStation market and then speak to someone at Sony, what would you need to adjust to be successful with that audience? What would the platform need to offer to justify the effort?

And you can play those questions out for any platform that you decided was not an initial target because they could become an opportunity in the future.

Being Open to the Outlandish

Furthermore, you should directly work to build relationships with these platforms as you network in the industry. A platform that is not a fit for your current project could be ideal for your next, and fostering meaningful connections with the industry insiders you meet today will put you in a better position to capitalize on those opportunities tomorrow.

Depending on the context, there is nothing wrong with making a longshot pitch. If you happen to secure a meeting with a particular platform as part of a networking event, make that time productive by delivering a great pitch and asking thoughtful questions after. As we discussed in Chapter 9, you might not be aware of an upcoming strategy shift that would make your game more relevant for a particular publisher or platform, but even if this is not the right project, how you conduct yourself and the information you gather can be highly valuable for your long-term goals.

While it can be rare, some indie games eventually see mobile ports as well, even if they don't seem like great mobile titles at first glance. *Divinity: Original Sin 2* is a vast and complex RPG experience that plays beautifully with a keyboard and mouse, but many game designers would be skeptical about the iPad being able to support the full scope of the *Divinity* experience.

Based on the user and critic reviews, Larian tackled the challenge handily. While we don't have access to the exact sales numbers, we can say with reasonable certainty that the launch was another facet of Larian's effort to continue monetizing their IP in a way that genuinely brought value to players. The *Divinity* series has seen a steady stream of updates and ports, and whether those are motivated by minimum guarantees or market analysis (likely both), we feel it is safe to estimate that these decisions have been profitable even if they do not seem immediately intuitive.

The *Divinity: Original Sin 2* iPad port came post-release, yes, but we highlight it here because the momentum you build on your way to release could open doors in your immediate or your distant future. To make the most of those opportunities, you should tap into that indie creativity and think about what might be possible, even if it's as ambitious as porting a large CRPG to an iPad.

Whether that door leads to an Apple Arcade exclusive, funding for a mobile port, or simply the opportunity to launch on an additional console that was not originally in your budget, you should keep an open mind and try to imagine what it would take to make the outlandish a reality.

Wishlist Momentum

Back in Chapter 4, we talked extensively about the Wishlist economy in indie games and how, because of their consistency in predicting future sales, Wishlists are often the foundation for minimum guarantees. The industry's largest platforms are data-minded, so they can estimate with reasonable accuracy how many units they are likely to sell on their platform relative to the number of Wishlists the game has on Steam.

These negotiations can happen at any stage leading up to the official launch, but they are most productive when you have a sizeable pool of Wishlists (relative to your target genre) and have six to eight weeks (at a minimum) before your launch so that the platform has enough time to vet the opportunity and integrate it into their calendar.

A word of caution: If you have a publisher for your game, have an open conversation about how they approach this process and what platforms they intend to target. An unusual email from a well-meaning indie can disrupt the relationship a publisher has built with a platform. Receiving two pitches for the same game makes all parties appear disorganized and any difference in the platform ask can undermine your credibility as well as the publisher's credibility.

We strongly believe that indie developers should have as much agency in their destinies as possible. The less time you spend on the sidelines and the more time you spend proactively creating new opportunities the better, but your publisher is on your team too. You will accomplish far more if you work together.

That disclaimer aside, talking about how to leverage Wishlists before we have fully explored how to generate Wishlists may feel premature, but like the structure of this book, we want you to see the end-goals first and work backward to understand the full scope of your journey.

A platform negotiation will likely not be a day one opportunity, but here's how you should think about platforms over the lifecycle of your development.

Establish Relationships

Industry events are the most organic way to strike up a casual conversation with a platform manager or scout, but at a distance you can start to build these by entering contests, showcases, and industry webinars. In all of these cases, a relevant stakeholder is likely to be present, and if you can follow up with a genuine question related to what they spoke about or to what they offered, you can start to build rapport even if your game is not ready for a full pitch.

Talk to Your Network

If you took our advice and started to participate in one or several indie development communities, the trusted peers you meet in those contexts might be able to point you in the right direction if you are trying to learn more about a specific platform. You may learn, for example, that an active poster in your favorite indie Discord channel previously launched a title on Xbox. Requesting a brief chat for their insights and their recommendations with this person can help you to prepare your own plan of attack and may lead to an introduction. Remember, a good network is built with two-way streets, so you should look for ways to actively add value where you can as well.

Ask Your Platform Representative for Help

When you secure a development kit for a console, you are typically assigned a point of contact at the same time. Though you should be incredibly selective about how often you message this person because they are not there to be your teacher or your mentor, a casual question to the tune of:

> I'm new to this, so I hope you don't mind my asking: Do you have any advice for how I should think about pitching an exclusive release window to your platform? We are a ways away from that being relevant, but is there a target Wishlist number or an ideal timing for that kind of conversation? My thought is that having an idea of what that goal is ahead of time will save me from needlessly bothering you or your team in the future. Thank you for your help.

This does not always work as every platform representative will have a slightly different approach to managing indies, but a polite and respectful request is worth a try.

Follow up a Splash with Another Splash

The gaming community can behave in unpredictable ways, so you can never quite predict when a viral moment or a well-timed announcement will shine the spotlight on your project. When it happens, however, look for ways to springboard into even bigger moments. If your #screenshotsaturday post showcasing an amazing pixel art boss battle trends on Twitter and hits the top of r/gaming, a games journalist might feature your work in an article. That could generate a nice boost in Wishlists, but you can dig deeper.

Look at all the accounts that interacted with your #screenshotsaturday tweet. Any notable insiders, like a publisher or a journalist or a platform stakeholder? If so, message those individuals, thank them for their support, and ask them if they have advice on what you should do to make it worthwhile to work with you in the future. You may not always receive a reply, but these moments can be the spark that begins new relationships.

For the relationships you already have, a big piece of press coverage is a good reason to follow up with a publisher or platform you pitched previously, provided they gave you permission to do so. You may have learned your game was too early in development for a particular publisher in your first meeting, so polite and well-timed follow-ups that show the excitement your game is generating can reopen talks.

Think Bigger than Minimum Guarantees

A minimum guarantee is typically the biggest possible win for an indie studio as far as platform relationships go, but there are other kinds of wins as well. We have mentioned exclusive promotions and preorder windows already, but you might also be able to secure the following:

- Placement for your console announcement trailer on the platform's official YouTube channel

- Introductions to key press contacts that typically cover news for that console

- Varying level of event support, from a spot in a showcase booth down to hardware for running your own booth

- Alternative funding sources, such as grants for developers from underrepresented backgrounds

- Other in-kind forms of marketing support like advertising credits, store placement, social media amplification, and influencer connections

Asking, "Will you give me this instead" may be too blunt of a followup for when a platform declines to give you a minimum guarantee, but you could ask, "If a minimum guarantee is not a fit, do you have a process for how you decide to provide other kinds of support? Having a better idea of what your goals are will make it easier for me to circle back at the right time with the right materials prepared."

If this sounds like our recommendations for negotiation with a publisher, that's intentional. Publisher and platform conversations can sometimes be very similar, so don't be afraid to apply what you've learned about talking with publishers to talking with platforms.

Launch Day Is Not Always Ideal

As exciting as it can be to launch simultaneously on PC, Xbox, Nintendo, and PlayStation, indies more often stagger platform releases for a variety of reasons. Development timelines and budget constraints may not support that much prelaunch work. One platform may have negotiated exclusivity, delaying the others. Or the interest of a platform may be unclear to all parties until sales data and game reviews are available.

For our part, we are fortunate to have a good relationship with our console representatives, and many of the indies we publish through Graffiti Games have received support from the consoles. As a result of that effort over years of working in the industry, we pitch the best fits to our contacts and often launch on PC and one console first to lean into the console's playerbase.

Then, post-launch, we start to rollout porting to other platforms, which may include more translation and localization as well.

But that's us. For you and the kinds of games you want to make, it might make mor sense to launch on PC first, multiple platforms at launch or a new console that is announced. Regardless of where you initially release your game, a platform that did not make business sense on launch day could be profitable six-months post-release because of the traction you earned.

Marketing from Zero

Though the games industry is more accessible than ever for indies, the competitive landscape is far from level. Not only are you competing against other indies – many of whom are as rabidly passionate about their goals as you are – but you are also competing with AAA studios as well. On any given day, the frontpage of Steam is a hodge-podge of featured promotions, recommendations curated based on user data, and notable bestsellers. As we write this chapter, our Steam frontpage features *Call of Duty*, a new *Final Fantasy* bundle, *Far Cry 5*, a promo for the Valve Index, and a price discount for *Stardew Valley*.

Three AAA franchises, a Steam initiative, and an indie goliath–and that's just part of the "Featured & Recommended" slider. If you're new to indie video game development, you and your 10 Twitter followers (Hi, Mom!) and your empty Discord server will somehow have to compete for attention in this hyper competitive market.

A publisher will help, but no matter how much support a publisher may provide, it is always worthwhile for indies to manage some form of their own marketing and to build their own communities. Publishers won't do everything. They have limitations, and though it may sound like a contradiction, they often want to see that you already have a community of some kind before making an offer, so to get marketing help you need to be marketing your game effectively already.

Starting at the beginning is hard, and instant success is a fairytale for the vast majority of developers.

The quality of your game will always be paramount, but if no one hears about it, all of the effort, time, and money you have invested into bringing it to life will go to waste, putting you farther behind in your resources for your next game idea. You have to make marketing your game a priority, no matter how much you dislike the process or how uncomfortable it may make you feel. You need to promote your work. You need to build a community. You need to attract the attention of press and gaming tastemakers.

If you don't know how to do that, learn, and take it as seriously as you take your game design or your code or your art because marketing is one of the pillars that will sustain your business for the short- and long-term.

DOI: 10.1201/9781003215264-17

Hello, World! Hello, Twitter!

The marketing for your game should begin the moment you commit to developing it. While you might think of marketing as a series of paid ad campaigns or elaborate booth experiences at gaming conventions, nearly everything we have discussed thus far is part of an effective marketing process. If you use this book as a blueprint for your business plans, you will have already completed a great deal of key marketing tasks.

In Part 1, we unpacked the inner workings of how the business side of the games industry typically operates and talked extensively about how to think about Wishlists, how games generate revenue, and how to think about what paths may be most profitable for your game and your studio as a whole. That math gives you targets that you can break down into monthly and quarterly goals to guide the progress and measurement of your marketing.

In Part 2, we dove more deeply into the pre-development choices that define the bones of your game, from choosing an engine based on genre and publisher-fit to identifying a scope that is practical for your team. Mapping this small mountain of comparable title and industry analysis to budgets and development milestones is a form of market research. You now have a clearer idea of who your competitors are, what they have done to be successful, and the creative choices you might make to carve your own niche. This legwork will surface again and again as you market your game.

In Part 3, your efforts in the previous section to identify what made your game unique and how it would stand apart from existing titles became the basis for a knockout pitch deck and negotiation approach. The choices you make in building a pitch deck – refining the way you describe the vision for your game, choosing great visuals, telling the story of you and your team and why you're the ones to bring this project to life–are all classic marketing tasks. Your pitch deck can be the basis of your store pages and the foundation for how you position your game when you talk to players, whether that's directly at a demo station or indirectly with social media posts.

You might not think of yourself this way, but congratulations, you are a games marketer. Now, we need to start using these pieces to attract and retain interested players.

The cornerstones of an indie marketing strategy are as follows:

1. **Key assets** – The art, text, and other media that communicate the game experience and target your ideal players.

2. **Digital on-property marketing** – Marketing channels that bring players to you, such as your Steam page, social media profiles, Discord server, and website.

3. **Digital off-property marketing** – The channels you use to bring your games to players, entering the places and communities where they gather, like Reddit, Twitter, and Facebook.

4. **Gaming events** – Both digital and physical, these gatherings of players, press, and industry insiders are an opportunity to engage future customers and to build business relationships.

5. **Press engagement** – Finding opportunities to regularly pitch news about your project to games journalists, pushing your work into the feeds of their loyal viewers and readers.

6. **Pre-release accolades** – Leveraging the strength of your demos and early progress to earn attention in indie showcases and contests or to garner the support of accelerators, grants, and scholarships.

7. **Streamer engagement** – Finding opportunities to have streamers play your game (demo during the pre-launch phase), pushing your work into the feeds of their loyal viewers.

We recommend that you begin these efforts in the order in which they are listed, but once development of your game is fully underway, each of these marketing tasks should be a perpetual part of your business routine. You will come back to them repeatedly on your road to release, applying the same mindset that you use for quality assurance: Gradual improvement over time is the most practical and effective, and the opportunities that these efforts facilitate are more impactful if you chase them throughout development rather than at the very end, right before launch.

Key Assets: How to Create Memorable Marketing

Key art is the visual that is most strongly associated with your product. It is often your first—and perhaps only—chance to get the attention of a consumer.

In film, a singular movie poster or image will become the anchor point for ad campaigns, thumbnails in streaming services, and box art for DVD cases. If you think of the Batman film *The Dark Knight*, you can likely picture the fiery Batman logo outlined by burning windows with Batman standing defiantly in the foreground. The visual is compelling in its own right, and the repetition of that image being used throughout the marketing for *The Dark Knight* seared it into our collective memories.

The same happens in games. Master Chief stands on a precipice with guns drawn when we think of *Halo*. We see Commander Shephard poised for action when we think of *Mass Effect*. If we think of *Ori and the Blind Forest*, we see Naru cradling Ori on a tree branch with a large tree glowing a cool blue in the background.

Key art is important for several reasons. Consistency in visuals and presentation, even if they evolve as the game evolves, tethers your marketing back to a memorable homebase. If your game releases 12 months from today, your target audience should have several encounters with your content. Whether they see your game on TikTok or on Reddit or in a YouTube preview, effective key art will help them to associate those various touchpoints with the same game.

If players see pieces of your game on five separate occasions but don't realize they are seeing the same game, you miss out on the opportunity to steadily build a player's interest over time. If you are an Ori fan today, you were likely exposed to the game on several occasions in a range of formats before you actually wishlisted or bought the game. Though you weren't shown the same key art every single time, the key art is strong enough that you start to associate characters, art direction, and gameplay with the title.

Much of this happens unconsciously for consumers as we are bombarded with content each day, but it all adds up to the feeling that you have seen this game permeating the indie scene and your curiosity has grown to the point that you are willing to give it a try.

Like a movie poster, great key art is a visual representation of what people can experience and for video games it captures the feel and experience. This is a lot to ask for a single image, so here are some guidelines:

- Use your comparable title research to look for trends or themes in how your genre signals to players that a game might fit their tastes.
- Apply the same color palettes, tones, and moods of your gameplay to your key art.
- Be thoughtful about font selection for your game title, ensuring that it is easily readable and captures the personality of your game.
- Have a focal point to the key art that draws people to a main element and the logo.
- Test various applications of your key art, adjusting elements and layout as necessary to retain the same impact.
- Don't limit your logo in one place because it will make it difficult to convert you key art into various image sizes.
- Don't use only text because chances are no one knows what your game is.
- Think about the various banner sizes that you might need to convert your key art into.

To expand on that last point, your key art will appear in several formats, so your design has to be versatile and thoughtful. Your key art will be used in the following places:

- As cover art for featured store listings
- As the endslate for trailers and promotional videos
- As thumbnails in store searches
- As social media and press graphics
- As the basis for event posters and banners

Sometimes your key art will take up most of a desktop screen. Other times it is a tiny tile in a stream of search results. Sometimes players are looking at your key art on their phones. Other times they are seeing it from the other side of a convention hall. That means one idea has to translate into multiple resolutions, sizes, and use cases.

Great key art takes time and is a worthy investment. Just as many Hollywood blockbusters outsource poster creation to expert designers, so many indies commission art and design specifically for their key art. This is too important to be slapped together in a few minutes in Photoshop. It's the face of your game and the first and possibly the only thing many players will see.

You should approach your other key assets with a similar commitment to quality and consistency. A great piece of key art is important, but that key art will also be supported by text describing your game as well as additional supporting screenshots, trailers, and GIFs. Stitching these pieces into one cohesive experience will make every piece of your marketing more powerful, and that effort should be applied to any promotion of your game.

The pitch you give a publisher about what makes your game interesting should feel similar to how your team members describe the game to first-time players at your booth. When they visit your Steam page later, it should feel like an extension of that first moment, rooting them in the familiar visuals while giving them access to more information about your game than they may have gleaned from an elevator pitch and a few minutes of gameplay.

When they talk to a friend about an interesting indie game they saw at MomoCon, that friend should be able to recognize the game based on a description if they saw it as well.

Lean on your pitch deck here to guide you because you already used the process to identify the most interesting and compelling elements of your game. From there, evolving your key assets as development progresses (and perhaps as you unlock additional funding), but make sure every part of your marketing evolves to match so everything stays connected and cohesive. The easiest way to do this is to create brand guidelines that outline rules including what font, colors and theme to use when creating key assets.

On-Property Digital Marketing: Attract and Retain Interested Players

On-property marketing consists of tactics that organically bring customers to you. Optimizing your website so that Google recommends your company for certain keywords is on-property because you control the content, as is a well-optimized Steam page. Through your efforts to be compelling in places where you have direct control – what you post on your blog–customers come to you.

Modern gamers discover new games through a variety of channels, and your game needs to be where players are. Indies often start with the right idea for on-property marketing by registering every social media handle they can think of and setting up a website for their studio, but they also often misunderstand the idea of bringing customers to them. Great on-property marketing is an active, ongoing process.

A Steam page, for example, looks like a static piece of marketing. Once you create your game listing, is there really that much more to do?

Yes, a lot. Updating your Steam tags on a regular basis, sometimes referred to as "tag hacking," is a strategy where you monitor trending searches in Steam and adjust your tags so that your game appears alongside currently relevant games. Most indie publishers adjust these tags on a weekly basis (roughly), but we have also met indies who change those tags several times a day to capitalize on their high volume of organic Steam traffic.

From there, you can use Steam's expanding suite of creator tools to publish news and updates about your game, injecting a feed of fresh content into your store page to signal to players that your project is alive, that you're devoted, and that more and more cool developments are moving through your pipeline. If you're featured in a festival or an event, you can further enhance your page with a live or pre-recorded developer stream so that Steam users can see your game in action and connect with you directly.

None of these tactics involve you entering a community outside of your control, but a great deal of work and thoughtfulness goes into making a piece of on-property marketing meaningful for your game.

For any on-property marketing tactic that you implement, you should keep these principles in mind:

- Aim to leverage the full range of tools and options available to you to get the most out of an effort: Leaving parts of a simple profile unfilled on any platform can hurt your search rankings and signal a level of amateurishness to your work.

- Understand the opportunities of the algorithm or dynamic: If you want to be successful on a platform such as Instagram, you should research the fundamentals of Instagram hashtags, etiquette, and best practices so that you can maximize the reach of your content.

- Make consistent updates: Some inbound marketing vehicles need daily updates to be effective while others may have less aggressive update cadences: Identify the balance between what is effective and what is reasonably practical for your team and stick to that schedule.

- Stay on brand: If you update the key art on your Steam page, for example, you should update it everywhere: That will require several adjustments to profile pictures and cover photos on your range of inbound platforms, but that effort will make it easier for players to associate your various efforts with your singular game.

- Point everything to a clear call to action: Wishlist this game on Steam, and make the link to do so easy to find at all times.

AAA studios have entire teams devoted to managing marketing on a full-time basis, so a solo indie or a small indie team cannot reasonably do *everything*, but you should at least do the following:

- Set up a website for your studio that includes your game. For most indies, managing a central studio presence is more practical than launching and maintaining entirely new properties for every game they make, but it may be wise to register a unique domain name for your game and set it point to the game listing on your studio page.

- Register Twitter, YouTube, Facebook, TikTok, Tumblr, and Reddit handles for your studio. Even if you don't plan to use them yet, reserving your username for Instagram, Snapchat, Imgur, and Twitch is a good idea also.

- Create a Steam page for your game. In the future, when you are an established studio, you may decide to withhold an official reveal of your game for marketing purposes, but if you are new with no audience, capturing every Wishlist and follower you can is important since you have no existing community to draw from. Connect Google Analytics to give you more insight into the traffic coming to your page.

- Use a professional contact e-mail, make it discoverable on your studio webpage and potentially your social media profiles, and check it regularly.

- Create or update your LinkedIn profile to include your studio, and request that your team members do the same. Players likely won't see this part of your marketing, but potential publishers and investors will.

- As soon as you have a playable demo available, submit your game to IGDB.com so that you get an extra search result when players Google your game and so that your game is available for Twitch users to follow or tag in their streams when they go live.

From here, stay active on a regular basis and use content that matches your team's unique strengths. If you have a video production background, livestreams and regular video devlogs might come naturally to you, making that kind of contact easier. Writers might blog or contribute articles to gaming publications. Artists might show progress timelapses of work-in-progress. And so on.

If you can post updates at least weekly – and it's okay to schedule evergreen content to automatically post ahead of time – that's a great start for an indie.

Off-Property Digital Marketing: Injecting Your Game Into Player Communities

You may have to play by Facebook's terms of service, but you have complete control over what you post on your page and how you position your studio and your game within that page. As soon as you enter a Facebook group devoted to indie games, you are "off-property" and are no longer in total control of what appears and how it appears. Each group has its own rules, its members have their own preferences, and moderators have the discretion to remove posts they feel do not fit their group's mission.

We make this distinction between on-property and off-property because even though both may occur within the Facebook ecosystem, how you use them will be very different. Great content, no matter where it appears, should be interesting, entertaining, and bring value to the user, but when that content is injected into someone else's community, you have to be careful to serve the specific needs of that audience.

Philip Barclay, Co-Owner and Executive Producer at Sabotage Studio (the team behind *The Messenger*) regularly posts GIFs and clips from *Sea of Stars* in Indie Game Developers IGD, a Facebook group with 120,000+ members. Though no one can argue that his posts are not promotional in nature, he reserves his posts for #screenshotsaturday (a time when indies are encouraged to promote their work), and he is careful to post only when he has high quality content to share.

Barclay respects the decorum of the community and does not post unless he has something worthwhile to highlight. He never posts simply for the sake of posting. He follows the rules and adds value.

You can follow this example to be a productive member of any player community, and these best practices will help:

- Read the rules and follow them. Gaming communities recoil against obvious shills, so comply with the standards of a community if you intend to be active there.

- Give, don't just take. An old marketing adage for community engagement says that you should give 80% of the time, and only take 20% of the time. For off-property engagement, that means that four out of five of your posts should be aimed at being a good community member and not be direct promotions of your product. In other words, be an actual member, not just a marketer.

- Listen before you speak. Spend time reading and consuming content in a community before participating so that you can understand the tone and culture of a group. Pay attention to what posts perform well and what posts don't so that you can get a sense for what content that audience prefers.

- Share your best. The competitiveness of social media marketing has created a trend where creators share content because they feel that they have to. While that can sometimes be passable on a platform like Twitter, only push great content to an off-platform community. In this context, you are better off posting only one great screenshot a month rather than weekly screenshots that are dull and bland.

You are likely to find off-property marketing opportunities on the following platforms:

- Facebook Groups – Though Facebook is not as popular with the up-and-coming generation of gamers, Facebook Groups devoted to indie games, consoles, gaming genres, and game engines are going strong and are incredibly active.

- Reddit – In addition to subreddits like r/gamedev, r/indiegaming, and r/pixelart, Reddit has vibrant communities devoted to specific consoles and genres. Your target players are likely here, and you can win their support by being a sincere supporter of what these communities aim to achieve.

- Imgur – A platform that originally rose to popularity by making it easy for Redditors to share images, this community now has its own standalone user base who often respond positively to in-depth posts about indie games, especially if they are from solo developers or small teams.

- Twitter – #Screenshotsaturday is a regular haunt for players and journalists looking for something new and eye-catching, but if your studio has a distinct perspective or mission, perhaps vocally supporting a particular social cause or a certain approach to game development, you can find Twitter conversations where you can contribute your voice. These replies won't be direct promotions of your game in most cases, but it means your studio and viewpoint will be more familiar to your target audience.

- Discord – Whether as standalone communities or extensions of communities that exist on other platforms, you can find a Discord server for just about any target audience in gaming and their cultures are as varied and diverse as gaming communities elsewhere.

- Message boards – Though they are not as popular as they once were, some genres still have active bulletin-board-based communities where you can post content and interact with players.

Off-property marketing will always be relevant for indies, and it is especially important when your studio is new and you have not yet built a community. If you only stay on-property when you have zero followers, relying solely on organic discovery of your content is likely a waste of resources. Audience growth will be minimal if not non-existent. If you take the time to make great content, also take the time to find the communities that welcome and crave that kind of content to create a steady trickle of players looking to learn more about your game.

Even as your community grows, off-property marketing will continue to be valuable, as we demonstrated in our Sabotage Studio example. Getting accustomed to it early in your career will put you on a good trajectory for long-term success.

Gaming Events: Entering the Epicenter of the Industry

Historically, conventions and expos have been a major hub for video game marketing and that trend has grown as gaming communities have grown worldwide. Reed Pop's Penny Arcade Expos (PAX) have blossomed into several events in the U.S. as well as internationally with PAX Australia. The Game Developers Conference (GDC) has become an industry staple for the global game development community. In Europe, events such as Gamescom and Devcom are flourishing, and in Brazil, the Brasil Game Show (BGS) and Gamercom have found success as well.

Even though the distribution of games and the majority of fan interactions are now digital, gaming events have continued to be the go-to channel for game promotion and for building industry relationships. In the age of Steam and Xbox Game Pass, that surprises many indies as they sometimes assume that the strength of their creative and a few cold e-mail s will put them on the same playing field as the indies who exhibit at events, but we have consistently found that indies who can incorporate event marketing into their promotional calendar perform better, over all, than those who don't.

Here's why:

- Direct interactions still matter: Whether it's with players or with future business partners, talking to someone in person while they have a controller in their hand is more memorable and impactful than an e-mail or a Zoom meeting.

- Players are open to new ideas: Trying a game online is an arduous process of downloading and installing demos, but at a convention trying a game is easy as picking up a controller, so more players are likely to try your game in-person than would online.

- Events spark social media engagement: All event attendees, from players to press to executives, become prolific social media posters during events, which can be a springboard for your game reaching players beyond the event.

- Press interest and coverage spikes: A range of journalists and creators attend gaming events and the volume of content they generate for an event gives you a high chance of being highlighted in an article or video: This is also a great way to build contacts, practice your messaging and become comfortable doing interviews.

- Major events come with digital tie-ins and promotions: Though event attendees are the primary target, larger gaming events often do platform tie-ins, so a Steam user not attending PAX is likely to see the games featured there, which often means a big spike in Wishlists or sales.

- Gaming events do their own marketing: You may not be able to guarantee inclusion in an event's marketing beats, but the volume of promotion a reputable event does to attract attendees and to generate interest can mean additional promotion for your game as well.

- You might win an award: Many events include a form of official awards for games in attendance, and these pre-press accolades have several uses: More on that later in this chapter.

Based on our analysis and anecdotal conversations with our partners, we expect events to continue to be an important piece of games marketing for all of the reasons listed above. However, you should assess current trends before committing your budget as COVID-19 or a future worldwide event may influence what is most relevant by the time you read this. As of 2021, we anticipate events to return in force when the virus has been addressed, and as a bonus, we also anticipate that digital-only events and showcases are likely to evolve from being a COVID workaround to being a regular part of promoting new games.

That disclaimer aside, we also recognize that the costs of attending an event can be prohibitive for indies. Even if you are lucky enough to live in a city where a major gaming convention takes place, badges and booths and promotional materials are not cheap. If you also have to account for travel, lodging, and the income you stand to lose by not being at your day-job, the amount of budget you need to attend even one event can simply be impractical.

We hear this from U.S. developers who might be a long drive away, and we have heard no shortage of frustration from the developers we work with in Europe and South America. We agree that the pay-to-play nature is unfair and puts otherwise great games at a disadvantage.

The good news is that the games industry is rapidly recognizing that great game developers can come from anywhere, not just major metros or tech hotspots. As a result, more publishers are taking digital submissions, and larger events are exploring ways to give resource-strapped indies better access to the industry. For example, PAX Rising and Indie MEGABOOTH are both programs to give solo developers or small teams a presence at a major convention.

And those programs can open other doors as well. For example, Creative Victoria, a government organization for Victoria, Australia, has offered scholarships for Victoria-based developers who were accepted to PAX Rising, giving them additional funding to cover event costs. The Indie Games Foundation Poland has brought Polish games to PAX East, PAX West, and PAX Online on several occasions, and many countries, regions, and cities are expanding access to creative grants and tax breaks for indie game developers.

This side of the industry was already evolving rapidly, but the surprise of COVID makes it difficult for us to give you a precise list of resources. Programs and organizations are changing quickly, and even the beloved Indie MEGABOOTH is still on hiatus as we write this.

We hate to give you more homework, but you should:

- Look for indie game development organizations, clubs, or accelerators in your area to unlock funding and potential event support.
- Explore potential grants and tax credits available in your country, region, and city: If Google does not bear fruit, contact your local Chamber of Commerce or Small Business Association and ask where to learn more about grant availability.

- If an event does not clearly offer an initiative like PAX Rising, reach out to ask if they have such a program or offer any support to new indies.

- Get scrappy and collaborate with other indies to lower your event costs, which could mean sharing booth space (if the event permits), carpooling, and splitting an AirBnB.

- Network remotely by using the exhibitor list as a way to discover new potential publishers or partners.

Though it might feel like a far-off possibility right now, access to events will get easier once you have a publisher because many major publishers consistently exhibit at conventions. They might not be able to fund your travel expenses, but they can at least have a playable version of your game at the booth and support it with posters and press coverage.

Whether you have a publisher yet or not and you plan on attending an event, you can take several steps to make the event more impactful for your investment. A common indie misstep is to underestimate the work that goes into a great event showing and to overlook opportunities to make that event as impactful as possible for the business.

In Part 2, we noted that you should plan for the development time you will need to make an event-worthy demo–one of the most common indie mistakes – so you should already have a headstart on your event plans. Next, add the following to your checklist:

- Know what the event does or does not provide. Does your booth come with a table? Chairs? How many outlets do you get? Does the event provide displays or stands? There are no universal answers to these questions, and few feelings are more demoralizing than arriving at an event and discovering that an essential piece of your booth experience (like power) is not provided by default.

- Get the setup and teardown schedule. To manage logistics effectively, don't guess at when you can arrive and when you should leave.

- Invest in reusable assets. Printing a big beautiful banner for your booth will not be cheap to begin with, but also account for how you will transport the banner to and from the event to keep it in good condition. A wrinkled and torn banner reflects poorly on your game, and having to print a new one for each event is a waste of budget.

- Bring help. Even if you are a solo developer, invite a trusted friend to join you so that your booth always has someone available to talk to players. This is a better experience for players, makes each day less taxing for you, and will also keep your favorite controller from disappearing while you wait in line at the bathroom.

- Make a cheat-sheet for controls available. To make the experience as easy as possible for players, set up a placard or a small display that clearly shows the buttons and what they do in your game. That way players can pick up a controller and immediately see how to play.

- Use handouts. Players will see dozens of games at even a small event, so even players who loved your game can struggle to remember the name. Crisp, glossy postcards are relatively affordable from online printers like Vistaprint, so repurpose your key art, include your website, and include a call to wishlist on the card.

- Have business cards. Just as players will forget a game, press and business contacts are not likely to remember all of your information, so come stocked with professional business cards for these moments.

- Bring tools, tape, extension cords, and surge protectors. A short power cable or a loose screw can derail your perfect booth experience, so having an emergency kit can save you from scrambling.

- Keep water and other necessities on hand. You'll be talking a lot, so stay hydrated instead of surviving off of free energy drinks, pack a few healthy snacks, and if you are prone to headaches, have aspirin available as well. Always have hand sanitizer with you because even before a pandemic, many people became ill at conferences.

- Be prepared to improvise. Something unexpected always happens. Hardware breaks. Pieces get lost. The stress can be intense, but you can problem-solve on the fly. Ask nearby booths for help. Uber to Best Buy to get a new screen. Rig a new hanger from tape and hooks if yours breaks.

If you have an opportunity to attend an event prior to exhibiting at one, spend some time taking notes on what your favorite indie booths include in their setups. Make a list of every component, from displays to hardware to giveaways, to give yourself a more accurate idea of what you need to deliver the experience you want.

As the event draws near, you should plan to do the following to make the most of your presence before and during the show:

- Engage press ahead of time with a memorable e-mail. If your event includes a press list, blast your game to them and invite them to schedule a demo time. Use your elevator pitch and your key gameplay hooks to get their attention.

- Create a press kit. To make it easier for journalists to talk about your game, create a centralized package of screenshots, videos, game descriptions, and information about your team. Link to it on your website during the event (more on this in the next section).

- Book meetings with publishers. Exhibitor lists are generally made public in advance of an event, so you can use that to identify who might be worth pitching to at the event. Add them on LinkedIn and use their online submission forms and contact e-mails.

- Look for complementary events. Groups like the Media Indie Exchange (MIX) and GamesIndustry.biz often hosts summits and showcases in tandem with major gaming events, providing even more return on your investment in attending.

- Be outgoing. Even if you are not naturally an extrovert, hiding behind your booth table can mean missing out on worthwhile conversations. Invite passersby to play your game. Talk to players who voluntarily walked up to try a level. Go to networking sessions and mixers and actually mix, even if it feels goofy and awkward. You spent a lot of money to be there, so don't waste it.

- Diligently follow up. As you make contacts and collect business cards, our sales and pitching tips from Part 3 will help, but don't forget about the follow through. If you meet someone new, write down a few notes in your phone or in a notebook to remind yourself what you discussed, and send them a note that evening or at the end of the day to solidify the connection. A LinkedIn invite is also a good idea.

- Practice and train your elevator pitch. Try to give each player who visits your booth the same experience and same level of enthusiasm, no matter how tired you are. If you have someone helping you at the booth, teach them the elevator pitch and have them follow a similar script to keep your booth experience consistent.

- Take notes. Players often make surprising observations, and a conversation with a fellow developer can give you a new idea. Write these down as they happen because your brain will be soup by the end of the convention.

- Make social media posts and use event hashtags. The attention and activity an event generate is a great way to grow your social following, so try to share a few pictures a day and use event hashtags so that attendees stumble upon your game while they are on social media themselves.

As you are starting to see, event marketing can be a complex and arduous endeavor. Some marketing agencies exclusively specialize in experiential marketing, the industry term that encompasses booth design and event planning, so give yourself room to learn and grow. Your first event will not be your best event, but you will get better with time.

Doing your best to capitalize on the many opportunities a gaming convention presents is most important. Even if you are not the ultimate salesperson or the perfect booth manager, if you are making the effort to step outside your comfort zone, to create and seize new business opportunities, you are on the right path and well-ahead of the average indie.

Press Engagement: Earning Media Coverage

Press coverage is always beneficial for an indie game, but it is especially important when your following is small. When someone writes about your game, even if they are not the world's biggest blogger, they share your project with their following, so one journalist can mean access to dozens if not thousands of players.

A great press pickup in isolation will not make your game a hit, but we consistently see spikes in Wishlists and game sales when an article, YouTube review, or podcast interview is released. Those spikes are even larger when they are integrated into a broader marketing plan where a press moment happens in conjunction with social media activity, a Discord promotion, Twitch streams, and presence at an event.

On the one hand, the growth of the games industry has meant an increase in the number of outlets and journalists who cover games. On the other hand, games journalism is highly competitive, so their own budgets are limited and requests from indie developers like yourself flood their inboxes on a daily basis.

Press engagement is difficult, which is why even juggernaut gaming companies like CD Projekt Red hire specialized game PR firms to enhance their marketing efforts. For indies, this is another point where a publisher can be a big help because they have likely built a network of relationships from releasing several games a year, but you should still be proactive about press engagement whether you have a publisher or not.

The best indies find creative ways to generate press coverage throughout the development of their games, not just at launch. Launch coverage is crucial, of course, but a steady trickle of coverage for a game is part of building anticipation (and Wishlists) over time to make the actual release more successful.

A press beat is a planned moment where you expect to get coverage, and a typical calendar of press beats for an indie game likely includes stories about:

- A new publisher relationship
- A reveal of a major game feature
- The announcement of the release date
- Launch
- The reveal of new platform support
- A new trailer release
- Attendance at an event
- Receipt of an award or recognition
- A new partnership or brand integration
- Plans for a physical edition or DLC
- Notable talent joining the project
- A charity initiative tied to the game

Not every story will hit the frontpage of *IGN*, but over the course of your game's development, you should work to generate a stream of press moments. If at first that coverage only comes from niche bloggers and YouTubers with only a few hundred subscribers, that's okay, and that's to be expected. Every piece of press can matter, and those smaller pieces of coverage can make it more likely for a bigger publication to write a story about your game because they see that your game is already generating interest.

Standard press beats can give you a framework to start from, but know that all of your competitors will be following a similar structure. Looking for and creating new press-worthy moments can lead to a significant marketing advantage.

If we revisit our earlier story about the *Sea of Stars* Kickstarter campaign from Sabotage Studios, the press beats for that campaign alone included:

- The announcement that the Kickstarter was live.
- The reveal of the *Sea of Stars* trailer.
- The news that Yasunori Mitsuda was contributing music to the game.
- The project reaching its fundraising goal.
- The stretch goal for adding DLC being met.
- The final total raised at the end of the campaign

The beautiful part of this campaign is that we can't tell from the outside what coverage was organic and what coverage came from previous press relationships. Each beat was notable, interesting, and gave journalists room to focus on the elements that made the most sense for their audience. A general gaming news site might share the trailer as these kinds of publications often do, but a retro-focused publication could tell the story of Mitsuda's contributions to *Chrono Trigger* and share their sincere enthusiasm around his involvement.

When you find yourself preparing for press engagement, be thoughtful about what your press contacts care about. A broad, general press blast can generate some traction, but we have found that understanding the kinds of stories a journalist or an outlet prefers to cover makes it easier to build relationships and generate meaningful coverage. If you're announcing that your game is coming to Xbox, pull your friend at *Nintendo Enthusiast* from your contact list but circle back when you have confirmed support for the Switch. Reporters receive dozens of e-mail s a day and if you send them irrelevant information, they may block you. Look at *Rock Paper Shotgun*, they specifically call out on their site that they are PC only.

The basic philosophy of how to build beats and the suggestion to target certain journalists with certain kinds of stories is helpful, but the value of the knowledge is low if you don't have press contacts. If we continue with the assumption that you are at the beginning of your indie journey (or at least this part), you have a great deal of work ahead of you, but the challenge is surmountable.

To build your press list, start with the following:

- Choose an organizational structure for tracking and managing your press contacts. Eventually, you may want to invest in a relationship management system, but for now a spreadsheet that includes the journalist's name, the publication(s) they write for, their Twitter handle, and tags about their major content focuses (like PlayStation RPGs).

- Gather press contacts at gaming events. If you take our advice and are friendly with everyone who visits your booth, you will meet several creators organically. Ask for their card, add them to your database, and follow up with them.

- Follow target journalists and interact with them. If you see a great article about retro twin-stick shooters and your game is also a retro twin-stick shooter, add that writer on Twitter and send them an e-mail with a genuine reaction to their article (not a request for coverage) to start building a connection.

- Build a list of platform-specific publications and general gaming publications who have default e-mails for news tips or specific processes for submitting stories for coverage.

- Set up Google Alerts for your studio name and game name so that you get a notification when someone covers your game.

- If a journalist or creator does a piece on your game, send them a thank you note. Ask them if you can help them in any way and offer to send them the next big build or a review key when they are available.

- Maintain a log of press coverage and share those moments on social media. Reamplify the coverage you receive by promoting it on your own social media, and keep a library of the stories written about your game. Your activity on social media can bring you more followers, and a collection of press clippings is a great item to include in your pitches.

The only shortcuts for press engagement are to rely solely on your publisher or to invest in an agency with a great track record for games PR. Both options can be great additions to your strategy under the right circumstances, but remember that our goal with this book is to help you find financial success with your game and to help you build a sustainable business.

A marketing agency can get you great coverage, but once you part ways, they take those press relationships with them. The same is true of a publisher's press connections. The quick wins are great, but unless you make an effort to grow your own network, you will find yourself back at the beginning of the process for your next game.

Lastly, your press engagement strategy should include a press kit that you regularly update over the course of your game's development and release. The goal of a press kit is to simplify the legwork that goes into writing about an indie game by packaging up key assets and information for journalists. Not only does this make your project more accessible for creators, but you can also use the press kit to steer the narrative about your game and to curate what assets are included in articles.

When you have a library of screenshots, trailers, and GIFs premade for a journalist, they are likely to pick from that collection for their article's cover image and body photos, which is far more ideal than relying on the journalist to pull a great shot from a trailer or from a demo.

The exact execution can vary, but an indie game press kit typically includes:

- A fact sheet (game name, developer name, publisher name, target release date, planned platforms, store links, website URL, social media URLs, short game description and a list of key features)
- Game description (a consumer-friendly version of your elevator pitch that describes major features and mechanics)
- Press release (a pre-made article about the game's development and release, written in such a way that a publication can copy and paste it as is and publish it)
- Key art (cover graphics, logos, icons)
- Videos (trailers, longplays)
- Screenshots (curated moments from the game)
- Gifs
- Contact information (who to talk to for more information and how to reach them)

In addition to linking to the press kit from your website, using a platform like IGDB or presskit() can give you a preformatted structure to follow as well as a place to host your assets. Your website or a PR platform can also be useful content hosts.

If you are new to the world of journalism and do not consider yourself a writer, deconstruct the press kits attached to the comparable titles you identified. Many of them will still be online and publicly available, and you can use their approach to guide your own decision making.

Pre-Release Accolades: Building a Body of Social Proof

Your game is one of hundreds of indie titles vying for player and publisher attention each day, and both audiences look for easily identifiable signals that your project might be more remarkable than the rest. Polished key assets and great art direction are a start, but any opportunity to standout could be a competitive advantage. Social proof – in short, someone respectable vouching for your game – can be that shortcut.

You have seen this before even if you did not realize it. On the Steam page for *Spelunky*, the sidebar highlights a few of the several awards *Spelunky* has earned, such as the Excellence in Design Award from the Independent Games Festival and Gamespot's Best of 2012 award. If you had never heard of *Spelunky* in 2012, seeing that award might convince you to spend more time learning about the game instead of clicking away.

Nearly all indie games feature awards like this in some way, utilizing the Steam awards section as well as highlight those awards in trailers and in the body of store pages.

Regardless of the value you might personally assign to game awards of any kind – we recognize that they can be controversial at times – they quickly communicate that someone is willing to stand behind your game, and the more respectable that person or organization is, the more powerful the award.

Social proof comes in many forms beyond awards, such as:

- Placement in an exclusive festival or showcase

- Notable press coverage

- Steam Curator reviews

- Promotion from a popular influencer

- Grant funding from a respectable organization

If you were accepted into PAX Rising or Indie MEGABOOTH, that's notable. It's not a Game of the Year Award, but industry gatekeepers decided that your game warranted a spot at a major event. That matters, and making the effort to submit your game to these kinds of indie initiatives could net you additional awards and recognition as well as indie-friendly events often include a batch of awards distributed by a panel of industry veterans.

Though a big streamer *might* discover your game organically and rave about it on stream, most forms of social proof will not organically fall into your lap. You have to go hunting for them and insert your game into the right events, shows, contests, and conversations.

Try this approach:

- Start local – Most regions, especially near major cities, have local gaming conventions, gaming groups, and grant programs that aim to showcase great hometown developers: Participating in these can help you to build momentum for your social proof campaign.

- Trade up – When you enter larger and larger contests or events, highlighting your previous accolades can show organizers that they should give your game more consideration: After all, it has already won awards, so it might be a safe bet to include in their event.

- Make a press beat – A significant award often becomes a press-worthy moment by default as the organizations distributing them typically work to promote their awards as well: Even if they do this consistently, sharing your latest award with the right press contacts could earn you additional coverage.

- Prioritize your time – Chasing social proof can be a drain on your energy and your time, so while another award for your Steam page would be great, be selective about where you submit, focusing on the events, contests, or communities most relevant to your game.

- Watch your budget – If an award is tied to an event that mandates your attendance, travel costs alone can be significant: Do your best to group opportunities together, attending a great event, submitting to awards and showcases tied to the event, and attending a publisher networking session at the event so you get the most from your investment.

- Find creative workarounds – While awards have straightforward submission processes, less formal forms of social proof, like a positive review from a respected journalist, can come from building rapport or a clever stunt.

- Don't share too early to the wrong audience – Some avenues of social proof are more appropriate for particular stages of development: If a contest favors games nearing release, hold off on submitting your demo.

- Regular players matter too – Make sure to not lose sight of the everyday player, the one who excitedly plays the full demo at your booth and welcomes everyone to your Discord: Highlighting positive reviews from non-celebrities can be impactful, so try cutting highlights of happy players at your booth and shouting-out the great members of your community.

In the hands of a savvy marketer, social proof is another part of an ongoing marketing mix, a piece of the bigger picture that draws more and more attention to a game. This part of your marketing should be woven throughout your pre-launch and post-launch efforts.

Other Marketing Channels

The marketing material we explored thus far encompasses the fundamental marketing tactics relevant to nearly all indies, but they are far from the only marketing channels that might impact the success of your game. Just as 3D modeling can be an artist's specialization or one piece of their general skillset, so too can marketing be a deep specialization for someone in the games industry. That depth is more than we can include in this book, but we can give you a brief primer on the other marketing channels you may encounter as an indie.

Paid Advertising

Ad campaigns are prevalent for games. AAA titles and big-budget mobile games are common sights on primetime television, and nearly every website or platform connected to the internet includes some form of advertising, whether that's search ads, social media ads, banner ads, YouTube pre-roll ads, or featured placement in a feed. For the right game and the right budget, any one of these could bring new players to your game and into your community.

The good news: Digital ad services provide incredibly powerful targeting so that you can deliver your ads to the users that match your ideal player profile.

The bad news: Learning to run digital ads can be an expensive process of trial and error.

When we launch a game, paid ads of some form are typically a part of the campaign. We use them to bring more attention to key press beats and to increase the splash of a release week. In all cases, they are one piece of a larger effort, and we rely on a specialist in digital ads to run those campaigns because staying up to date on platform changes and interface updates is a full-time job.

You can certainly teach yourself to run Facebook ads, Reddit ads, or Google Search ads, but this is yet another skill that takes time, practice, and budget. If you have a small budget and no advertising experience, be cautious with any form of paid advertising. If you do make an investment here, you should strive to spend $1 to $2 USD (or less, ideally) per Wishlist/sale conversion.

Influencer Marketing

Twitch streamers, YouTubers, and TikTokers of varying sizes often pick up indie games organically. They see a game that interests them or their fans recommend one, and they try it on their channels. *Among Us* is the ultimate success story in this corner of marketing because a few Twitch streamers sparked a wildfire of interest in this social deduction game, long after its initial release.

Organic influencer engagement is awesome, but it is also unpredictable and unreliable, so many studios and publishers pay influencers to promote their games. For a pre-agreed amount of activity – such as hours-streamed, videos produced, or tweets made – the influencer charges a pre-agreed fee.

The benefits of influencer marketing are as follows:

- You can find influencers who have already captured and retained your target audience.
- Great influencer content is more interesting than a traditional ad.
- The highly social nature of influencer-created content can extend your reach on social media as well.
- Streamer reactions and memorable gameplay moments can be used for social media clips and highlight reels (if you have permission).

Unfortunately, there are drawbacks to influencer marketing:

- The reach of an influencer is easy to estimate, but predicting at how effective an influencer will be at driving Wishlists or sales is more difficult.
- Finding, recruiting, and coordinating streamer launch streams can be a laborious process of cold e-mails, follow ups, and contract negotiations.
- The return on an influencer spend is more difficult to measure than more straightforward marketing channels, like digital ads.
- Influencer rates can be cost-prohibitive for many indie marketing budgets.

To elaborate on that last point, influencers charge wildly different rates, but a general rule for Twitch streamers is that you should expect to pay $1 per concurrent viewer (CCV for short) per hour streamed. So, if you go to SullyGnome.com or TwitchTracker.com and look up TheBlacktastic, your favorite retro streamer, you can see that he averages 100 viewers, which means you should expect to pay him $100 per hour streamed.

We say this is a general rule because you can often negotiate bulk rates if you are respectful and book the streamer for several hours or sessions of stream time, and the agreement can also include a set number of tweets and permission to use their gameplay footage in social media posts later.

If you manage your own influencer marketing, you are likely to encounter some streamers who overvalue their hourly rate, and you will find streamers who may have a modest Twitch following but command higher rates because they have a knockout TikTok following and a great Twitter presence. All of those variables matter, and you should take them into account when estimating the value of hiring a specific influencer.

For reference, Twitter and Instagram influencers typically charge per 1,000 followers at a rate ranging from $10 to $25. For an influencer with 3,000 followers, therefore, you can expect to pay between $30 and $75 per post or tweet. That's a broad range, but this space varies significantly.

TikTok looks to be trending in this direction as well, but as a platform and as a marketing tool it is still rapidly evolving. At this moment in time, TikTok is looking to be an important part of games marketing, and the early data we've seen TikTok drive for Wishlists and sales suggest that TikToker may ultimately command a higher premium than a comparable Twitter or Instagram following.

YouTube is more difficult to give an average rate for because production value and content length can quickly inflate budgets for even small YouTubers, but expect them to be more costly than Twitch streamers because pre-recorded content can take more time to create, and unlike a Twitch stream that ends when the streamer logs off, a YouTube video is a relatively permanent marketing anchor that can drive traffic for months to come.

The larger an influencer, the less likely they are to conform to these averages. An agent's commission likely becomes a factor, and the volume of paid opportunities a popular influencer receives gives them the negotiating power to command a higher rate and to be selective about what they promote. From a marketing perspective, that's a good thing overall, but you should be careful about betting all of your budget on one influencer.

Don't be afraid to be creative on this front to garner organic or in-kind influencer marketing. Mega Cat Studios, the creators of *Bite the Bullet* successfully partnered with LA Beast, a competitive eater-turned YouTuber with over 2.7 million subscribers and racked up 20 million views for drinking a 20-year-old Crystal Pepsi on video. Mega Cat pitched LA Beast on being an Easter egg (a hidden piece of game content) in *Bite the Bullet* to celebrate his food stunts. LA Beast, and several other competitive eaters, loved this idea and helped to promote the launch on social media.

A similar arrangement can be made with games themselves. *Shovel Knight* has cameoed in over 35 other games, sometimes as an Easter egg and other times as a playable character. For Yacht Club, the cameo is a shoutout *Shovel Knight* to fans while also being a potential avenue to reach new players. For the developer hosting the cameo, the discovery or addition of *Shovel Knight* can be a marketing moment and press beat that targets the sizable community of players that follow *Shovel Knight*.

Just because budgets are tight, don't totally rule out your ability to access influencer marketing.

Curators and Key Distributors

Steam provides a built-in Curator platform where content creators build structured lists of reviews for their followers and receive key offers from developers via the Steam dashboard. Many Steam users follow curators who review certain genres of games so that they can discover more of the kinds of titles that interest them, and they also often follow their favorite content creators.

Fans of *Zero Punctuation!*, produced by Ben "Yahtzee" Croshaw, can follow an unofficial "Yahtzee Recommends" curator on Steam to quickly see Croshaw's recent positive reviews directly in their Steam feed. These fans have come to trust Croshaw's perspective and are happy to discover a new game because of his journalism.

Though Valve does not share the specifics of their algorithm, the way reviews and recommendations influence how often and how high in a search a product will appear in other major ecommerce platforms suggests that Steam likely does something similar. If your game has positive reviews and positive curator recommendations, players are more likely to buy it, so Steam would – in theory – be motivated to show players the games that best meet that criterion.

Even if that's not the case, the organic boost in traffic and sales that curators, as well as individual reviewers, can provide makes them a typical part of a games marketing strategy. The power of reviews of all kinds is also why many developers and publishers distribute large batches of free keys. A higher live player count looks good on Steam, and players who are happy about getting a free game might feel compelled to leave a review, which can then convince a future player to buy the game.

Handing out large batches of keys yourself or via a key distribution service can be beneficial, but it could also torpedo the profitability of your game. As soon as your game page is live on Steam, expect to receive an ongoing deluge of key requests. A few will be well-meaning content creators, but many will be feeders for key resellers that profit at the expense of creators. We recommend sending codes to curators via Steam's Curator Connect program because instead of receiving a key, the curator has the game added to their library.

Be selective with mass key distributions, and carefully vet a key service before making an investment. When you do try a service like that, run a small trial first to see how effective that vendor is for reaching your target players. On services you can also set parameters that penalize people who take a code and don't post content for your game, which helps weed out the nefarious actors. If you see a boost in Wishlists, reviews, and coverage, consider investing more.

Just as we recommend building your own press list, we also recommend building your own pipeline for reviewers and curators. The idea is not to manipulate the quality of your reviews, a practice often described as "astro-turfing," but rather to find consistently engaged reviewers so that you can roughly predict how many reviews you can expect for every 100 keys you give away. When you own and control the list, you can prune the names who take keys but never review, and you can grow it specifically with reviewers who are most relevant for your genre.

However, there are times where you might want to hold off allocating keys for reviews. For instance, if you launch and a major bug pops up and you're seeing mixed reviews. Hold off until you patch that bug and then start allocating keys.

Giveaways

Sometimes a form of key distribution, giveaways use free products or offerings to incentivize reviews, press coverage, and word of mouth. You might partner with Alienware Arena to promote beta keys for your game to their community of users. You know they have an engaged list of players and based on your research you believe that many of those users also match your target player profile. If a player likes the demo, they may Wishlist the game and encourage their friends to check out the game. And, since it's a beta key, you can disable access at your discretion and not give up a sale. Or you can create keys for a demo, which eliminates the need for disabling access.

Alternatively, you could give away a custom controller to grow your e-mail list and Discord server. If someone subscribes or joins, they are entered to win.

Giveaway promotions of any kind almost always lead to a surge of traffic and activity. People will go to your site. They will follow you on Twitter. They will give you their e-mail. But will they ultimately support your work?

No, so be judicious about your giveaways and don't mistake a jump in Twitter followers as a sign of success because they may unsubscribe in droves a few weeks after the giveaway ends or when they get flagged for bot activity. A good giveaway campaign will directly excite your target audience and be slightly less interesting to the wrong audience, so you will often see prominent indies leaning on game-specific products.

While nearly anyone would accept a free game code or a gift card, more of the players who might actually buy your game will be just as excited for a custom pin featuring your main hero because they place value on what the pin represents, not just what it is worth on eBay. That will not entirely eliminate scummy freeloaders, but it helps.

If you choose to runaway giveaway, be thoughtful about your target goal and measure it closely so you are smarter about future giveaway budgets. Also, follow the terms of service for the platforms where you promote the giveaway, and be careful to comply with local and national laws around raffles and collecting user information.

Charity Activations

Using your game to give to a good cause can be an avenue for winning the hearts and minds of players. That can sound self-serving at first, but many indies stumble into cause-marketing just by virtue of wanting to make the world better. If you know what causes matter, you can skip right to using your game for good. Along the way, the players you attract because they like your games and what you stand for will give your business the support it needs to continue giving to charities in the future.

As an experiment, we ran a small charity Twitch campaign to celebrate *The Adventures of Chris*, and through a combination of luck and great input from streamers and viewers, one of the fundraising streams hit the frontpage of Twitch. For the cost of a few keys, we reached several thousand new players, but more importantly, we raised over $4,500 for No Kid Hungry, enabling them to give 45,000 meals to kids in need. We recruited the streamers. We distributed the keys. We set up the Tiltify campaign. And we got to help a lot of children.

And that's a small-scale example of what's possible if you make the effort to do good with your work.

When Extremely OK Games (formerly Matt Makes Games) saw that *Celeste* was gaining popularity amongst speedrunners, they actively supported the scene. They exchanged Discord messages with speedrunners and used their feedback for game updates and improvements. To date, the *Celeste* community has donated thousands to charities because of speedrunners. In one Summer Games Done Quick (2018) race, runners TGH and yoshipro inspired over $8,000 in donations to Doctors Without Borders. That's almost $4 *per second*.

The enthusiasm of the *Celeste* speedrunning community and their resulting generosity is due in large part to Extremely OK Games taking the effort to engage their players directly. The runners deserve a great deal of credit here, but there would be far fewer of them if Extremely OK Games was less active. In addition to being great community leaders, Extremely OK Games has directly supported charities in a number of efforts, including lending *Celeste* to a Itch.io bundle featuring 1,391 creators to benefit NAACP Legal Defense and Educational Fund and Community Bail Fund.

In sum, 814,526 players donated a total of $8,149,814.66 to the Bundle for Racial Justice and Equality, which is an average of $5,858.96 for every creator in the bundle.

That's a lot of players. That's a lot of good to a worthy cause. Everyone wins: Players get to discover new games, developers get to reach new players, and non-profits get more resources to devote to their missions.

Example Calendars and Schedules

Theory and principles are great, but the application of these marketing ideas is a consistent challenge for indies. Maintaining a regular cadence of activity, creating enough content, and regularly managing a community requires an investment of time and potentially budget. Making the game is the most fun for developers, and it's where they feel more comfortable, so they often put-off marketing under the premise of the game itself being more important.

We hope having an example plan gives indies a template for planning their own campaigns. With a schedule in place and a clear plan for each month, we can raise your likelihood of giving your marketing the attention it needs.

Our example schedule is for a hypothetical indie studio with a reasonable amount of funding, enough to pay five team members for 18 months.

Example Launch Calendar

Target Launch Month: March 2023

- Oct. 2021 through Dec. 2021: Team begins development
- January 2022: Social media and Reddit activity begins
- February 2022: Regular social and Reddit engagement continues
- March 2022: The game debuts a a demo at PAX East, which includes a press push, a small ad spend, custom pins, and attendance at a publisher networking event
- April 2022: Finalize publisher deal, announce partnership to press and social media with publisher's network
- May 2022: New gameplay trailer reveal with press and social push to publisher's network
- June 2022: The team exhibits at a regional gaming convention and continues social media activity
- July 2022: The game is featured in a Steam indie game festival
- August 2022: Discord members and select content creators are invited to an exclusive alpha test and are permitted to share the experience
- Sept. 2022: The team reveals a new demo at PAX West, announces a Switch release to go with the PC release, debuts a Switch trailer, reconnects with previous press and pushes to new press, targets Switch fans with a paid campaign
- Oct. 2022: Beta showcase with organic streamers and Discord members
- Nov. 2022: Alienware Arena beta key giveaway, promoted with small ad spend
- Jan. 2023: Official release date push to press and social media
- Feb. 2023: Curator and early reviewer key distribution

- March 2023: Launch campaign that incorporates a press blast, curator and reviewer outreach, a giveaway, launch streamers, Reddit ads, and YouTube ads is coordinated to coincide with exhibiting at PAX East

Even with broad strokes, you can see that this marketing plan is relatively aggressive even for having modest scope. Almost every marketing month has an anchor activation to promote the game, placing a significant amount of demand on you and your team to keep up and still meet development deadlines.

With a larger budget, the team could add GDC, Momocon, and Gamescom to their event schedule. They could run ads on a monthly basis to amplify their social media and drive steady traffic to Steam. They could run developer streams on Steam and Twitch. They could tether every press beat to an accompanying paid influencer effort on Twitch, YouTube, and TikTok. They could post weekly development blogs and monthly Steam updates about their progress.

And on. And on. And on.

Marketing can be a bottomless budget item, so even if you can't afford our example template, you can still benefit from noting the structure and key features. Few activations occur in isolation, and the plan steadily builds toward a grand finale moment of the launch.

And then the team will kick off post-launch efforts to wrangle reviewers, support customers, listen to feedback, and potentially transition into promoting a DLC, a physical collector's release, and a charity event.

If we zoom in, we can also map out what a typical week would look like for this schedule.

Example Social Media Calendar

Daily

- Twitter engagement (replies, likes, and retweets)
- Social media monitoring (your profiles or mentions of your game)
- Community monitoring (reading gaming news and fan posts related to your target player base)
- Marketing e-mail inbox check and management

Weekly

- One screenshot or GIF (gameplay, art, streamer reaction, etc.)
- One community question
- One behind the scenes post (in-progress art, engine view, progression view)
- Reddit community activity (being an active community member)

- Original post to a Reddit community (targeting relevant subreddits no more than once per month)
- Screenshot Saturday participation on Twitter, Facebook, and Reddit
- Optional: Periodically hosts developer streams or uploads development videos

Post volume increases

- During events
- Around major press beats
- As launch nears

With more budget and resources, your team might be able to generate enough original content to post daily and to plan regular collaborations with influencers and creators. You could also mix in periodic ad spends to grow Wishlists and community members and host development streams and Steam streams on a consistent basis.

As a rule, try to make each post a meaningful piece of content. Avoid posting just to check the box of having posted that day. Though volume does matter, engaging and retaining your audience is more important, and uninteresting content will drive them away.

Budget and Measurement

Like every other aspect of indie development, marketing budgets can be highly variable. With persistence and grit, you can personally manage almost everything in our example calendars instead of paying a team member or agency to do it for you. Additionally, your dream publisher might take over many of these items, doing them for you so you can focus more on development, but those costs may also be recoupable, potentially impacting your total revenue potential.

With so much at stake, budgeting carefully is important, but you should also consistently measure and evaluate your marketing to ensure that your marketing budget (both the dollars you spend and the time you spend) is worthwhile.

Example Marketing Budget Breakdown

If we mapped a budget to our example launch calendar, the math might look like this:

- **October 2021**: Team begins development, buys a domain name, and hires a freelancer designer to make a website and logo [$1,000]
- **January 2022**: Website launches. Social media and Reddit activity begins [Part-time community manager begins]

- **February 2022**: Regular social and Reddit engagement continues [Community manager]
- **March 2022**:
  - ○ The game debuts a demo at PAX East [$1,500 + $1,000]*
  - ○ Press push [Community manager]
  - ○ Ad spend [$500]
  - ○ Custom pins [$515]
  - ○ Entry into a publisher networking event [$200]

  Estimate based on historical Indie MEGABOOTH minibooth fees plus lodging and food costs for 2

- **April 2022**: Finalize publisher deal, announce partnership to press and social media with publisher's network [Publisher activation, may be recoupable]
- **May 2022**: New gameplay trailer reveal with press and social push to publisher's network [Publisher activation, may be recoupable]
- **June 2022**: The team exhibits at a regional gaming convention and continues social media activity [$600]
- **July 2022**: The game is featured in a Steam indie game festival [Organic]
- **August 2022**: Discord members and select content creators are invited to an exclusive alpha test and are permitted to share the experience [Organic]
- **Sept. 2022**: The team reveals a new demo at PAX West, announces a Switch release to go with the PC release, debuts a Switch trailer, reconnects with previous press and pushes to new press, targets Switch fans with a paid campaign [Publisher activation, may be recoupable]
- **Oct. 2022**: Beta showcase with organic streamers and Discord members [Organic]
- **Nov. 2022**: Alienware Arena beta key giveaway, promoted with small ad spend [$1,000]
- **Jan. 2023**: Official release date push to press and social media [Organic and Publisher]
- **Feb. 2023**: Media, streamer and early reviewer key distribution [Organic]
- **March 2023**: Launch campaign that incorporates a press blast, curator and reviewer outreach, a giveaway, launch streamers, Reddit ads, and YouTube ads is coordinated to coincide with exhibiting at PAX East [$2,000 for ads, $4,000 for influencers, Publisher supports as well]

Part-time community manager cost for the total duration of the campaign $25,000

All of that adds up to a marketing budget of $38,315, and the delayed costs of a publisher recoup could increase that number as well.

As far as video game budgets go, a marketing budget of approximately $40,000 is not that ambitious, but that is highly relative. Sure, Epic invested $146 million in the *Borderlands 3* exclusive window. That figure encompassed a $80 million minimum guarantee as well as $15 million for marketing. For a solo indie developer scraping together a budget with friends-and-family loan, $40,000 could represent a huge financial risk.

Good marketing is a smart investment as it helps to ensure that players actually hear about your game, but every indie should be as judicious as possible with how and where they put their money. We said that about your development budget, and it applies to your marketing as well. Learning when cutting costs is smart business versus when it hobbles your potential is all about educated bets, and unfortunately that can mean learning from mistakes.

To make a marketing mistake less painful, avoid betting all of your budget on a singular marketing channel or marketing tactic. The material we covered briefly in this chapter all requires great execution to be the most impactful, so the first press release you write won't be perfect. Your first convention booth might be awkward and missing a few pieces. Your first Facebook ad spend could have mixed returns.

That's normal, so spread it out and inject as much manual, organic marketing activity into your plan as your schedule allows. Finding and contacting indie game YouTubers one by one, politely asking them to review your game, is time-consuming and tedious, but it's free. Networking with community leaders and being consistent with social media and Reddit can be equally laborious, but they are also free.

The more you can find clever ways to cross-promote and to collaborate with partners to reach new players without additional budget, the farther your game can go. At the same time, be sure to measure the returns on your efforts so that you can get smarter and smarter about where you spend time and budget for marketing. Remember, it takes trial and error – along with time – to have success with paid avenues.

Crash-Course in Marketing Metrics

We live in the age of big data. Modern marketers deploy an arsenal of tools to track, target, measure, and refine digital marketing to maximize returns. When you can identify the demographics of the perfect customer and move them through a highly optimized sales experience, every marketing dollar becomes more profitable.

One famous story of data-driven marketing is Target's algorithm for recommending products to customers. Based on a teen girl's purchase history, the algorithm correctly predicted that she was pregnant and started to send her coupons and mailers aimed at expecting mothers. The twist is she hadn't told her parents yet, triggering several angry and uncomfortable conversations for both the brand and the family.

In another story, a clever roommate used the versatility of the Facebook ad platform to target his roommate–and only his roommate–with creepy ads. The prank played out over several weeks and has become a marketing industry example of how effective digital ad targeting can be.

The best gaming companies in the world blend their creativity with their understanding of data and metrics to consistently drive sales for their products. Your marketing may never need to be as elaborate as Target's algorithms, but knowing how deep marketing can go is important for your ability to understand new opportunities.

For now, here are the primary key performance indicators (KPIs) that are most relevant to your game:

- Unit sales
- Steam Wishlists
- Steam Follows
- Game Reviews

No matter how many people saw your ad, the effort is wasted if no one actually buys your game, so no matter what marketing you use, evaluate it against these three metrics. An ad that reaches 10,000 players is great in theory, but an ad that reaches 1,000 players and generates 100 sales is better.

The secondary KPIs that are worthwhile to measure and grow are as follows:

- Traffic to store pages
- Newsletter subscribers
- Discord membership
- Social media followers
- Press pickup

We classify these as secondary metrics because they are still valuable to track, but focusing solely on the "high score" of these metrics is a common mistake. You can buy thousands of Twitter followers to jump your follower count over night, but it is ultimately meaningless. Yes, having a large Twitter following is useful, but that's only if those followers are actively supporting your work. When you only chase secondary metrics and don't assess how they drive primary KPIs, you can do a lot of marketing that does not help your business.

Think of secondary metrics as clues that you are on the track, and then take the next step to see how they are affecting Wishlists and sales.

The other metrics that are relevant but are not necessarily KPIs, are as follows:

- Impressions or views (how many people saw an ad or a post or a story?)
- Clickthroughs (how many people interacted with the piece of marketing to learn more?)

- Time-on-page (how long did they stay on your website or store page?)
- Shares (how many people shared your content with someone else?)
- Demographics (who is interacting with your marketing and your products?)

If you took our advice and connected Google Analytics to your Steam page, you have probably already seen that digital analytics can be far more granular than what we have described here. In short, your overall marketing spend should generate more profit than you invest, and metrics help you to make that determination.

Anything you can track has the potential to be useful, but if you are new to marketing, the metrics here are the best place to start.

But there is bad news: Most distribution platforms in our industry provide very little data. The Nintendo eShop will share sales data, but not in real time or with attribution. You can broadly estimate how much traffic an ad, for example, sent to your Switch game, but you will have no way of knowing for sure how many of the sales (if any) came from the ad itself. In the flurry of a launch where several marketing channels are pumping traffic at once, definite conclusions are nearly impossible.

Steam is making an effort to provide more data transparency to developers and publishers, but the rollout is slow. Recently, they added UTM tracking support (the ability to attribute Steam actions to referral URLs), but that support is limited to web purchases. If your player sees your game and their click automatically opens the Steam app, the attribution disconnects.

Between limits on conversion data and the complexity of an indie game marketing campaign, how can you tell if you are being effective?

Try the following:

- Use the lead-up to launch to run a series of tests. If you refer back to our example marketing schedule, you can see that many marketing efforts are initially launched in isolation or in small batches. That approach helps you to better correlate changes in Wishlists to your recent marketing, giving you a way to identify what is effective and what can be improved.

- Look for trends. Few marketing campaigns are fully optimized at the beginning, especially if you are starting with a small organic audience. If your audience growth and Wishlist rates steadily improve over time, you are on the right track.

- Centralize your analytics. Tools like Google Data Studio enable you to centralize your reporting to one dashboard, a handy time-saver for a busy indie. When you can see your KPIs at a glance, checking them with more regularity is much easier.

- Delegate to experts. Early-on, hiring an agency or a full-time marketer may not be possible, but as you generate revenue, consider handing off marketing to a dedicated resource. You should still monitor your KPIs when you do this, but having a specialist run the execution can increase your returns.

An Extension of Your Game

Just as adjusting your scope to match the math of your sales projections can feel dirty, like it is contradictory to the creative passion that may have drawn you to indie game development in the first place, marketing can feel that way as well. Asking people for money is an odd feeling for many creatives. If that sentiment applies to you, reframe how you think about marketing relative to your game.

If you think back to how you discovered the games you love, you will likely find that you actually enjoyed being marketed to. You were happy to have found a new game to experience, and the marketing actually felt like an extension of that experience rather than a slick way to open your wallet.

For fans of the *Monster Hunter* series, waiting in line at E3 to pose with a comically large weapon and a giant dragon is an exciting part of being a fan. Yes, Capcom is marketing the next expansion with their booth presence, but they are doing it in a way that expands and elevates the fan experience. For these players, they are grateful for the marketing because it speaks to what they love about the games they play and enhances it.

A Discord community is not so different. It's a marketing vehicle, yes, but interacting with fellow fans and building friendships also adds value. Your players are better for having participated because your marketing genuinely brought them joy.

Even a tactic as classically manipulative as an advertisement can be approached this way. If your Facebook ad is well targeted and speaks truthfully about what players can expect if they buy it, the transaction that follows is just as beneficial to the player as it is to you. Players want to discover and support great games. You made that easier so that they can spend less time shopping and more playing.

PART 5

Post-Release

DOI: 10.1201/9781003215264-18

Sabotage Studios and *The Messenger*

From Lackluster Sales to $1.6 Million on Kickstarter

———

The Messenger, developed by Sabotage Studios and published by Devolver Digital, is highly regarded in the indie game community. Their trajectory was not a rocket-propelled ascension into record sales, however. *The Messenger* earned its success over the long tail of their game sales.

The Messenger is a stunning action-platformer that was inspired by the classic game series *Ninja Gaiden*, which was originally released in 1988 as an arcade game and later migrated to the NES. In *The Messenger,* you play as a ninja who is making his way through a cursed world to deliver a scroll that will save his people.

Between the art, the story, and the gameplay, the game offered a memorable, unique gameplay experience, and the reception upon release was incredibly positive.

Destructiod called it "The Switch's best indie yet" and went on to say "it's safe to say this is a cut above the rest."

Nintendo World gave it a 10/10 saying *The Messenger* is a "Masterful and Smart Adventure."

With critical acclaim like this, (and many more positive reviews) Sabotage Studios co-founder Martin Brouard anticipated a smash hit.

In an interview with *Gamesindustry.biz*, Brouard shared, "Seeing how the critical reception is, I was expecting [sales to be] a little higher. We are just under 50,000 units on all platforms after a little more than a week, which is really a good start. But if we compare ourselves to some of the other indie hits recently, it might be a little under them."

Brouard was not alone in his surprise as passionate players and indie evangelists found the sales number puzzling also.

However, the game went on to be very successful. According to Steam Spy it sold between 200,000 and 500,000 copies. And that's just on Steam! It's also available on Nintendo Switch, PlayStation 4, and Xbox One.

Of course, every game wants to be successful at launch, but launch performance is not always the best indicator of how successful a game will actually be. In addition to devotedly nurturing your community as excitement for your game grows, the

234

long slope of sales extending long beyond release day can be the most profitable part of a game. Consider how many units you will sell over time, plus the opportunities from DLC's, console releases, physical releases, and even your game's soundtrack (if you own the soundtrack rights). Sabotage Studios leveraged the praise of early reviewers to tap into several revenue channels while continuing to find new players.

The long-term success of Sabotage Studios' *The Messenger* helped to fund another game within the same universe, *Sea of Stars*. It raised $1,628,126 on Kickstarter.

With the combination of their own creative business insights and the support of publisher Devolver Digital, *The Messenger* has given Sabotage Studios momentum and stability that has enabled them to continue growing.

https://www.gamesindustry.biz/articles/2018-09-12-the-messengers-special-delivery

https://www.destructoid.com/reviews/review-the-messenger/

https://www.kickstarter.com/projects/sabotagestudio/sea-of-stars

https://store.steampowered.com/app/764790/The_Messenger/

https://steamspy.com/app/764790

What about Second Launch?

You did it! You released your game. Congratulations on the monumental achievement. Getting to this point is difficult, and many aspiring indies lose motivation and abandon their projects long before they are ready for a release.

The journey is not over. In Part 2, we highlighted the fact that many indies overlook the amount of work that comes after a launch. They don't have a plan for tackling post-launch activities effectively, and they forget that they need a budget for that work as well.

To recap, you should assume that a typical post-launch campaign for a game will include the following:

- Bug fixes and content updates
- Review management
- Community engagement
- Ongoing marketing and press
- Discount promotions and bundle participation
- Facilitating more revenue opportunities

The first four items on that list are self-explanatory. Players will find bugs that you missed in QA, and fixing them helps to ensure the long-term success of your sales by making every future play through more enjoyable. Whether reviews are positive or negative, you should monitor them for actionable opportunities.

If a negative review is a result of a bug, you can follow up with a polite message when the bug is fixed, inviting them to play the game again and to message you if they continue to encounter problems. For positive reviews, amplifying them and connecting with excited creators can turn one happy player into dozens of new players.

Along the way, your social media marketing efforts will continue and new chances to generate press coverage may arise as well.

DOI: 10.1201/9781003215264-19

The larger post-launch activities, the ones that require more coordination and planning than having developers available to fix bugs, are also significant revenue opportunities.

Discounts and Bundles

Valve told *GamesIndustry.biz* that 51% of Wishlist conversions "occur during discount events, including discounts applied to launch." That insight may not be mind blowing because that is how many of us have come to use Steam. If we are on the fence about buying a game, we add it to our Steam Wishlists and revisit it when we get the e-mail that it is on sale.

That behavior is why, to take us all the way back to where we started in Part 1, "19 percent of all #ishlist adds convert to sales within 12 months" (according to Valve).

If you stop promoting and supporting your game at launch, you immediately eliminate a great deal of potential revenue. Even if you are not actively adding content, you should plan to leverage your game for at least 12 months after its release so that you can reach as many players and move as many units as possible.

Discounts are one of the most common long-term tactics for generating revenue, and it is also one that is applied very differently across the spectrum of the games industry.

Tom Giardino of Valve shared this with *GamesIndustry.biz* in 2020: "There is no single correct discounting strategy [for Steam]." He points out that the platform hosts highly successful developers who have never discounted their titles while other developers who frequently offer large discounts have also been successful.

That is not very helpful, but it echoes a persistent theme in the business of games, which is that there is no blueprint for guaranteed success, so you have to be thoughtful about making the choices that are right for you, your game, and your players.

If you have a publisher, they will take on the responsibility of managing discounts and promotions in all likelihood. They have the benefit of seeing sales trends from all of their titles and will have had more experience with every part of the discount process. Their recommendation is likely worth following, but if you find yourself in a position where you have input into (we recommend having some input if you're working with a publisher) or total control over your discounting strategy, these best practices can help.

A Launch Discount Is Probably a Good Idea

Players have come to expect a launch-day discount from indie Steam releases. In some ways, you consider it a small "thank you" to the players who supported your game up until that point, rewarding them for having Wishlisted and for showing up on a day one to buy. At the same time, that launch day discount is a simple way to convert early players, so don't be afraid to offer a 10%– 15% discount on release.

Gradually Increase Discounts over Time

The temptation to cut your game price by 50% a few months after release will be strong. You can be assured it will move units, which can be highly attractive as you stare down the budget for your next project, but those quick sales could come at the cost of reducing your overall revenue potential. If you jump to big discounts, smaller discounts in the future will look less enticing, slowing your overall sales momentum for the laggards on your Wishlist. They saw you did 50% once before, so why buy now at 20% when they could just wait?

Additionally, a large portion of your unconverted Wishlists may not need a giant discount to convince them to buy. If you could convert them at a 20% discount instead, you preserve more of your profit margin. Over the course of a 12-month period, the few extra dollars you might capture with this mindset can result in a substantial amount of revenue.

Therefore, steadily trend toward a large discount over time, and use your sales data to decide whether you offer a bigger discount for the next sale. If you run a 15% discount twice in a row and convert roughly the same number of Wishlists, you may be able to wait a few promotional periods before going lower.

Steam Sales Are Not the Only Sales

Official Steam sales are big marketing moments, but they should not be your only promotional windows. You should look to coordinate your own Steam promotions outside of the Valve calendar, and you tap into your other platforms for sales opportunities as well. Every platform has its own promotional calendar, and even if they serve the same types of players (such as GOG serving PC gamers alongside Steam), the difference in audience and marketing support can be enough that a sale on Steam followed by a sale on GOG puts you in front of different customers.

Then extend that mentality to Xbox, PlayStation, and Switch. Look for natural spikes in player enthusiasm, including a new hardware update or a surge of interest in a comparable title (where your game may appear as a similar title within the store). You can also participate in themed sales in collaboration with other developers to make each discount more profitable.

Account for Sales Fatigue

Players have learned to anticipate major sales events, so if Valve has announced the dates for it's next big promotion, sales are likely to dip in the immediate weeks prior to the event. After the event, sales are likely to dip again as consumers recover from the excitement and the expense.

Therefore, you should avoid running an independent promotion in these periods, and you should also be ready to see those fluctuations reflected in your sales trends. The humanity here – players only have so much money and so much energy – is important and extends into your frequency of discounts as well. If you are constantly pushing another great discount, your audience will begin to lose interest in you and your game.

If your game is always on sale, a sale is no longer a special moment. If you are always talking about sales, you are likely talking less about the things your community actually cares about. That matters, and handling it poorly can alienate players.

Be Strategic with Bundle Promotions

Gamers love to buy bundles. They come with great discounts, and the mix of getting games you know you want while also getting to discover games you aren't familiar with is fun and rewarding. For developers and publishers, the bundle experience makes them a different kind of opportunity.

Your game is not just on sale; it's packaged with a batch of other games. Some players will get the bundle because they want your game, but if you are 1 out of 10 games in the bundle, you can safely assume that most of the sales were not motivated by your game specifically. These are, potentially, entirely new players that you may not have touched with your previous marketing efforts.

The immediate sale is a win, but this exposure to new players is a chance to tie a bundle promotion to a secondary effort. On Steam you can also organize your own bundles with fellow developers to ensure that your title doesn't get lost in a larger bundle. These bundles can be of any size and you can even create one with just your games, if you have a few on your roster.

If you are releasing a DLC, timing it in conjunction with a bundle can get new players into your community who may then pay full price for the DLC. You could also pair the bundle with any number of social or community activations designed to retain those new players. That could be a giveaway, a contest, or an event.

Charity Activations

Thanks to the success of Humble Bundle, many bundle programs include a charity initiative where a developer donates a portion or the totality of proceeds to a good cause. Beyond bundles, you can coordinate your own fundraiser or contribute to established events such as SpeedGaming's annual marathon to benefit No Kid Hungry or RPG Limit Break's event to benefit National Alliance on Mental Illness (NAMI).

For events like these, a batch of free keys can motivate streamers to participate and can be given to donors who contribute. In this format, you are not selling keys in any way, so there is no immediate profit. However, for the effort of generating a few keys, you can win over new players using an approach similar to the bundle philosophy just described. New players will discover your game, giving you a chance to win them over permanently.

Secondary Platforms

Steam, Epic, Xbox, PlayStation, and Switch are not the only places where players buy games. If you release your game on additional platforms, even if they still target PC gamers, you can access new players. Depending on the platform and the trajectory of your game, these secondary platforms may offer minimum guarantees. More often, however, they are more open to providing marketing and promotional support for a new title because they are smaller and willing to negotiate.

In some cases, these platforms can be a part of your primary launch, but many indies end up migrating to them 6–12 months after their initial release. Oftentimes, these platforms are territory-based and releasing on them after your initial launch will help with the game's long tail sales. Some examples of platforms include:

- GOG
- Green Man Gaming
- Fanatical
- Genba
- Buka
- Plug in Digital
- Nuuvem

Each platform has its own selection criteria submission process, so read up on their guidelines and expect to work through a pitch and sales process. Aim to begin talks shortly after your launch if you can. The excitement surrounding your release will give you an advantage during negotiations.

Not all of these platforms will be the right fit, nor will they all accept your game, so be prepared to have several pitch sessions to find new platform partners.

Unlocking Additional Revenue Channels

Finding more revenue beyond sales is highly circumstantial. As we discussed in Part 1, you have several options for generating more profit from your game, from DLC to merchandise, but one size does not fit all. Revisit Chapters 1–3 for a refresher on potential revenue channels and the major considerations that might make a revenue source a viable option, such as having a notable musician produce your soundtrack and releasing that as a separate download and physical collectible.

If music is not a standout part of your game – or, perhaps, you do not have the rights to distribute it in other commercial forms beyond your game – that option is not a fit for you.

Our emphasis on pre-release planning should help you to anticipate what avenues are most likely a fit, so now we have to decide if they are ultimately worthwhile. Additionally, keep yourself open to opportunities. During your pre-release planning you might have a T-shirt or other merch planned to release post-launch, but if you have successful sales, you'll likely have new opportunities arise that you didn't think were possible.

The Size of Your Customer Pool

The marketing associated with any post-launch activation will always have the potential to attract new players, but the majority of post-launch products and content expansions target existing players. If you loved *Cuphead*, you likely can't wait to play the DLC, *The Delicious Last Course*. Passionate players want more, and DLC is one way to give them more.

Because DLC – or merchandise, or soundtracks, or physical releases – rely heavily on existing players, we can roughly estimate the profit potential of a follow-up activity.

If we operate under the assumption that the reception for your game has been positive, we can guess that 15–30% of your current players will buy DLC. We say "guess" because publicly available data is limited on this front, and the data we do have is murky at best.

A 2020 study from the NPD Group (and reported on by *SegmentNext*) found that 28% of players have paid for additional content, but the study notes that players were "more likely to buy microtransactions rather than DLC."

Back in 2010, Jim Sterling, writing for *Destructoid*, reported that only 15% of gamers buy DLC. Granted, that's a long time ago in the context of gaming, and no one can deny that microtransaction and ongoing content monetization models have exploded in the last decade, but we want you to make careful choices about investment into more development.

If you look, you can find studies that report that as many as 62% of players will buy DLC, but none of these estimates indicate whether or not players will buy *your* DLC even if they are likely to buy DLC in general. More comparable title research can help you to benchmark how popular DLC is within your target genre, but even then, do not let optimism mislead you.

If 5% of your players bought your DLC, would you turn a profit? How does that math look if you consider a dire scenario of a 1% conversion rate? Those numbers may sound small, but in most realms of digital marketing, a 5% conversion rate is a legendary level of performance. The games industry is more complicated, but advise developers to prepare for best- and worst-case scenarios.

That logic should apply to any monetization effort that relies on reactivating your current player base, whether that's $0.99 microtransaction or a special edition physical Switch release.

Player Demand

The math around your customer pool is a quick way to eliminate unprofitable choices, but if the math works in your favor, your diligence is not yet complete. Even if you have a strong player base, are you sure that they actually want your followup offering? Hundreds of indie games have successfully marketed DLC or T-shirts or plushies, and even more have failed.

Before you begin to pursue another form of monetization, consider taking these steps.

Assess Your Level of Access to Players

Using your total player base to estimate the viability of another product is a good start, but you should also consider your ability to market to them. Selling 10,000 units is great, but how many of those players are you directly connected to? Are they on your e-mail list? Are they in your Discord? Do they follow you on Twitter? If you don't have a reliable way to talk to your players, you should consider that too few will hear about your new merchandise to justify the investment.

Listen to Your Players

Gamers are not shy about sharing their opinions, directly or indirectly. If players want more content or want to buy a T-shirt, they will often say so, but that means that you and your team need to be present to listen. Monitoring player reactions across the web can help, as can directly asking players what they would like to see next from your team. That does not mean you should always do what players request because oftentimes it's a vocal few talking the loudest. But if you spend a weekend at a convention having players ask about plushie versions of your cute protagonist, you may want to explore that opportunity.

Start with Small Tests

Unless you really love (like really really) a T-shirt design, no indie needs four boxes of unsold shirts stuffed into their closet. Before you invest in a big merchandise order or in building a full-featured expansion, use smaller, less risky tests to evaluate player's true interest. For merchandise, that could mean preorders for, or a small limited run of, a product. For DLC, that could mean releasing a free cosmetic.

For a vinyl album, that could mean releasing the digital soundtrack on Steam. If players place preorders, if they log in to get the cosmetic, if they pay for the digital soundtrack, you have data to support that a bigger effort could be profitable. Another option is to poll players to see what they might be interested in. We've done this with posters, which helped us print the posters fans actually wanted and not what we thought they wanted.

Find a Partner

The right partner can help you solve the conundrum of player access and post-launch production. Though DLC is usually done in-house, your publisher may be open to funding a portion of the development, whether that was the publisher you launched with or a publisher you engage to port your game to consoles. On the merchandise front, working with an established vendor can reduce your financial risk, simplify execution and management, and also give you an additional marketing channel. Retailers such as The Yetee and Fangamer have established communities in their own rights, so working through them can give you access to more customers along the way. Just like platforms, some retailers will need pitching and this is where you'll need to leverage your game's success in order to secure that partnership.

Deciding Scope

The size of your followup effort should be right-sized to the market opportunity while fitting within your larger business plan. If your team does not have motivation or interest in releasing a DLC, that matters. If you are already working on your next game or want to move onto your next game, you could still do a DLC, but you may see more opportunity in your next project so you scale back the size of your DLC.

For merchandise, just because you sell one plushy does not mean that you always have to sell plushies or that you have to add new plushies to your line. You can capitalize on fan excitement with a limited edition release to avoid manufacturing too many units, and then you can move on. Merchandise is one of the easiest ways to overextend a budget, so moving cautiously is a smart approach.

Understand the New Business

You are running an indie game studio, adding a merchandise line does not change that, but it does mean learning another type of business with rules and considerations different from gaming. Selling T-shirts is not the same as selling games, so you should take the time to research the commitment you're making and how your new products typically generate revenue before you order thousands of shirts and boot-up a Shopify store.

Most of the themes in this book still apply. Know your margins. Look at production timelines. Consider fulfillment costs and logistics. Build a business and marketing plan specifically for those products if you are making a large investment. And look for common traps and pitfalls that surprise new business owners in that space.

For example, merchandise looks deceptively simple to incorporate and manage, but several hidden costs and responsibilities can suck up your profits. Many new businesses look to outsource manufacturing to save on costs, often shipping in products from China, but they do not factor in important processes and requirements, many of which can require a specialized attorney.

Using a third party fulfillment service to manage your orders and customer service also looks straightforward, but many of these services charge "per pick" (for each product they ship on your behalf) and also charge storage fees. The more palettes of products you have sitting in their warehouse, the more you get charged each month. If you do not sell merchandise quickly, those fees can cannibalize your hope for profits.

Your work in games will open many doors for you, but that does not mean you have to personally walk through all of them.

Open for New Opportunities

Our industry changes quickly, so you are likely to encounter a range of startups and new product ideas in the course of your work. We cannot predict what one of those new opportunities might look like, but in the past we have seen indies partner with board game companies, incorporate their games into other product campaigns, and be one of the first to release a game on a new platform.

At one point, the Epic Games Store was a new idea. One indie had to go first, and the chance to be that indie is commonly a result of great business practices. You develop relationships with the right contacts so they think of you when they see something new, and you have the credibility of an established, trustworthy studio. If you continue to look at the industry through a creative lens, you are likely to find revenue channels that may not be as typical as selling T-shirts but can be another way to profit from your game.

The Next Game

We began this book with the goal of arming you with the knowledge and the tools you need to build a successful, sustainable indie games business. That emphasis on sustainability underpinned every major idea we covered because we don't want your first game to be your last game. We want you to be in a position where each project gives you access to more resources and gives you more freedom to fully explore your creative ideas.

For your first game, that means finding and securing funding to get you through development and into a position where you can generate revenue with game sales. That process is difficult and often painful because you may have to go months without an investor or publisher providing support, so each month is a *Mission Impossible* dance around bills and surprise expenses.

Do not go back to that same starting point to face the same challenges for your next game. Use your first game to give you a headstart on developing and funding the next so you can spend fewer months desperate for funding and more time focusing on making games.

Stay Lean. Stay Scrappy.

If you are fortunate enough to have a highly successful first game, do not let a deluge of short-term profits obscure your long-term vision. We have given you multiple strategies for extending the profitability of your game, but the average indie game sees a steady dwindle in sales, month over month, no matter how savvy they are. Few indies make a game so successful that they do not have to make another to stay in business.

A big paycheck can make all of the careful budgeting and planning practices you worked to put in place seem less important. Resist that temptation. Take care of your people. Pay your bills. File your taxes. And then set aside the remaining profits for an emergency fund or as a direct reinvestment into your studio. You have

DOI: 10.1201/9781003215264-20

another development cycle ahead, and that capital will make it less frantic and give you more leverage to negotiate.

Get a Headstart

The publisher side of your business experience hates this advice because we self-ishly want our indies to have 100% of their focus on the game they are launching with us, but when it comes to running a games studio, beginning development on your next game as you near the launch of your current game can be a savvy way to maintain momentum.

When you work on one game at a time, you risk having a large gap between the launch of one game and the beginning of funding for the next. When you overlap development timelines, you can have the materials you need to build a new pitch deck and begin talking to publishers.

While your team gets players excited for the release of your game on the convention floor, you can be across the street in the hotel lobby reconnecting with the publisher you met last year. Your first pitch to them was not a fit for their focus, but your next project is. You know them. They know you. They saw your game make headlines. They stopped by your booth and saw a line of gamers waiting to play.

The immediacy of those feelings is exciting for everyone. At a minimum, you get a few months ahead of the pitch cycle. At best, your next injection of funding comes alongside your first royalty checks, allowing you to staff-up and add better tools for your team. As development picks up speed on the upcoming title, you can continue to generate profits from the first as well.

With careful planning and a dash of luck, the success of your games will grow from title to title. Your existing fans support your next project and new players join them. You make smarter business decisions, so you get more from your budget while you also have a larger network of connections to collaborate with.

Nothing is easy about this. You know that most new businesses fail, and that failure rate is particularly high in games, but everything we covered will help you skip over dozens of painful–and very expensive lessons.

The Merits and Pitfalls of a Sequel

The obvious choice for your next game might appear to be a sequel. Your first game explored only a portion of your game universe, and the foundational characters and gameplay mechanics are established and reasonably polished.

Reconsider

Returning to your beloved game world may feel good for you, but it can erect a barrier between you and your next opportunities. When players see a sequel, they assume that they need to have played the first to fully enjoy the second, so a large chunk of your player base will have to come from your existing community, bringing us back to the same conundrum we faced when evaluating the business merits of producing DLC.

In the case of the sequel, that same barrier that deters players can also deter new investors and publishers. They see the challenges of marketing a follow up, and they might feel that they missed out on the full potential of their investment by not being part of the first game. As we've said before, do the math. Just because someone bought your game doesn't necessarily mean they will purchase the sequel.

Exceptions exist for this advice, of course. Even if you do not have a sequel, ask the publisher for your first game if they would like to support your next project. If your relationship has been positive and sales have been healthy, they may be interested in continuing to grow alongside your studio. If your publisher believes in the sequel potential and helps to fund its development, your combined resources could address the typical challenges of marketing a sequel.

Likewise, when sales of the first game are high enough, a sequel or ongoing content development can be an obvious choice.

InnerSloth, the team behind *Among Us*, trashed their development for *Among Us 2* when they saw their first installment suddenly finding massive traction. Because of the nature of the game, the pivot to focusing exclusively on supporting *Among Us* gave InnerSloth the bandwidth to fully capitalize on the new wave of interest. They could improve gameplay, fix bugs, and add content, retaining the player count the game needs to be fun so that it could continue to attract new players.

Conversely, Moon Studios immediately followed *Ori and the Blind Forest* with a sequel, *Ori and the Will of the Wisps*. Published by Microsoft Studios (now known as Xbox Game Studios), Moon Studios had the advantage of a great partner, but the strength of the game itself was remarkable. *Game Rant* reported that *Ori and the Blind Forest* turned a profit for Microsoft Studios in its first week and has gone on to sell more than 2 million copies in its lifetime.

Not surprisingly, Microsoft returned to publish the sequel, so between the massive sales momentum and the support of a large partner, the business merits of a sequel were likely clear for Moon Studios.

That could be the case for you, and we hope it is, but no matter what, we hope that whatever decision you make is carefully considered.

It's Dangerous to Go Alone

The indie community has a long tradition of supporting and sharing with each other. To date, this spirit of collaboration has been largely on the development side of the industry with very little knowledge about the business of games changing hands.

We Want That to Change

If this book helps you to find indie success, we urge you to pay it forward. Share your experiences–your failures and your triumphs – with your peers. Mentor young indies. Volunteer to give talks at events and schools. Any success we have enjoyed has come as a result of the great people around us, whether that's our own mentors or our teammates or our partners. Those people made our careers possible, so we believe we have a duty to do our part to build the next link in that chain.

And now it's your turn. Make great games, and make a difference.

REFERENCES

Side quests

1 (Supergiant Games and Bastion)

Noclip. (2019, December 23). *The Making of Bastion - Documentary*. YouTube. https://www.youtube.com/watch?v=uo7TcJ2E0-I.

J. Michael Leon's LinkedIn. LinkedIn. (n.d.). https://www.linkedin.com/in/j-michael-leon-4388731/.

2 (Ori and the Will of the Wisps)

Doolan, L. (2020, February 28). *The project AM2R creator now designs levels for the Ori developer Moon Studios*. Nintendo Life. https://www.nintendolife.com/news/2020/02/the_project_am2r_creator_now_designs_levels_for_the_ori_developer_moon_studios.

Dring, C. (2020, March 10). *Building Ori and the Will of the Wisps with 80 people working from home*. GamesIndustry.biz. https://www.gamesindustry.biz/articles/2020-03-10-building-ori-and-the-will-of-the-wisps-with-80-people-working-from-home.

Lane, G. (2021, January 1). *Moon Studios on Ori and the Will of the Wisps' journey from Xbox to Switch*. Nintendo Life. https://www.nintendolife.com/news/2021/01/feature_moon_studios_on_ori_and_the_will_of_the_wisps_journey_from_xbox_to_switch.

Square Enix to make work from home permanent as of December 1. Square Enix. (n.d.). https://www.jp.square-enix.com/company/en/news/2020/html/df9995782da2d516db9ebac425d02d4019665f70.html.

3 (Enter the Gungeon)

Sinclair, B. (2016, May 9). *Dodge Roll's speedrun to indie success*. GamesIndustry.biz. https://www.gamesindustry.biz/articles/2016-05-09-dodge-rolls-speedrun-to-indie-success.

4 (Risk of Rain)

Cameron, P. (2019, August 14). *How moving from 2D to 3D shaped the design of Risk of Rain 2*. Game Developer. https://www.gamedeveloper.com/disciplines/how-moving-from-2d-to-3d-shaped-the-design-of-i-risk-of-rain-2-i-.

DevBlog #1 - Our Next Project. Hopoo Games DevBlog. (2017, May 8). https://web. archive.org/web/20180118042945/http://hopooo.tumblr.com/post/160452455554/ devblog-1-our-next-project-weve-been-working.

Fenlon, W. (2019, April 4). *Risk of Rain 2 devs talk hitting 500,000 players, mod support, and what's coming next.* PC Gamer. https://www.pcgamer.com/uk/risk-of-rain-2-devs-talk-hitting-500000-players-mod-support-and-whats-coming-next/.

Kerr, C. (2019, May 3). *Risk of Rain 2 crosses 1 million sales in first month.* Game Developer. https://www.gamedeveloper.com/business/-i-risk-of-rain-2-i-crosses-1-million-sales-in-first-month.

McAloon, A. (2019, March 27). Risk of Rain 2 is running a buy-one-get-one free launch promo. https://www.gamedeveloper.com/console/-i-risk-of-rain-2-i-is-running-a-buy-one-get-one-free-launch-promo.

Meet our team. Hopoo Games. (n.d.). https://hopoogames.com/meet-our-team/.

Risk of Rain 2 on Steam. Steam. (n.d.). https://store.steampowered.com/app/632360/ Risk_of_Rain_2/.

Rodriguez, J. (2021, April 30). *Risk of Rain 2: An interview with Paul Morse of Hopoo Games.* PC Invasion. https://www.pcinvasion.com/risk-of-rain-2-interview-paul-morse/.

Stadia Team. (2020, September 24). *Interview with Hopoo Games on Risk of Rain 2, Arriving Sept. 29 on Stadia.* Stadia. https://community.stadia.com/t5/Stadia-Community-Blog/Interview-with-Hopoo-Games-on-Risk-of-Rain-2-Arriving-Sept-29-on/ba-p/30595.

Wood, A. (2017, December 22). *We finally get our first look at Risk of Rain 2.* PC Gamer. https://www.pcgamer.com/we-finally-get-our-first-look-at-risk-of-rain-2/.

5 (The Messenger)

Meister, R. (2018, September 1). *Review: The Messenger.* Destructoid. https://www. destructoid.com/reviews/review-the-messenger/.

The Messenger on Steam. Steam. (n.d.). https://store.steampowered.com/app/764790/ The_Messenger/.

The Messenger. SteamSpy. (n.d.). https://steamspy.com/app/764790.

Sea of Stars Kickstarter. Kickstarter. (2021). https://www.kickstarter.com/projects/ sabotagestudio/sea-of-stars.

Sinclair, B. (2018, September 12). *Making a retro indie game stand out from the crowd.* GamesIndustry.biz. https://www.gamesindustry.biz/articles/2018-09-12-the-messengers-special-delivery.

Sources

About BostonFIG. BostonFIG. (n.d.). https://www.bostonfig.com/about/.

Barclay, P. (2021, March 6). *A short preview of lighting-based puzzles in Sea of Stars!* Indie Game Developers IGD - Facebook Group. https://www.facebook.com/ groups/IndieGameDevs/posts/10157590282116573.

Biazzo, J. (2020, June 25). *Ori and the Will of the Wisps sold over 2 million copies*. Gameranx. https://gameranx.com/updates/id/202848/article/2-million-ori-will-wisps-sold-detailed-xbox/.

Birkett, J. (2018, May 24). Using Steam reviews to estimate sales. Game Developer. https://www.gamedeveloper.com/business/using-steam-reviews-to-estimate-sales.

Bundle for Racial Justice and Equality. itch.io. (n.d.). https://itch.io/b/520/bundle-for-racial-justice-and-equality.

Cameron, P. (2019, August 14). *How moving from 2D to 3D shaped the design of Risk of Rain 2*. Game Developer. https://www.gamedeveloper.com/disciplines/how-moving-from-2d-to-3d-shaped-the-design-of-i-risk-of-rain-2-i-.

Carless, S. (2020, August 3). *How that game sold on Steam, using the 'NB number'*. The GameDiscoverCo newsletter. https://newsletter.gamediscover.co/p/how-that-game-sold-on-steam-using.

Carless, S. (2021, June 29). *Game localization for discovery: Trickier than you think?* GamesIndustry.biz. https://www.gamesindustry.biz/articles/2021-06-29-game-localization-for-discovery-trickier-than-you-think.

Carter, C. (2018, February 4). *Celeste sold best on Switch according to its creator*. Destructoid. https://www.destructoid.com/celeste-sold-best-on-switch-according-to-its-creator/.

Clement, J. (2021, March 3). *Share of gamers buying microtransactions in the u.s. 2019*. Statista. https://www.statista.com/statistics/1104738/video-gaming-dlc-share/.

Dealessandri, M. (2020, June 10). *How to price your game and thrive during Steam sales*. GamesIndustry.biz. https://www.gamesindustry.biz/articles/2020-06-10-how-to-price-your-game-and-thrive-during-steam-sales.

Dealessandri, M. (2020, May 18). *A game developer's guide to Steam Wishlists*. GamesIndustry.biz. https://www.gamesindustry.biz/articles/2020-05-15-a-game-developer-guide-to-steam-wishlists.

DevBlog #1 - Our Next Project. Hopoo Games DevBlog. (2017, May 8). https://web.archive.org/web/20180118042945/http://hopooo.tumblr.com/post/160452455554/devblog-1-our-next-project-weve-been-working.

Diaz, A. (2020, October 17). *Make love, NOT War: Five years Of 'Undertale'*. NPR. https://www.npr.org/2020/10/17/924581553/make-love-not-war-five-years-of-undertale.

Dillard, C. (2009, February 1). *Team meat interview - Super Meat boy*. Nintendo Life. https://www.nintendolife.com/news/2009/02/team_meat_interview_super_meat_boy.

Doolan, L. (2020, February 28). *The project AM2R creator now designs levels for the Ori developer Moon Studios*. Nintendo Life. https://www.nintendolife.com/news/2020/02/the_project_am2r_creator_now_designs_levels_for_the_ori_developer_moon_studios.

Dring, C. (2020, March 10). *Building Ori and the Will of the Wisps with 80 people working from home*. GamesIndustry.biz. https://www.gamesindustry.biz/articles/2020-03-10-building-ori-and-the-will-of-the-wisps-with-80-people-working-from-home.

Fenlon, W. (2019, April 4). *Risk of Rain 2 devs talk hitting 500,000 players, mod support, and what's coming next*. PC Gamer. https://www.pcgamer.com/uk/risk-of-rain-2-devs-talk-hitting-500000-players-mod-support-and-whats-coming-next/.

Fields, S. (2015, April 10). *'Ori and the Blind Forest' turned a profit within a week*. Game Rant. https://gamerant.com/ori-blind-forest-sales-profit/.

Gach, E. (2018, January 15). *Super Meat Boy is the latest port to sell better than expected on the Nintendo Switch*. Kotaku. https://kotaku.com/super-meat-boy-is-the-latest-port-to-sell-better-than-e-1822056498.

Games Done Quick. (2018, July 1). *Celeste race by TGH v yoshipro in 36:26 - SGDQ2018*. YouTube. https://www.youtube.com/watch?v=KS0QeQ1zXxI.

Gibson, E. (2009, March 25). *GDC: Braid cost 200k to MAKE, says Blow*. Eurogamer.net. https://www.eurogamer.net/articles/gdc-braid-cost-200k-to-make-says-blow.

Grayson, N. (2018, November 28). *Steam Spy is back, but not as accurate as before*. Kotaku. https://kotaku.com/steam-spy-is-back-but-not-as-accurate-as-before-1825608646.

Hades (2018) Credits. MobyGames. (n.d.). https://www.mobygames.com/game/windows/hades/credits.

Hill, K. (2012, February 16). *How Target figured out a teen girl was pregnant before her father did*. Forbes. https://www.forbes.com/sites/kashmirhill/2012/02/16/how-target-figured-out-a-teen-girl-was-pregnant-before-her-father-did/?sh=27f3c5ef6668.

Hruska, J. (2016, December 27). *Star Citizen developer Chris Roberts clarifies engine change to Amazon's Lumberyard won't delay the game*. ExtremeTech. https://www.extremetech.com/extreme/241674-star-citizen-developer-chris-roberts-clarifies-engine-change-promises-move-amazons-lumberyard-wont-delay-game.

Hudgins, A. (2016, July 26). *Next up for the creator of TowerFall, a game about climbing a mountain*. Kill Screen. https://web.archive.org/web/20180105123149/https://killscreen.com/articles/celeste/.

iCue Dev. Corsair. (n.d.). https://www.corsair.com/us/en/icue-dev.

Indie Megabooth Submissions. Indie MEGABOOTH. (2019, November 26). https://indiemegabooth.com/about/submissions/#:~:text=PAX%20East%20and%20West%3A%0A,your%20equipment%20and%20one%20badge.

J. Michael Leon's LinkedIn. LinkedIn. (n.d.). https://www.linkedin.com/in/j-michael-leon-4388731/.

Kerr, C. (2019, May 3). *Risk of Rain 2 crosses 1 million sales in first month*. Game Developer. https://www.gamedeveloper.com/business/-i-risk-of-rain-2-i-crosses-1-million-sales-in-first-month.

Khan, A. (2017, March 15). *Interview with Oculus' Jason Rubin - Part 1: The Unpublisher*. Shacknews. https://www.shacknews.com/article/99385/interview-with-oculus-jason-rubin---part-1-the-unpublisher.

Krupa, D. (2013, February 19). *Hotline Miami coming to PS3 and PS Vita*. IGN. https://www.ign.com/articles/2013/02/19/hotline-miami-coming-to-ps3-and-ps-vita.

Lane, G. (2021, January 1). *Moon Studios on Ori and the Will of the Wisps' journey from Xbox to Switch*. Nintendo Life. https://www.nintendolife.com/news/2021/01/feature_moon_studios_on_ori_and_the_will_of_the_wisps_journey_from_xbox_to_switch.

Lawler, R. (2021, May 4). *Epic vs. Apple TRIAL reveals the cost of exclusives and 'free' games*. Engadget. https://www.engadget.com/epic-apple-app-store-trial-023401781.html.

Lindell, M. (2021, June 23). *Tweet by Martin Lindell*. Twitter. https://twitter.com/martinlindell/status/1407924045425881090.

Marks, T. (2020, March 5). *Inside EXOK Games: The brand new studio that's already sold a million copies*. IGN India. https://in.ign.com/celeste/145619/feature/inside-exok-games-the-brand-new-studio-thats-already-sold-a-million-copies.

McAloon, A. (2019, March 27). Risk of Rain 2 is running a buy-one-get-one free launch promo. https://www.gamedeveloper.com/console/-i-risk-of-rain-2-i-is-running-a-buy-one-get-one-free-launch-promo.

McMillen, E., & Refenes, T. (2011, April 14). *Postmortem: Team Meat's Super Meat Boy*. Game Developer. https://www.gamedeveloper.com/audio/postmortem-team-meat-s-i-super-meat-boy-i-.

Meet our team. Hopoo Games. (n.d.). https://hopoogames.com/meet-our-team/.

Meister, R. (2018, September 1). *Review: The Messenger*. Destructoid. https://www.destructoid.com/reviews/review-the-messenger/.

Meitzler, R. (2020, January 10). *Disco Elysium's full script is over a million words long, according to developer*. Dualshockers. https://www.dualshockers.com/disco-elysium-script-length-one-million-words/.

Meunier, N. (2009, April 5). *Indie queue: Meat boy gets supersized*. The Escapist. https://www.escapistmagazine.com/v2/indie-queue-meat-boy-gets-supersized/.

Miche, H. (2020, October 26). *New survey on DLC and microtransactions shows gamers' feelings*. SegmentNext. https://segmentnext.com/dlc-and-microtransactions-survey/.

Monthly summaries. SteamSpy. (n.d.). https://steamspy.com/year/.

Nelius, J. (2019, March 29). *Google Stadia has game Developers Confused, excited, and worried*. PC Gamer. https://www.pcgamer.com/google-stadia-has-game-developers-confused-excited-and-worried/.

Noclip. (2019, December 23). *The Making of Bastion - Documentary*. YouTube. https://www.youtube.com/watch?v=uo7TcJ2E0-I.

PAX East 2020 Fee Schedule. Scribd. (n.d.). https://www.scribd.com/document/501106408/PAX-East-2020-Fee-Schedule.

PAX Rising Grants. Creative Victoria. (n.d.). https://creative.vic.gov.au/grants-and-support/programs/pax-rising.

Retrospective on Undertale's popularity. (2016, September 14). [web log]. https://undertale.tumblr.com/post/150397346860/retrospective-on-undertales-popularity.

Risk of Rain 2 on Steam. Steam. (n.d.). https://store.steampowered.com/app/632360/Risk_of_Rain_2/.

Rodriguez, J. (2021, April 30). *Risk of Rain 2: An interview with Paul Morse of Hopoo Games*. PC Invasion. https://www.pcinvasion.com/risk-of-rain-2-interview-paul-morse/.

Sea of Stars Kickstarter. Kickstarter. (2021). https://www.kickstarter.com/projects/sabotagestudio/sea-of-stars.

Senior, T. (2011, October 17). *Project Zomboid robbery delays latest update, Zomboid "will come back stronger" says dev*. PC Gamer. https://www.pcgamer.com/project-zomboid-robbery-delays-latest-update-zomboid-will-come-back-stronger-says-dev/.

Shea, B. (2020, April 7). *Chrono Trigger composer contributing to Sea of Stars soundtrack*. Game Informer. https://www.gameinformer.com/2020/04/07/chrono-trigger-composer-contributing-to-sea-of-stars-soundtrack.

Sinclair, B. (2016, May 9). *Dodge Roll's speedrun to indie success*. GamesIndustry.biz. https://www.gamesindustry.biz/articles/2016-05-09-dodge-rolls-speedrun-to-indie-success.

Sinclair, B. (2018, September 12). *Making a retro indie game stand out from the crowd*. GamesIndustry.biz. https://www.gamesindustry.biz/articles/2018-09-12-the-messengers-special-delivery.

Smith, E. (2016, January 14). *Keeping it human: The story of Fullbright's 'Gone Home' success*. VICE. https://www.vice.com/en/article/kwxjjv/keeping-it-human-the-story-of-fullbrights-gone-home-success-200.

Spelunky. Spelunky Wiki. (n.d.). https://spelunky.fandom.com/wiki/Spelunky.

Stadia Team. (2020, September 24). *Interview with Hopoo Games on Risk of Rain 2, Arriving Sept. 29 on Stadia*. Stadia. https://community.stadia.com/t5/Stadia-Community-Blog/Interview-with-Hopoo-Games-on-Risk-of-Rain-2-Arriving-Sept-29-on/ba-p/30595.

Statt, N. (2020, June 11). *Itch.io's amazing 1,500-game charity bundle surpasses $5 million goal*. The Verge. https://www.theverge.com/2020/6/11/21287909/itch-io-bundle-for-racial-justice-equality-five-million-dollar-goal-hit.

Steam: The dynamic of games languages. Nimdzi. (2020, April 29). https://www.nimdzi.com/steam-the-dynamic-of-games-languages/.

Stein, Z. (2015, May 25). *This is how big the script was for The Witcher 3: Wild Hunt*. IGN. https://www.ign.com/articles/2015/05/29/this-is-how-big-the-script-was-for-the-witcher-3-wild-hunt.

Sterling, J. (2010, January 9). *Survey: 15% of gamers actually buy DLC*. Destructoid. https://www.destructoid.com/survey-15-of-gamers-actually-buy-dlc/.

Square Enix to make work from home permanent as of December 1. Square Enix. (n.d.). https://www.jp.square-enix.com/company/en/news/2020/html/df9995782da2d516db9ebac425d02d4019665f70.html.

Sweeny, A. (2018, February 3). *'Celeste' sold the most units on Nintendo Switch*. Nintendo Enthusiast. https://www.nintendoenthusiast.com/celeste-sold-the-most-units-on-nintendo-switch/.

Swichkow, B. (2014, September 6). *How I pranked my roommate with eerily targeted Facebook Ads*. Ghost Influence. https://ghostinfluence.com/the-ultimate-retaliation-pranking-my-roommate-with-targeted-facebook-ads/.

Takahashi, D. (2021, July 8). *Amazon shifts Lumberyard to open source 3D game engine supported by 20 companies.* VentureBeat. https://venturebeat.com/2021/07/06/amazons-lumberyard-becomes-an-open-source-3d-game-engine-with-support-from-20-companies/.

The Messenger on Steam. Steam. (n.d.). https://store.steampowered.com/app/764790/The_Messenger/.

The Messenger. SteamSpy. (n.d.). https://steamspy.com/app/764790.

Thier, D. (2021, March 19). *Game Pass' massive growth is bringing developers some surprises.* Forbes. https://www.forbes.com/sites/davidthier/2021/03/19/game-pass-massive-growth-is-bringing-developers-some-surprises/?sh=316f292362b4.

Tinner, P. (2020, September 23). *Among Us 2 canceled to focus on current game's popularity explosion.* ScreenRant. https://screenrant.com/among-us-2-canceled-announcement-innersloth-puffballsunited/.

Tone Control. Tone Control - Idle Thumbs Network. (n.d.). https://www.idlethumbs.net/tonecontrol.

Wood, A. (2017, December 22). *We finally get our first look at Risk of Rain 2.* PC Gamer. https://www.pcgamer.com/we-finally-get-our-first-look-at-risk-of-rain-2/.

Yin-Poole, W. (2012, January 3). *Super Meat Boy sells over 1 million.* Eurogamer.net. https://www.eurogamer.net/articles/2012-01-03-super-meat-boy-sells-over-1-million.

Yin-Poole, W. (2021, May 4). *Epic's "fully loaded" Borderlands 3 deal cost $146m, secured six months of PC exclusivity.* Eurogamer.net. https://www.eurogamer.net/articles/2021-05-04-epics-fully-loaded-borderlands-3-deal-cost-usd146m-for-six-months-of-pc-exclusivity.

INDEX

A

AAA (triple-A) studio, 7, 8, 28, 33, 56, 94, 180, 199, 205
A/B marketing test, 188–189
Adjusted revenue share, 26
Amazon Web Services (AWS), 87, 91
Among Us, 67, 72, 73, 219, 249
Among Us 2, 249
Apollo, 45
Apple Arcade, 194, 195
Astro-turfing, 222
Attorney, working with, 168
    advocating for yourself, 171
    client–attorney relationship, managing, 170
    fair and clear rates, 169
    proven industry experience, 168
    publisher, taking changes to, 170–171
    relevant regional credentials, 169–170
    responsive and available, 169
AWS, *see* Amazon Web Services
Axiom Verge, 25

B

Barclay, Philip, 206
Bastion, 2–3, 9, 30, 71, 144, 194
Berry, Noel, 69, 71, 72
BGS, *see* Brasil Game Show
The Binding of Isaac, 51, 52, 67
Bioshock 2, 55
Bite the Bullet, 118, 220
Blasphemous, 71
Blizzard, 44
Blood Car 2000!, 52
Blow, Jonathan, 56, 78
Blue Fire, 59, 67, 184, 188
Bond, Sarah, 26–27
Borderlands, 101
Borderlands 3, 228
Borderlands 4, 101
BostonFIG, 59
Braid, 71, 78

Brasil Game Show (BGS), 208
Budget, 7, 9, 24, 29, 38, 99, 154
    breakdown, 126–127
    burn rate, 99–100
    development, 62, 66, 71, 228
    estimates, 97–99
    long tail, 100–101
    marketing, 226–228
    projected costs vs. actual costs, 99
    template, 102
Bundle promotions, being strategic with, 240
Bundle sales, 16, 34
Burn rate, 99–100
Business implications of QA, 179–180

C

Call of Duty, 16, 199
Carless, Simon, 69–70
Castle Crashers, 44
Castlevania, 33
Celeste, 25, 67, 68, 69, 70, 71–72, 78, 223
Charity activations, 223, 240–241
Chrono Trigger, 31, 214
Cinematic trailer, 122
Cloud-based systems, 108
Code freeze, 83
Community element of indie games, 5
Company funding, 11
Comparable titles, 67, 69, 72–73
Console certification, 16, 83, 96, 178–179, 193
Construct 3, 86
Content creators, 6, 221
Contract studios, 9
CORSAIR, 91
Course corrections, 108
COVID-19 pandemic, 209
Crash-course in marketing metrics, 228–230
Creative approaches to indie merchandise, 33
Crowdfunded projects, 51, 60–63

Crowdfunding, 13–14, 33, 60
Cruelty Squad, 86
Crunchyroll, 145
CryEngine, 87, 89
Culture-fit, 106
Cuphead, 242
Curators and key distributors, 221–222
Currency, Wishlists as, 37, 39–40
Customer pool, size of, 242–243
Cyber Hook, 184
Cyber Shadow, 86

D

The Dark Knight, 201
Deck content
    demo and GDD, 129–130
    marketing assets, 121
        game trailers, 122–123
        key art, 124–125
        screenshots and GIFs, 123–124
    product details, 117
        engine, 121
        game concept, 118
        game length and game price, 119–120
        launch timing, 119
        platforms, 120
    roadmap to launch, 125
        ask and budget breakdown, 126–128
        market analysis, 125–126
    team information, 128–129
The Delicious Last Course, 242
Dennaton Games, 30, 86
Developers, 5, 6
    challenges as, 13
    crowdfunding, 13–14
    definition of "indie" developers, 7–9
    financial success of, 5, 14
    investors, 9–10
        working of, 10–11
    large teams, 8
    mid-size teams, 8
    publishers, 9–10
        working of, 12–13
    self-publishing, 13–14
    small teams, 8
    solo, 8
Development funding, 166
Development plan for a game, 48
Devolver Digital, 30, 86, 110, 234, 235
Digital distribution, 13, 28, 29
Digital marketing
    off-property, 205–207
    on-property, 203–205
Disco Elysium, 83

Discord, 19, 44, 181, 183–184, 207, 231
Discounts and bundles, 238
    bundle promotions, being strategic with, 240
    charity activations, 240–241
    gradual increase of discounts over time, 239
    launch discount, 238–239
    sales fatigue, account for, 239–240
    steam sales, 239
Discovery call, 138, 148, 151
    asking your own questions, 156–158
    budget and timeline questions, 154–155
    engine selection and market fit, 155–156
    general preparation, 151–152
    preparing for specific publishers, 152–153
    preparing to answer questions, 153
Disney, 44
Distribution platforms, 15, 230
Divinity: Original Sin 2, 195
Dodge Roll, 110
DOTA, 33
Druckmann, Neil, 56

E

Early Access projects, 51
Engine selection, business perspective on, 85
    Construct 3, 86
    CryEngine, 87
    GameMaker, 86
    Godot, 86
    Open 3D Engine, 87–88
    Unity, 87
    Unreal, 87
Enter the Gungeon, 67, 110
Envelope math, 9
Epic Games Store, 16–17, 25, 27, 40, 91, 241, 245
Established engine, 85, 121
Eurogamer, 78
Events, 6
Extremely OK Games, 223

F

Facebook, 91, 205–206, 207, 228, 231
Fangamer, 32, 62, 244
Far Cry 5, 199
Final Fantasy, 199
Final Fantasy 6, 76, 77
Financial success of developers, 5, 14, 31, 40
First-person shooter (FPS), 16
Fish, Phil, 7
Follow feature, 41–42
Forbes, 26
Fortnite, 126
FPS, *see* First-person shooter
The Fullbright Company, 55

Full-scope publishers, 12
Funding
    additional, 209
    company funding, 11
    crowdfunding, 13–14, 33, 60–63
    development, 166
    investment firm/fund, 10
    milestone-based, 141
    project funding, 11

G

Galyonkin, Sergey, 68
Game design document (GDD), 21, 48, 51, 57, 158
Game Developers Conference (GDC), 208
The Game Discoverability Now!, 69
Game Informer, 96
GameMaker, 47, 50, 86, 155
Game of Thrones, 33
Game Pass service, 17, 27
Gameplay trailer, 122
Gamercom, 208
Game sales, 23–26
GamesIndustry.biz, 37, 44, 110, 234, 238
Game testers, sourcing, 182–184
Gaming events, 183, 201, 207–212
Gaming Outfitters, 32
Gaynor, Steve, 55, 56
GDC, *see* Game Developers Conference
GDD, *see* Game design document
Genre and market evaluation, 65
    sales success, predicting, 66
        ins and outs of sales data, 68–71
        trends and traps, 71–73
    stepping back for the big picture, 73–74
Genre trends, 89–90
Giardino, Tom, 238
GIFs, 59, 117, 123, 203
Giveaways, 222–223
Godot, 86
GOG, 16, 24, 39–40
Gone Home, 55, 56, 71
Google, 26, 41
Google Analytics, 205, 230
Google Drive, 108, 129
Google Slides, 117
Google Stadia, 194
Graffiti Games, 17, 59, 198
Graveyard Keeper, 73
Gross profit, 23, 30

H

Hades, 3, 8–9, 144
Halo, 16, 201

A Hat in Time, 67, 87
Hobby game projects, 51–53
Hobby projects, 50
Hollow Knight, 32, 67, 68
Hopoo Games, 11, 87, 174, 175
Hotline Miami soundtrack, 30, 86
Humble Bundle soundtrack, 17
Hyper Light Drifter, 86
Hypnospace Outlaw, 86

I

iCUE, 91
Imgur, 207
Incomplete recoup, 142
Indie Game: The Movie, 7
Indiegogo, 13, 60
Indie MEGABOOTH, 209, 217
Industry stakeholders, 7, 14, 90
Influencer marketing, 219–221
InnerSloth, 249
Instagram, 28
Intellectual property (IP), 13, 31, 54, 78, 144–146
Investment firm/fund, 10
Investment scout, 10
Investors, 6, 9–10
    private, 10
    professional, 10
    working of, 10–11
IP, *see* Intellectual property
Itch.io, 13, 16, 17, 34, 53, 223

K

Katana Zero, 71, 155
Key performance indicators (KPIs), 229
Kickstarter, 13–14, 29, 31, 60, 61, 62, 214
Korol, Gennadiy, 44
Kotaku, 68
KPIs, *see* key performance indicators

L

Languages chosen for game, 81–82
Large teams of developers, 8
Launch discount, 238–239
Lazy Bear Games, 73
The Legend of Zelda: The Wind Waker, 30, 67
Leon, Michael, 2
Letter of intent (LOI), 166–167
Levine, Ken, 56
Licensing deals, 11, 30, 33–34, 90
LinkedIn, 152
Living document, 63
LOI, *see* letter of intent

Long tail, 100–101
Lumberyard, 87, 91

M

Mahler, Thomas, 44
Marketing, 199
    budget and measurement, 226
        crash-course in marketing metrics,
            228–230
        example marketing budget breakdown,
            226–228
    channels, 218
        charity activations, 223
        curators and key distributors, 221–222
        giveaways, 222–223
        influencer marketing, 219–221
        paid advertising, 218–219
    example launch calendar, 224–225
    example social media calendar, 225–226
    extension of game, 231
    gaming events, 207–212
    media coverage, earning, 212–216
    memorable marketing, creating, 201–203
    off-property digital marketing, 205–207
    on-property digital marketing, 203–205
    pre-release accolades, 216–218
    press engagement, 212–216
Mass Digi Challenge, 59
Mass Effect, 201
Massively multiplayer online games (MMOs), 76
Master Chief, 201
Math, 21, 24, 39
    for actual profit, 23
    envelope math, 9
Matt Makes Games, 25, 223
McMillen, Edmund, 51, 52
Meat Boy, 52, 79
Media coverage, earning, 212–216
Media rights, 144
Mega Cat, 118
Memorable marketing, creating, 201–203
Mentor feedback, 183
Merchandise rights, 144
Merchandisers, 6, 18–19
Merchandising, 31–33
Message boards, 207
The Messenger, 31
Metacritic score, 39, 70
Metroid II, 44
Metroidvania, 187–188
MGs, *see* Minimum guarantees
Microsoft, 17, 27, 45
Microsoft Studios, 249
Mid-size teams of developers, 8

Milestone-based funding, 141
Milestone schedule, 141
Milton "DoctorM64" Guasti, 44
Minimum guarantees (MGs), 13, 24–26, 35,
        39–40, 91, 142, 197–198, 241
Miscreated, 87
Mission Impossible, 247
Mitsuda, Yasunori, 31
MMOs, *see* Massively multiplayer online games
MomoCon, 203
Monster Hunter series, 231
Moon Studios, 44–45, 249
Music, 22, 29–31
My Friend Pedro, 87

N

NAMI, *see* National Alliance on Mental Illness
National Alliance on Mental Illness (NAMI), 240
National Football League (NFL), 18
Netflix, 26, 33, 145
Net profit, 23–24
NFL, *see* National Football League
Nintendo, 13, 15, 16, 28, 35, 40, 52, 178
Nintendo Enthusiast, 214
Nintendo eShop, 15, 16, 35, 178, 179, 229
Nintendo Switch, 15, 69, 89, 178, 179
Nordhagen, Johnnemann, 55

O

OCRemix, 29
Oculus, 91
Off-property digital marketing, 205–207
On-property digital marketing, 203–205
Open 3D Engine, 87–88
Orbiting stakeholders, 18–19
Ori and the Blind Forest, 44, 45, 124, 201, 249
Ori and the Will of the Wisps, 44, 45, 71, 249
Outlast, 87
Outside brands, 7

P

Paid advertising, 218–219
Partner, advantages of working with, 28–29
Pathologic 2, 87
PAX, *see* Penny Arcade Expos
Pay-per-hour, 26
Penny Arcade Expos (PAX), 207
    PAX East, 58, 59
    PAX Rising, 209, 217
People and project management, 107
    backups, 107
    organization and communication, 108
    version control, 107

Photoshop, 203
Physical releases, 27–29
Pitch, failure of, 133–135
Pitch, presenting, 130
    preparing your own questions, 131
    rehearsing your pitch, 131
    time constraints, accounting for, 131
Pitch deck perfection
    basics, 114–117
    deck content
        demo and GDD, 129–130
        marketing assets, 121–125
        product details, 117–121
        roadmap to launch, 125–128
        team information, 128–129
    failure of pitch, 133–135
    pitch delivery, 132–133
    presenting a pitch, 130
        preparing your own questions, 131
        rehearsing your pitch, 131
        time constraints, accounting for, 131
Pitch delivery, 132–133
Planning, 48
Platformer, 76
Platforms, 6, 14
    distribution, 15, 230
    GOG, 24, 39
    incentives, 90–92
    indie mindset for, 19–20
    primary, 15–17
    secondary, 17, 35
    tertiary, 16
Player demand, 243
    assessing the level of access to players, 243
    finding a partner, 244
    listening to your players, 243
    starting with small tests, 243–244
PlayStation, 15, 16, 17, 28, 239, 241
PlayStation 3, 30
Porting, 121, 178, 191, 192, 193
Porting efficiency, 85
Porting publishers, 12
"Postmortem" project analyses, 80
Pre-development decisions, 47–50
Pre-release accolades, 201, 216–218
Press, 6
Press engagement, 178, 201, 212–216
Primary platforms, 15–17
Private investor, 10
Professional investor, 10
Profit
    gross, 23, 30
    net, 23–24
Projected costs vs. actual costs, 99
Project funding, 11

Project management, 107
    backups, 107
    organization and communication, 108
    version control, 107
Project types and project goals, 50–51
    crowdfunded projects, 60–63
    hobby game projects, 51–53
    living document, 63
    pre-development decisions, 47–48
    retroactive pre-development, 49–50
    self-published projects, 53–56
    traditional publishing, 56–60
    true pre-development, 48–49
Project Zomboid, 107
PS Vita, 30
PUBG, 72
Publisher, 2, 6, 9–10, 12, 37, 137, 138–139
    attorney, working with, 168
        advocating for yourself, 171
        client–attorney relationship, managing, 170
        fair and clear rates, 169
        proven industry experience, 168
        relevant regional credentials, 169–170
        responsive and available, 169
        taking changes to the publisher, 170–171
    full-scope, 12
    game development, juggling business development with, 172
    indie publisher deal structure, 140
        advances, 143
        intellectual property (IP) terms, 144–146
        milestone schedule, 141
        recoup, 141–142
        revenue share, 143–144
    key background insights, 139–140
    negotiation process, 146
        general sales tips, 149–150
        meeting context, 148–149
        pitch context and rapport, 147–148
        revisiting pitch deck, 146–147
    Nintendo-savvy, 15
    offer, 148
    porting, 12
    preference, 88–89
    publisher-to-project fit, 12
    regional, 12
    review, 148
    right-royalty-only, 12
    royalty-only, 12
    working of, 12–13
Publishing deal, stages of, 151
    approaching a publisher
        who has made you an offer, 165
        who has not made an offer, 164–165

Discovery Call, 151
    asking your own questions, 156–158
    budget and timeline questions, 154–155
    engine selection and market fit, 155–156
    general preparation, 151–152
    preparing for specific publishers, 152–153
    preparing to answer questions, 153
how to counter, 162–164
letter of intent (LOI), 166–167
publisher review, 158–159
receiving an offer or an LOI, 159–162
shopping offers, 165–166
walking away, 165–166

Q

QA, *see* Quality assurance
Quality assurance (QA), 177
    business implications of, 179–180
    feedback, gathering, 184–186
    game testers, sourcing, 182–184
    implementing QA feedback, 186
        recognizing own biases and limitations,
            187
        revisiting comparable title research,
            187–188
        run tests, 188–189
        understanding the root issue, 188
    management for indie games, 180–182
    as a skill, 189

R

Rao, Amir, 2
Real-time strategy (RTS) games, 16
Recoup, 141–142
Reddit, 201, 207
Regional publishers, 12
Release window, picking, 95
    avoiding Q4 and major holidays, 95–96
    being aware of other game releases, 96
    launching one month later than you think, 97
    "slow" season, releasing in, 96
    tradeshow launches, 96
Revenue, 8, 11, 18, 20, 21, 36, 42
    adjusted revenue share, 26
    bundle sales, 34
    game sales, 23–24
    licensing deals, 33–34
    merchandising, 31–33
    minimum guarantees (MGs), 24–26
    physical releases, 27–29
    scope of, 36
    secondary platform sales, 35
    share, 143–144

soundtracks, 29–31
subscriptions, 26–27
Revenue channels, 241
    customer pool, size of, 242–243
    new business, understanding, 244–245
    player demand, 243
        assessing the level of access to players,
            243
        finding a partner, 244
        listening to players, 243
        small tests, starting with, 243–244
    scope, deciding, 244
"Right of first refusal" clause, 145
Right-royalty-only publisher, 12
Riot, 44
Risk of Rain, 174
Risk of Rain 2, 87, 174–175
Robi Studios, 59, 60
Rock Paper Shotgun, 214
Rogue State Revolution, 86
Royalty-only publishers, 12
RPG Maker, 88
RPGs, 16, 31
RTS games, *see* Real-time strategy games
Rubin, Jason, 91

S

Sabotage Studios, 31
Sales, 13
    bundle sales, 16, 34
    game sales, 23–26
    secondary platform sales, 35
    steam sales, 239
Sales fatigue, 239–240
Salesmanship, 39, 130
Sales success, predicting, 66
    ins and outs of sales data, 68–71
    trends and traps, 71–73
Sanshee, 32
Schafer, Tim, 56
Scope, assessing
    assessing additional development needs,
        83–85
    by assets and length, 77
        ask another developer (exercise), 79–80
        learn from your old projects (exercise), 80
        prototype (exercise), 79
        reverse engineer an existing game
            (exercise), 78
    business perspective on engine selection, 85
        Construct 3, 86
        CryEngine, 87
        GameMaker, 86
        Godot, 86

Open 3D Engine, 87–88
    Unity, 87
    Unreal, 87
  by genre, 76–77, 89–90
  licensing fees and other terms of use, 90
  platform incentives, 90–92
  publisher preference, 88–89
  time estimates, mapping scope to, 94–95
  translation and localization, 80–83
Scope of investment, 11
Scope of revenue, 36
Screenshots, 123–124, 203
Sea of Stars, 31, 62
Secondary platforms, 17, 35
Second launch, 237
  additional revenue channels, unlocking, 241
    customer pool, size of, 242–243
    deciding scope, 244
    new business, understanding, 244–245
    player demand, 243–244
  discounts and bundles, 238
    account for sales fatigue, 239–240
    being strategic with bundle promotions,
      240
    charity activations, 240–241
    gradual increase of discounts over time,
      239
    launch discount, 238–239
    steam sales, 239
  new opportunities, 245
  secondary platforms, 241–242
Self-published projects, 50, 53–56
Self-publishing, 13–14
Sequel, merits and pitfalls of, 248–249
Sequel rights, 144, 145
Service, games as, 26–27
Shacknews, 91
Shopping offers, 165–166
Shovel Knight, 71, 187, 221
Simon, Gavin, 2
Simple recoup, 142
The Sinking City, 87
Skype, 45
Skytorn, 71–72
Slack, 44
Small teams of developers, 8
Snoozy Kazoo, 59, 60
Solo developers, 8
Soundtracks, 22, 29–31
  Hotline Miami soundtrack, 30
  Humble Bundle soundtrack, 17
Spelunky, 155
Spelunky 2, 71
Stadia, 26
Staggered recoup, 142

Stakeholders
  indie mindset for, 19–20
  industry, 7, 14, 90
  orbiting, 18–19
Starcraft II, 44
Stardew Valley, 32, 73
Star Wars, 144
Steam, 241
Steam algorithm, 16, 34, 35
Steam page, 204
Steam sales, 239
Steam Spy, 68–69, 113
Steam store, 55
Steam Wishlists, 19, 24
  as a crystal ball for future sales, 37–39
  as currency, 39–40
  Follow feature, 41–42
  revenue, 42
  and Steam algorithm, 40–41
Storefront algorithms, 41
Streaming services, 6, 26
Strictly Limited Games, 28
Subscription services, 26–27
Supergiant Games, 2–3, 144, 145
Super Mario Bros, 33
Super Mario Maker, 71, 72
Super Meat Boy, 44, 51, 52, 72
Switch, 239, 241
Switch box set, 31
Switch porting, 13, 15

T

Tax, 23
Team building and management, 102
  agreements and equity, 104–105
  recruiting and hiring, 105–106
  team member relationships, types of, 103–104
Team dynamics, 106
Technical tests, 16
Teespring, 33
Tertiary platforms, 16
Thomas Happ Games, 25
Thorson, Maddy, 69
TikTok, 201, 220, 225
Time estimates, mapping scope to, 94–95
Timeline gap/overage, assessing, 97
tinyBuild, 73
Tone Control, 56
Towerfall, 71
Traditional publishing, 51, 56–60
Trailers, 203
Translation, localization, and porting, 191
  change of plans, 193–194
  launch day, 198

new porting opportunities, opening, 194
    being open to the outlandish, 195
    wishlist momentum, 196–198
    preparation, best practices for, 191
        getting the tools needed, 192
        planning for the unexpected, 193
        potential obstacles, flagging, 192–193
        routinely assessing the workflows, 192
        testing, 193
Trello, 44
T-shirts, 32, 33
Turnip Boy Commits Tax Evasion, 53, 59, 60, 72, 129
Twitch, 6, 205, 213, 219, 220, 223, 225
    integration, 18, 87
    and YouTube creators, 183
Twitter, 5, 28, 37, 207

U

Undertale, 33, 62–63, 71, 86
Unity, 87
Unreal, 87, 89

V

Valve, 238
ΔV: Rings of Saturn, 86

W

Walking away, 165–166
Warner Brothers, 2, 9
War of Rights, 87
Wishlist, 37
    as a crystal ball for future sales, 37–39
    as currency, 39–40

Follow feature, 41–42
math, 66
momentum, 196
    asking platform representative for help, 197
    following up a splash with another splash, 197
    good network, 196–197
    minimum guarantees, 197–198
    relationships, establishing, 196
revenue, 42
and Steam algorithm, 40–41
The Witcher 3: The Wild Hunt, 83
Wolcen, 87
Word freeze, 83
"WORK-for-hire" development studios, 9
Wright, Chris, 194

X

Xbox (Microsoft Store), 16, 40, 239, 241
Xbox Game Pass, 26
Xbox Game Studios, 249
Xbox Live Arcade, 2, 9

Y

The Yetee, 32, 33, 244
YouTube, 6, 183, 201, 213, 220, 225
Yu, Derek, 56

Z

Zenimax, 17
Zero Punctuation!, 221
Zimonja, Karla, 55–56
Zoom, 44, 131, 151, 208

9 781032 104225